D0612510

Florida Weather

Second Edition

Florida A&M University, Tallahassee
Florida Atlantic University, Boca Raton
Florida Gulf Coast University, Ft. Myers
Florida International University, Miami
Florida State University, Tallahassee
University of Central Florida, Orlando
University of Florida, Gainesville
University of North Florida, Jacksonville
University of South Florida, Tampa
University of West Florida, Pensacola

Florida Weather

SECOND EDITION

MORTON D. WINSBERG

with the assistance of James J. O'Brien, David F. Zierden,
and Melissa L. Griffin, Florida Climate Center

University Press of Florida
Gainesville · Tallahassee · Tampa · Boca Raton
Pensacola · Orlando · Miami · Jacksonville · Ft. Myers

Copyright 2003 by Morton D. Winsberg
Printed in the United States of America on acid-free paper
All rights reserved

08 07 06 05 04 03   6 5 4 3 2 1

Library of Congress Cataloging-in-Publication Data
Winsberg, Morton D.
Florida weather / Morton D. Winsberg; with assistance of James J. O'Brien,
David F. Zierden, and Melissa L. Griffin.—2nd ed.
p. cm.
Includes bibliographical references and index.
ISBN 0-8130-2684-9
1. Florida—Climate. I. Title.
QC984.F6W56 2003
551.69759—dc21   2003054091

The University Press of Florida is the scholarly publishing agency for
the State University System of Florida, comprising Florida A&M University,
Florida Atlantic University, Florida Gulf Coast University, Florida International
University, Florida State University, University of Central Florida, University
of Florida, University of North Florida, University of South Florida, and
University of West Florida.

University Press of Florida
15 Northwest 15th Street
Gainesville, FL 32611-2079
http://www.upf.com

NORTH BREVARD PUBLIC LIBRARY

Contents

Tables

Text

Appendix

Acknowledgments

A deep debt of gratitude is owed to a number of the state's residents with profound knowledge of its weather and climate who read early versions of the first edition carefully and made numerous suggestions. Those whose counsel was greatly valued are, in alphabetical order: Earl Jay Baker, associate professor of geography, Florida State University, Tallahassee; Fred M. Craller, meteorologist in charge, U.S. National Weather Service, Tallahassee; Thomas A. Gleeson, professor of meteorology, Florida State University, and state climatologist, Tallahassee; Paul J. Hebert, meteorologist in charge and Florida area manager, National Weather Service Forecasting Office, Miami; James A. Henry, associate professor of geography, Tennessee Technological University, Cookville; Charles L. Jordan, service professor of meteorology, Florida State University, and former state climatologist, Tallahassee; Donald J. Patton, professor of geography, Florida State University, Tallahassee; Dewey M. Stowers Jr., professor of geography, University of South Florida, Tampa.

Two climatologists from other states read the manuscript in later drafts and made many helpful comments: Peter J. Robinson, Department of Geography, University of North Carolina, Chapel Hill; and Philip W. Suckling, Department of Geography, University of Georgia, Athens.

Daniel C. Endrizzi, Peter A. Krafft, and James R. Anderson of the Institute of Science and Public Affairs, Florida State University, made cartographic contributions and designed the book. The institute also provided a grant, which partially defrayed the cost of production. Members of the Document Division of Florida State University's Strozier Library are recognized for their efforts to facilitate data collection, and David S. McCulloch merits thanks for his skill in data management. EarthInfo Inc. of Denver has placed a large share of the nation's weather data on

CD-ROM and devised programs to make those data easily accessible. Elizabeth Purdum, Institute of Science and Public Affairs, Florida State University, read the final draft of the manuscript. Recognition is given to George W. Bomar, David M. Ludlum, and George H. T. Kimble, whose books on weather and climate, written for laypersons, were inspirational. Finally, a deep debt of gratitude is owed to all the unpaid volunteers throughout Florida who for well over a century have reported its weather.

The revised edition benefited from the advice of James Elsner, professor in the Department of Geography, Florida State University; James O'Brien, director of Florida State University's Center of Oceanic and Atmospheric Prediction Studies as well as his assistants who are in charge of the center's Florida Climate Center, David Zierden and Melissa Griffin. The author is immensely grateful to Peter Krafft, staff cartographer for the Florida Resources and Environmental Analysis Center at Florida State University. He drew a number of maps and gave patient counsel to the author, who drew the rest. Also thanks are extended to Henry Fuelberg of the university's Department of Meteorology and Ron Block of the National Weather Service's station in Tallahassee, who got the author involved in the analysis of Tallahassee weather.

Full responsibility for all errors is, of course, assumed by the author.

Author's Note

The data used to construct most of the maps and tables found in the body of the book were temperature and precipitation averages. The value of averages for predicting future weather depends on the variation from them each year. If great variation from the average is frequent, the predictive power of averages is weak. In Florida, the degree of yearly variation from the mean for both temperature and precipitation differs greatly between seasons. This phenomenon will be examined closely in this book. Here it is important to warn the reader to exercise extreme caution in predicting future weather from temperature and precipitation averages, especially for periods within those seasons when one can expect great variation from one year to the next.

Although the state of Florida has a dense network of weather stations, their number is not sufficient for the construction of maps containing minute detail. Those maps that accompany the text in this work are, we hope, correct interpretations of the distribution of various elements of the climate. The lines that show this distribution are meant to suggest differences in climate throughout the state and should not be thought of as definitive boundaries. It should also be remembered that there is considerable local variation in both temperature and precipitation throughout the state that could not be captured on maps of such small scale, particularly in places along Florida's coasts and the Keys but also those near Lake Okeechobee and smaller lakes.

The march of the seasons from one end of the state to the other has been plotted on maps by selecting a temperature and determining when it reached that level at a certain place in the state. For example, the first week in winter was defined as falling on the first week after the end of November when the average maximum temperature fell to 75°F or below.

The selection of the temperature was subjective, and the reader's view of what constitutes the beginning of a season might not correspond. The maps do show that in an average year, because of the length of Florida's peninsula, a certain temperature will be reached in one part of the state before another.

Introduction

Climate is Florida's most important physical resource, a fact well recognized by its citizens, whose state government has officially designated it the Sunshine State. For the state to claim to be *the* Sunshine State is unfair to Arizona, California, and New Mexico. In their drier areas, the sun is visible from the ground longer than anywhere in Florida, where clouds frequently obscure it. Nonetheless, the southern half of Florida's peninsula does have milder winter weather than anywhere else in the 48 coterminous states.

Mild winters have been turned to great advantage by Floridians. Given that much of it is covered by infertile sandy soils, the state would never have attained national importance in farm production without these mild winters. Today it enjoys international fame for its oranges, and during the winter it supplies consumers east of the Mississippi River with a large share of their fresh vegetables. Nor would the state have become so attractive to tourists. Florida has approximately 60 million visitors annually. Though they now come as often during the summer as during the winter, Florida's tourist industry began as a refuge from the cold for people from the northern United States.

The state's mild winters appeal to many of the aged, and more have chosen to retire in Florida than in any other state. Florida ranks first nationally in the percentage of total state population aged 65 or older. Over 2.6 million immigrants, most from the Caribbean Basin, are now living in Florida, in part because of the similarity of its climate with that of the countries they left. Greater Miami today has the highest concentration of people from the Caribbean region of any large city in the nation.

Initially, nineteenth-century Florida boosters had to struggle to win favorable recognition of its climate. The long, hot, humid summer, when fatal fevers and what were then called "miasmas" afflicted the residents, was the source of much fear among those who lived in colder areas, inhibiting many from resettling there. These hazards, however, did not deter the Spanish, who maintained a small presence in Florida between the late sixteenth and early nineteenth centuries. They seemed to have accepted the oppression of its summers with little complaint, perhaps because most had become acclimated by first living in the Caribbean.

During the nineteenth century, many books and pamphlets extolling the state's climate were published to stimulate both immigration and tourism. These publications usually minimized or ignored the environmental problems that interfered with the maintenance of health as well as the pursuit of economic activity. Not until well into the twentieth century did modern technology bring under control diseases related to heat and humidity; widespread use of air-conditioning reduced discomfort, and the technological revolution in agriculture began to overcome problems in crop and livestock production.

Given the fact that today Florida's climate is a major factor in the decision to live in or visit the state, information about it should be available in a form that can be understood by the general public. This book is an attempt to describe the weather and climate of the Sunshine State through maps, tables, and narrative. Its purpose is to provide a useful reference for those who, for pleasure or profit, desire to know more about Florida's climate. It is not meant to be a scholarly work on the state's climate; for that, Henry, Portier, and Coyne's book *The Climate and Weather of Florida* is recommended.

Weekly and monthly mean temperature extremes as well as precipitation will be discussed at length. In any year, however, there can be great variations from these means. It is often when weather diverges from the normal that interesting weather events occur. Throughout the book a number of these abnormalities are examined.

In the first chapter, I discuss the major controls of weather and climate and how these controls apply to Florida. Thereafter, the organization of the book is temporal, treating in turn each of the four seasons. Visitors may want to read only the chapter related to the season of their visit. Consequently, topics related to the controls of weather and climate discussed in the first chapter may be repeated in a chapter on the season but in greater detail. I introduce important Florida weather events such as hurricanes, freezes, thunderstorms, and tornadoes with the seasons in which they occur most frequently.

Since Florida markets its weather to promote economic growth, it might seem inappropriate for a book published by the state of Florida to dwell on catastrophic weather events. My intention is not to frighten readers but rather to make them aware that, as anywhere else in the nation, at times there is a risk involved in the pursuit of outdoor activities.

I discuss air pollution only briefly, because Florida's atmosphere throughout most of the year is normally unstable enough, what with strong convectional air currents as well as prevailing winds off the Atlantic Ocean, that air pollutants are rapidly dispersed. Nonetheless, it cannot be ignored. Motor vehicles in Florida release enormous amounts of noxious gases into its atmosphere, as have a growing number of coal-fired electric plants. Although at times various cities have experienced levels of smog that are unacceptable, occurrences are rare compared with states like California and those of the northeastern United States. A serious irritant is pollen. Regrettably, information concerning the type, season, and distribution of pollen throughout the state is fragmented. Nonetheless, I address this important issue, albeit briefly.

Weather Stations

Florida's weather has been a topic of interest for centuries. Shortly after the United States acquired Florida in 1821, weather records began to be kept at the newly opened military posts. Within a few decades, weather became an economic issue with the growth of the state's citrus and winter vegetable industries. Consequently, weather stations became more common. Weather data for almost 300 stations are available, but fewer than 50 have more or less complete data for the past 30 years, an interval that those who study climate believe is acceptable to establishing meaningful averages.

A major effort has been made to select a sufficiently large number of stations that are well distributed to make an accurate analysis of the state's climate. Throughout most of the state the effort has been successful (fig. I.1). Unfortunately, there are large areas within the state that are lightly populated and in which stations are rare. This is particularly true of the Everglades and Big Cypress Swamp in South Florida, the Kissimmee River Valley in Central Florida, and the Apalachicola River Valley south of Blountstown.

Fig. I.1. The weather and wireless telegraph station at Jupiter, Florida, in 1910. *Source:* Florida State Archives.

While most National Weather Service stations in Florida are maintained in cooperation with individuals, as well as government and nongovernment agencies, the service operates twelve. These twelve stations produce far more elaborate data than the cooperative stations, most of which gather only precipitation and temperature data. While the twelve stations are too far separated from each other to cartographically display their many weather variables, some of the more important data have been collected and compiled into tables found in the book's appendix.

The Second Edition

Since climate is the average of daily weather, some might wonder why it is necessary after only 13 years to publish a second edition of *Florida Weather*. True, the weather of the 1990s differed significantly from that of

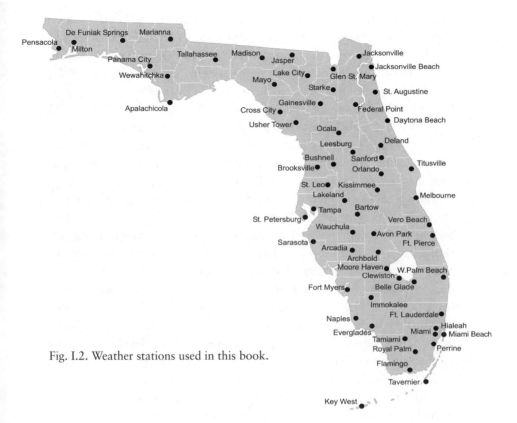

Fig. I.2. Weather stations used in this book.

some earlier decades, but climatologists don't examine climate by decade. The conventional interval for weather averages is 30 years. If one were to compare two 30-year weather averages for a station that were even 50 years apart, it is likely that the differences would be minor.

Several things, however, have transpired during the 1990s that merit a new edition. First, there has been remarkable progress in the science of weather, which continues to be a highly dynamic physical science. We can explain weather a great deal better today than even a decade ago. In this edition I have devoted far more attention to the phenomenon of the El Niño Southern Oscillation than in the previous one. Although the 1990s have produced little evidence to confirm long-term climate change, Florida, and for that matter much of the nation, has experienced an unusually large amount of weather extremes such as heat, drought, hurricanes, tornadoes, and heavy rain. Consequently, I have added to the book a section on torrential rain, expanded that of drought, and included a subsection on Hurricane Andrew, the most destructive weather event in the history of the nation. In part generated by the weather extremes of the 1990s, but also because of a growing concern over the issue of human impact on the physical environment, climatic change has become a much discussed topic. While global climatic change has generated much hyperbole, it cannot be ignored. As a consequence, I included a section on global climatic change and its possible impact on Florida. Also, since Florida continues to urbanize rapidly, urban heat islands are given greater attention.

The information revolution, which has had such a profound impact on the 1990s, has contributed greatly to this new edition. Most of the data used in the first edition were laboriously compiled onto computer spreadsheets by hand, and the software to manipulate the data was primitive compared with what is available today. Climate data today are available both on CDs and from the Internet, and can be directly imported onto spreadsheets where they can be manipulated far better than I was able to do when the first edition was being written. Virtually all climate averages in the new edition use data from 1972 through 2001. The computer also has been of benefit to the second edition because of its rich source of up-to-date weather information. While weather information for the first edition was primarily from books, journals, and newspapers, that for the second edition mainly came from the Internet. Far more information concerning the state's weather events was gleaned from the Internet, and in a much shorter period of time, than was possible from the information sources available for the first edition.

The Controls of Weather and Climate and Their Application to Florida

Before beginning a discussion of weather and climate, both words must be defined, as they are not interchangeable. *Weather* means the conditions in the atmosphere at a particular time and place. *Climate* represents weather averages or, as some climatologists would prefer to define it, the long-term state of the atmosphere. Both weather and climate depend on various controls such as latitude, altitude, mountain barriers, land and water distribution, ocean currents, prevailing winds and storms, and pressure systems. In Florida, to varying degrees and at different times, all the controls except mountain barriers influence its weather. Given the low elevation of the state, local variation in relief produces only small differences in temperature. Nonetheless, in the winter these differences may be sufficient to determine whether farmers have a successful harvest or a crop that has been destroyed by a freeze.

The Controls of Weather and Climate

Latitude

The sun is the earth's principal source of heat. The degree of heat received at a particular place is primarily dependent upon the angle of the sun's rays reaching it; the higher the angle the more intense the receipt. Each day at astronomical noon in a specific place, the sun attains its highest point above the horizon, but the angle is never the same on two successive days because the earth's rotating axis is inclined 23.5° from a plane between it and the sun. This inclination means that the place where the vertical rays of the sun strike the earth migrates during the year between 23.5° N, where it is on June 22, and 23.5° S, where it is on December 21. These two dates, which may vary by a day depending on the year, are known as days of the solstice.

South Florida and South Texas are as close to the equator as one can get in the coterminous United States. As a result, when the sun is highest in the sky on any given day, its rays strike South Florida and South Texas at a greater angle than elsewhere within the 48 states. For example, at noon on June 22, the summer solstice, the sun's rays reach Orlando at an angle of 85° whereas in New York City, 12° latitude north of Orlando, the angle of the sun would be 73°. On December 21, the winter solstice, the sun's rays hit Orlando at an angle of 38° whereas the angle would be only 26° in New York City. Since Orlando has a higher angle of the sun at its zenith on any given day than New York City, and they both are close to sea level, it has the higher average summer and winter temperatures. It should be added that the sun is above the horizon longer in Florida during the winter than farther north in the United States, which also contributes to its higher temperatures in that season. The duration of sunlight in winter is actually slightly over an hour longer in central Florida than in New York City. The reverse is true in the summer, when the duration of daylight in central Florida is about an hour less than in New York City.

Even within the state the annual receipt of energy from the sun varies, as 6.5° of latitude separate the extreme north of the state from that place farthest south. The input of the sun's energy, especially during the winter, is considerably more effective in the southern part of the state than the northern. Although other factors besides the angle of the sun contribute to the difference, Jacksonville in January has an average maximum temperature 10°F lower than that of Key West. The difference in the average July maximum temperature between the two cities, however, is only 1°F. This summer uniformity in heating throughout the state is, in part, because the length of the daylight hours in North Florida is slightly more than in South Florida, but the angle of the sun at its zenith in the northern part of the state is a few degrees lower than in its southern part. One variable compensates for the other in both parts of Florida, leading to approximately the same amount of solar radiation throughout the state.

People who come from farther north to visit or live in Florida frequently note that the period of twilight is much shorter than what they are accustomed to. Twilight results from the illumination of the higher levels of the atmosphere by the sun when it is below the horizon. The duration of twilight is shortest in the Tropics, where the apparent track of the sun down to the horizon is steepest. In fact, at the equator the period between when the sun sets and the first stars become visible in the night sky is so rapid that, with only slight exaggeration, one might think a light had been turned off. The length of twilight also varies with the season. It is shortest at the time of the equinoxes (March and September) and longest during June and December, the months of the solstices. Nautical twilight is defined as the period from sunset until the sun is 6° below the horizon. In every month of the year, nautical twilight is slightly over twice as long in New York City as in Key West, although Key West has acquired a national reputation for the beauty of its sunsets.

Land and Water Distribution

Although the sun is the earth's primary source of energy, for the air to be heated the sun's rays must first heat the earth's surface. Although land surfaces of the earth vary in their ability to absorb and to reflect heat, the most fundamental difference in heating of the earth's surface is between water and land. When water and land are exposed to the sun's rays of the same angle, the land surface will heat more rapidly than the water surface and will attain a higher temperature. There are several reasons for this difference: (1) land is opaque, and heat concentrates in a narrow layer near its surface, while sunlight penetrates water and thus heats to a considerable depth; (2) evaporation from water bodies also acts to keep the temperature of the water from rising very high; (3) at night or in the winter, radiation of heat from land is far more rapid than from water, since water of different temperature can circulate over a great depth, while solid land cannot move; (4) it takes much more heat to raise the temperature of water than land.

The temperature of air reflects the temperature of the surface it rests on. Consequently, if air moves from oceans onto the land, it is much the same temperature as the ocean's surface when it arrives. The same is true of air masses that, having been heated or cooled over land in the interior of continents, then migrate to other land areas, such as when frigid air invades the United States from the interior of Canada in the winter, or when warm air from the Gulf of Mexico is transported into the north in the same season. Air that moves onto the land from water is said to be maritime; that which moves out of the interior of continents is called continental air.

Florida is mainly a long peninsula, and with the exception of the northwestern part of the state, no place is more than 80 miles from both the Gulf of Mexico and the Atlantic Ocean. No part of northwestern Florida is more than 75 miles from the Gulf of Mexico, but that part of the state is far from the Atlantic Ocean. The surface water temperature in both the Gulf of Mexico and the Atlantic Ocean rises to about 84°F in the summer, but in the winter it falls to roughly 70°F. The water temperature of the Gulf of Mexico is a little warmer in the summer and slightly cooler in the winter than the Atlantic Ocean because the Gulf is shallower. This yearly range of water temperature is considerably less than that of the land surface along the same latitude but far from the sea. Although temperatures throughout Florida are heavily influenced by the Gulf of Mexico and the Atlantic Ocean, the greatest effects are seen nearest the coast (fig. 1.1a and 1.1b). The interior of the state normally gets higher temperatures during the day and lower temperatures at night, the result of land heating more rapidly than water during the day and cooling more rapidly at night.

It is difficult to measure the degree of influence of the ocean on the state's climate because in only a few places in Florida are there weather stations near the coast and also nearby stations farther inland. In Greater Miami, for example, we find a weather station on Miami Beach and several scattered throughout the city. When the climate of Miami Beach is compared with that of Miami International Airport, only eight miles away, there are notable differences in both temperature and precipitation. Miami Beach normally experiences lower maximum temperatures and higher minimum temperatures than the airport, and it receives less precipitation. By inference we can assume that the coastal climate throughout the state is slightly different from that even a short distance into the interior.

The maritime effect penetrates more deeply into the eastern than the western side of the peninsula because the most frequent regional-scale wind for both coasts of the peninsula, particularly during the warmer months, is out of the east (see table D.3, appendix). This wind reaches the east coast directly from the ocean but must pass over the peninsula before

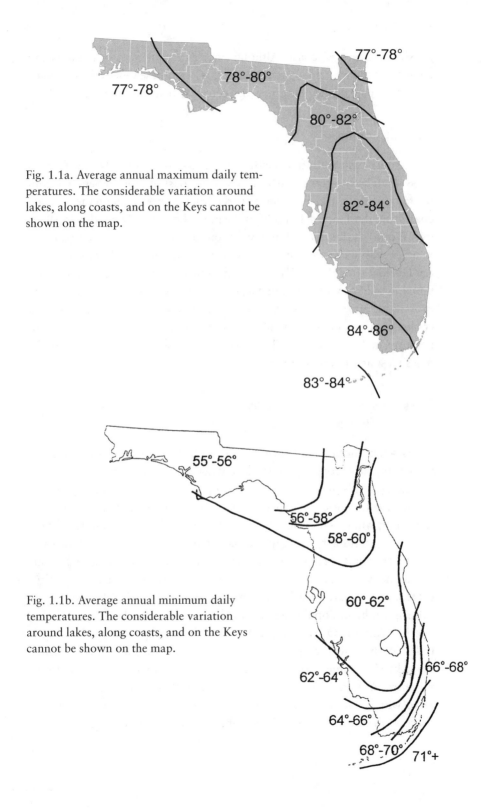

77°-78°

77°-78°

78°-80°

80°-82°

82°-84°

Fig. 1.1a. Average annual maximum daily temperatures. The considerable variation around lakes, along coasts, and on the Keys cannot be shown on the map.

84°-86°

83°-84°

55°-56°

56°-58°

58°-60°

60°-62°

66°-68°

62°-64°

Fig. 1.1b. Average annual minimum daily temperatures. The considerable variation around lakes, along coasts, and on the Keys cannot be shown on the map.

64°-66°

68°-70°   71°+

it exits on the west coast. Although not as frequent, strong winds can come from the west and reach the east coast. At these times the west coast is the first part of the peninsula to receive the maritime winds.

Ocean Currents

Ocean currents may influence the climate on land, but only when winds cross them before coming ashore. The east coast of Florida benefits from the famous Gulf Stream, a warm current that moves north up the Atlantic coast from the Tropics. It modifies the prevailing easterly wind that passes over it onto the land. Although winds out of the east are not so regular as in other seasons, in the winter this current of water helps keep southeastern Florida, roughly from Vero Beach to Key West, considerably warmer than it would be without it. In warmer seasons, when easterly winds truly prevail, the air that reaches the coast after passing over the Gulf Stream is cooler than the air over the interior of the state. The average high temperature in July at coastal Titusville is 2°F lower than at Orlando, 30 miles west and in the interior.

Pressure Systems, Prevailing Winds, Land-Sea Breezes, and Storms

Air is set in motion by moving from areas of high to low pressure. A global circulation of air is established when air rises over the heated equator and descends over the poles. The flow is not direct from the equator to a pole, because the earth's rotation on its axis causes belts of pressure and prevailing winds to develop along certain latitudes. The westerly winds, which are found between approximately 30° N and 60° N, and the easterly trade winds, between the equator and 30° N, are the most famous prevailing winds. They lie parallel to each other and diverge from a latitudinal high-pressure area located at approximately 30° N known as the subtropical high. Popular names for the well-developed subtropical high over the Atlantic Ocean are the Azores-Bermuda high and the horse latitudes. Within this high-pressure cell, air is descending and surface winds are light. The name "horse latitudes" was coined during the days of sailing ships. At times ships became becalmed in these latitudes, and to conserve water, livestock (including horses) sometimes had to be thrown overboard. In the Northern Hemisphere these two prevailing winds and

Fig. 1.2. Low- and high-pressure systems drift into the United States from the Pacific Ocean, drawing air into them in a counterclockwise manner in the case of cyclones and clockwise out of them in the case of systems of high pressure. Low-pressure systems often produce clouds and precipitation, whereas high-pressure systems produce clear skies. These systems usually follow paths of jet streams that dip deep into the southern United States in the winter. This photograph, taken from a weather satellite in October 1982, shows two low-pressure systems, one over California, the other passing into the Atlantic from North Carolina. They have followed jets streams that begin to dip southward as the continent enters its cold season. The center of the country is clear, dominated by a large high-pressure system. *Source:* NOAA.

the high-pressure belt that separates them and from which they originate lie between latitudes that include much of the United States. All three influence the weather and climate of Florida.

Within the belts of winds, low-pressure storms develop. These cyclones are of various sizes. The largest are midlatitude cyclones that often are hundreds of miles in diameter (fig. 1.2). Commonly they drift from west to east, carried along by both the polar and the subtropical jet streams, narrow, fast-moving air currents within the westerly wind belt. The paths of these jet streams are constantly changing, especially the polar. It nor-

Fig. 1.3. GOES image of Tropical Storm Diana, off the east coast of Florida, and a large tropical storm, off Baja California, on September 8, 1984. A frontal system over the Midwest extends to the lower Mississippi Valley. A low-pressure system was moving in from the Pacific, carried by the jet stream, and was hovering over Idaho. *Source:* NOAA.

mally takes a more polar route in the summer and often dips down to lower latitudes in the winter (fig. 1.3). Hurricanes, tornadoes, and waterspouts are systems of smaller diameter but with much greater differences in pressure between their centers and peripheries and as a consequence with more violent winds. More benign wind systems, also associated with low pressure but not part of the cyclone family, are land and sea breezes.

Although the process is of extraordinary complexity and only now is beginning to be understood, the origin of low-pressure systems is similar to that of the formation of whirlpools in moving water. Currents of air pass each other just as water currents do. A situation may arise where an eddy is formed. A low-pressure eddy that develops in the atmosphere of the Northern Hemisphere will have wind spiraling into it counterclockwise, but in the Southern Hemisphere it will be clockwise. As these large low-pressure systems move across the continent, they draw in air from different directions. When they pass a place, the wind direction changes, as does the temperature. Precipitation also may occur.

Especially in the north during the winter months, Florida experiences the effects of large low-pressure systems (midlatitude cyclones) that drift across the United States from west to east within the westerly wind belt. These low-pressure systems often form in the North Pacific. It thus can be said that Florida's weather results from events that take place thousands of miles away and sometimes are very minor at the time they occur. These low-pressure systems are often carried along in the aforementioned polar and subtropical jet streams. Since air spirals into these low-pressure systems in a counterclockwise manner, the direction of the wind over Florida depends on where their centers are at a particular time in relation to the state. The center could be positioned so that warm, moist air from the Gulf of Mexico is passing over all or part of Florida, or it could be delivering cold air to the state from Canada (fig. 1.4). In other seasons Florida also experiences smaller but more intense low-pressure storms, such as hurricanes, tornadoes, and waterspouts.

Masses of air with different temperatures, especially during the cooler months, frequently pass over Florida. The leading edges of these air masses are called "fronts." Thus, when a mass of cold air reaches Florida, it is described as a "cold front." Conversely, when a mass of warm air reaches the state, it is called a "warm front." During the winter, North Florida frequently experiences the chill of cold fronts, but these fronts rapidly lose their strength as they advance farther south, down the peninsula. On occasion, however, even Miami is invaded by a front that brings freezing temperatures behind it, and at least once snow has fallen on the city.

Hurricanes are tropical cyclones with extremely low pressures that form in the Atlantic, Caribbean, or Gulf of Mexico from early summer to late fall. They are far less frequent than midlatitude cyclones. Their winds, however, are a great deal stronger, and as a result these types of storms have the potential to be destructive and have been the cause of great loss

Fig. 1.4. Orange trees killed or severely injured during the 1894 "Big Freeze" in Central Florida. *Source:* Florida State Archives.

of life (fig. 1.5). On a smaller scale, but locally at least equal in their ability to do damage, are the tornado and waterspout, the latter being somewhat similar to a tornado but forming over water. Primarily spring and summer phenomena, both may occur throughout the state.

The fact that land both cools and heats more rapidly than water has created one of Florida's most important wind systems, the land-sea breeze. On a clear sunny morning, especially in summer, the ground near the shore heats rapidly, and as a result air above it is heated. Air expands and begins to rise, decreasing the surface pressure. The sea breeze commences when cooler air over the water begins to move toward the low-pressure system on the land created by the air that is rising. Because Florida is low and flat, its land-sea breeze is among the best developed in the world (Burpee, 1979; Burpee and Lahiff, 1984).

The strength of a sea breeze and the distance it penetrates onto the land depend on the difference in temperature between the water and land sur-

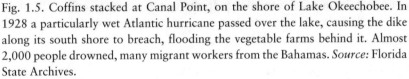

Fig. 1.5. Coffins stacked at Canal Point, on the shore of Lake Okeechobee. In 1928 a particularly wet Atlantic hurricane passed over the lake, causing the dike along its south shore to breach, flooding the vegetable farms behind it. Almost 2,000 people drowned, many migrant workers from the Bahamas. *Source:* Florida State Archives.

faces and the direction of regional-scale winds. Normally winds reach 15 to 20 miles into the interior of the peninsula, but may reach farther if pushed by a regional-scale wind. Along the northern Gulf coast of the state, strong southerly winds may push the sea breeze as far as southern Alabama and Georgia. The sea breeze is enthusiastically welcomed in summer by residents of Florida's coastal communities, since it brings relatively cool air from the ocean. As will be discussed later, sea breezes contribute greatly to precipitation over the state.

Land breezes occur at night. Because water retains its heat longer than the land, by evening the air above water becomes warmer than the air over the land nearby. Consequently, the gradient is reversed, the air moving from the higher pressure, now over the land, to the sea. Land breezes generally are weaker than sea breezes. In the summer they may not really be noticeable until early morning.

Prevailing winds are what the name implies: the most common direction from which the winds come. The direction of prevailing winds differs throughout the state, both geographically and seasonally (table D.3, appendix). These differences result primarily from changes throughout the year in the location of global pressure and wind belts. During the winter, winds throughout the state generally arrive from one of the northern quadrants, most commonly from the northwest. These northerly prevailing winds are of higher velocity than those in other seasons, particularly along the coast between Key West and West Palm Beach.

In the spring, as the Azores-Bermuda high moves northward, the prevailing wind direction over the state begins to change as well. Winds over Florida prevail out of the north in the winter, out of the south in the summer. The transition from the northern to the southern direction starts in South Florida and moves up the east coast. By midsummer, virtually the entire state has prevailing winds from the south. Unlike the winds that prevail in the winter, which often are only slightly more common than winds from other directions, the summer southeast prevailing winds truly prevail, especially in South Florida. By fall the prevailing winds begin their shift from the southern quadrants to the northern ones. The shift moves up the peninsula, arriving in North Florida by October. Average wind velocity also begins to increase.

ENSO's Effects on Florida

ENSO is an acronym for two physical environmental phenomena, El Niño and Southern Oscillation. El Niño is the name given to a warm ocean current that appears irregularly off the north Peruvian coast that overrides the normally cold current and temporarily converts the coast's desert climate into a humid one. It acquired the name, which refers to the Christ Child, during the sixteenth century when the Spanish colonists noticed that it usually arrived around Christmas. The Southern Oscillation refers to the early-twentieth-century discovery of an oscillation in surface air pressure between Tahiti in the southern Pacific Ocean and that in Darwin, Australia. When one was high, the other was low. No connection was made between El Niño and the Southern Oscillation until the middle of the twentieth century. Then meteorologists began to see how these two events contribute to the understanding of weather throughout a large portion of the world by the way they alter upper air currents and pressure belts.

El Niño proved to be more than just a warm current that periodically arrived along the Peruvian coast. It was established that the Peruvian current was associated with a general warming of the waters of the equatorial Pacific Ocean. Moreover, it was discovered that the equatorial Pacific Ocean would as frequently turn colder than normal. This phenomenon was given the feminine name La Niña. La Niña has the capacity to alter weather globally in the same manner as its brother, but with different outcomes. El Niño and La Niña return every two to seven years. Neutral years, however, outnumber the combined El Niño and La Niña years more than two to one. Oscillations in other parts of the world have been discovered that modify normal climate in the same manner as ENSO, but these oscillations do not appear to have the same degree of global impact.

Until the early 1980s, ENSO research proceeded slowly. However, the unusually long and strong El Niño of 1982–83 that was accompanied by an abnormally large number of weather aberrations throughout the world generated great interest in the degree to which the two were connected. An even stronger El Niño occurred in 1997–98, further intensifying research to unravel these connections. It is of interest to note that insurance claims in the United States for property damage that resulted from weather catastrophes were unusually high during the ENSO episodes of both 1982–83 and 1997–98. During the El Niño event of 1997–98, Florida and neighboring Georgia exceeded all other states in the number of weather catastrophes for which insurers had to pay claims of $25 million or more. Florida exceeded all other states in the number of weather catastrophes (three) that produced claims of $100 million or more. In fact, the damage to Florida property and crops during the 1997–98 El Niño was estimated at $500 million. One can appreciate why insurance companies are so enthusiastic about ENSO research, since it has the potential of advancing long-term weather predictions, which would reflect on the rates they charge.

The Center for Oceanic and Atmospheric Prediction Studies at Florida State University focuses much of its research on the ENSO phenomenon. While its primary interest is global, it has not neglected its impact on Florida. Although ENSO will be discussed in other chapters as it relates to specific weather events within Florida, what follows is a summary of how it amplifies certain climate-driven events. The operative word here is *amplifies* because all too often the popular press fixes the *cause* of catastrophic weather events on an El Niño or La Niña episode. Although

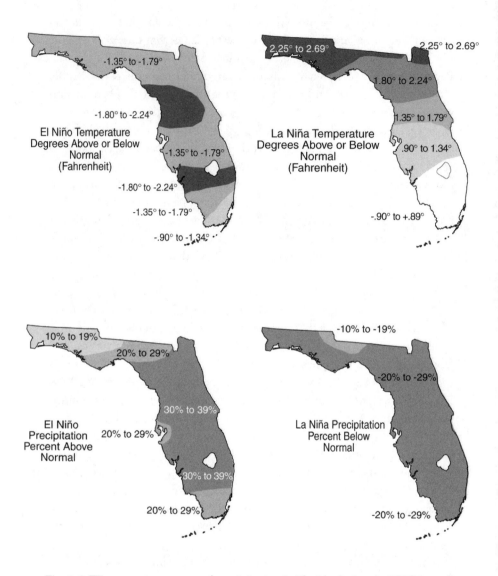

Fig. 1.6. Winter temperatures and precipitation in Florida during the El Niño and La Niña phases of ENSO. ENSO has an especially strong effect on Florida winters. *Source:* O'Brien et al., 1999.

ENSO amplifies weather events in the spring, summer, and fall, the amplification is not nearly as great as in the winter. In winter, pressure systems move jet streams and their accompanying storm tracks closer to Florida than in other seasons. Maps are also provided to show that winter temperature and precipitation in Florida during ENSO episodes differ from normal (fig. 1.6).

El Niño

- Winds and pressure: Jet streams that guide fronts and storms more frequently pass close to or over Florida.
- Rainfall: Above average.
- Temperature: Below-normal temperatures but lower frequency of severe freezes, though not those that are minor or moderate.
- Hurricanes: Reduced frequency of hurricanes.

La Niña

- Winds and pressure: Jet streams and their accompanying fronts and storms pass farther to the north and affect Florida's weather less than in El Niño and neutral years. High-pressure cells linger longer.
- Rainfall: Generally dry conditions prevail longer, but more torrential rain falls in North Florida. Prolonged droughts may extend into the summer. Wildfires greatly increase.
- Temperatures: Less cloud cover leads to above-average temperatures. Heat waves occur more frequently.
- Hurricanes: Chances increase substantially. Slight increase in tornadoes.

(Lists from O'Brien et al., 1999)

Precipitation

The only effective manner by which large quantities of moisture can be released from the air is to lower the air temperature until it falls below the dew point. The dew point is reached when water vapor in the air begins to condense into microscopic water droplets or, if cooled enough, tiny ice crystals. Clouds then start to form. Even then the conditions for precipitation have not been reached, for the water droplets and ice crystals usually are too small. They must grow in size before precipitation occurs. If they don't grow, they will simply evaporate and the cloud will disappear. In warmer regions, such as Florida, rain is often produced by the collision of water droplets and ice particles until they reach the size of raindrops. Then they fall from the cloud.

The best way air can be cooled quickly to the point of condensation is for it to be forced into higher altitudes. Air that rises expands as it reaches elevations of lower pressure, and this expansion in turn causes it to cool. There are four basic types of atmospheric lifting from which precipitation may occur: orographic, frontal, convective, and convergent.

Air forced up mountain barriers may rise to an elevation sufficient for precipitation to occur. This type of precipitation is called *orographic.* Some of the wettest places in the world are on the windward sides of mountains. Air also can be lifted aloft when a mass of air of higher temperature meets one that has a lower temperature (*frontal precipitation*). Since warm air normally is more buoyant and unstable than colder air, the warm air will rise over the cold. The warm air may be forced high enough to be cooled to the point where the water vapor within it condenses into water, clouds form, and precipitation occurs. Great amounts of warmer air are often forced over colder air during the passage of midlatitude cyclones. Air can be forced to rise during the summer when, locally, the ground is heated sufficiently that air above it becomes unstable and begins to rise. A convectional current of air may develop. If the air reaches a high enough altitude, water vapor condenses into water droplets and clouds form. In time, rain may fall from the clouds to the ground. This form of precipitation is known as *convectional.* Convectional rainstorms usually are accompanied by thunder and lightning. Air masses also can be lifted aloft when two masses of similar temperature meet (*convergent precipitation*). Uplift occurs because of crowding, in much the same way that toothpaste is squeezed from a tube.

Clouds assume different shapes, depending on how the water vapor in the air was cooled to the point of condensation (fig. 1.7). Various types of cumulus clouds are typically associated with convection and convergence, and in Florida they are most frequent in the summer months. Cirrus and stratus clouds are more associated with orographic and frontal precipita-

Fig. 1.7. Four types of clouds are commonly seen over Florida: (a) cirrus (high altitude, any time of year);

(b) stratus (low altitude, typical of winter, particularly in North Florida);

(c) cumulus (fair weather, most common in warm months); and

(d) cumulonimbus (cumulus clouds that have developed into thunderheads, most common in summer). *Source:* NOAA.

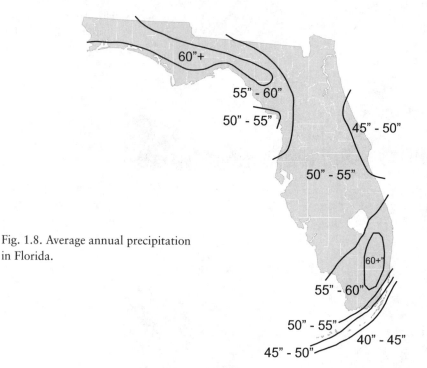

Fig. 1.8. Average annual precipitation in Florida.

tion. In Florida they are most common in the winter, in association with frontal activity, especially in the north.

Florida is among the wettest parts of the United States, most places getting at least 50 inches of rainfall annually (fig. 1.8). Although it is often assumed that there are many more days of precipitation in Florida than in states farther north, that is not the case. Throughout most of the state, a tenth of an inch or more of precipitation falls on 70 to 80 days in an average year. In New York, the average number is 76 days, in Cincinnati 77, and in Chicago 70.

Doesken and Eckrich (1987) provide further evidence that the length of time that rain falls in Florida is not unusually long. They have calculated for the entire nation the average share of hours during the year in which there was at least a trace of measurable rain or melted snow. In the area around the Great Lakes, the share is between 18 and 21 percent; in Florida, it is approximately 10 percent, a little higher in the north than in the south. In the United States, the lowest share of hours when there is

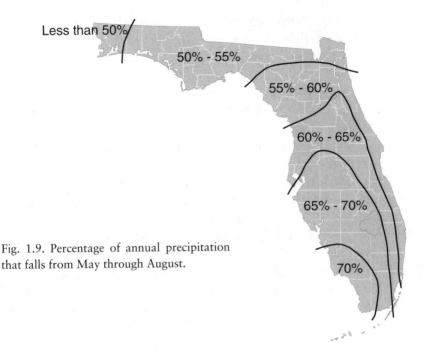

Fig. 1.9. Percentage of annual precipitation that falls from May through August.

precipitation is in the desert of the Southwest, where it is 3 percent of the time.

Except for North Florida, which gets winter rain from passing low-pressure systems, the rest of the state receives most of its precipitation during the warm months (fig. 1.9). Most of that rain is from thunderstorms, and these occur most frequently in the afternoon. The rest of the daylight hours are normally bright and sunny. Confidence that the sun will be visible from the ground sometime each day is so great in St. Petersburg that a local newspaper once had a policy of giving away free papers following any day in which the sun was never visible from the ground.

It is in the intensity of its precipitation that Florida differs from states farther north. Of the days in Florida in which there is measurable precipitation, between 30 and 35 percent have accumulations of half an inch or more, compared with 15 to 25 percent in states north of the Ohio River. On many of these rainy days in Florida, the source is a thunderstorm.

When it rains in Florida, it usually pours. This axiom applies best to the state's western panhandle and the area between West Palm Beach and Miami, known as the Gold Coast. They are the wettest places in the state, with approximately 60 inches of precipitation falling each year (fig. 1.8). Although there is little difference throughout the state in the number of days each year when there is measurable precipitation, there is a considerable difference in the number of days on which there is heavy rain. For example, in these two wettest portions of Florida, in an average year there are about 37 days in which the total rainfall is at least one-half inch. In each year there are normally about 21 days when rainfall is over one inch and two to three days when it is over three inches. The driest place in the state is the Keys, where annual precipitation averages about 40 inches. Compared to the panhandle and the Gold Coast, the Keys have only about half the number of days when rainfall is one or two inches or more.

Most of the torrential rain is produced by storms that enter Florida from either the Gulf of Mexico or the Atlantic Ocean, so the coasts receive a far larger share of their annual precipitation from these storms than does the interior (fig. 1.10). Along both panhandle and southeastern coasts, it is around 17 percent of their totals. In the peninsular interior it falls to about 8 percent. The annual frequency of tropical storms varies greatly, and these percentages are only averages.

Florida is too low in elevation for precipitation to occur through air being forced up by landforms to a higher elevation (orographic precipitation). There are excellent opportunities in the winter, however, for warm air masses to meet and rise over cooler ones (frontal precipitation), particularly in North Florida. Also, throughout the state in the summer, moist air above warm ground is constantly being heated during the day and lifted aloft. As it rises, the water vapor within it condenses, clouds form, and perhaps precipitation falls (convectional precipitation). Finally, during the summer, with sea breezes from the Atlantic Ocean and the Gulf of Mexico converging on the hot center of the state, conditions are ripe for massive amounts of air to be lifted aloft, followed by precipitation (convergent precipitation). Florida's peninsular shape and geographical situation provide some of the best conditions of any place in the world for convergent precipitation.

Whereas peninsular Florida receives a large quantity of rain, only a small share of it falls during the winter and spring. In part, as mentioned, this is because the peninsula rarely receives the full force of the winter frontal storms that bring rain and sometimes even snow to the northern part of the state. Another explanation for the lack of winter rainfall over

Fig. 1.10. An offshore rain shower from a squall line of cumulonimbus clouds off the beach at Boca Raton. *Source:* NOAA.

the peninsula, especially its southern half, is that the winds off the Atlantic Ocean that blow out of the Azores-Bermuda high-pressure cell in the winter and spring are usually stable. They actually acquire characteristics similar to those that flow throughout the entire year off the Atlantic Ocean onto the Sahara Desert. The vertical structure of these winter and spring air masses inhibits the growth of cumulus and cumulonimbus clouds, the principal sources of summer rain. (More will be said about this in chapter 3.) Northwest Florida, one of the state's wettest areas, gets rain from both winter frontal storms and summer storms of convective origin. This part of the state has a higher percentage of its annual rainfall in the winter than any other section.

Climates Similar to Florida's

Although some boosters would like to believe Florida's climate is unique, many parts of the world have similar climates (table E, appendix). All fit within the climatic classification known as *humid subtropics*. By some definitions, however, that portion of the peninsula south of Miami is regarded as a part of the true tropics. Humid subtropical climates are generally found on the southeastern sides of continents on both sides of the equator between latitudes 25° and 37°. Climates here are strongly influenced by the western portions of subtropical high-pressure cells that develop over oceans. The one that affects Florida is the Azores-Bermuda high. During the summer, the westward-moving air that flows out of the equatorward side of these high-pressure systems picks up much moisture as it moves across the oceans. When that air reaches a landmass whose surface is warm, through convectional heating the air rises and the moisture is released. Hot and humid summers are the most familiar characteristics of the humid subtropical climate.

In winter the high-pressure cell does not assert as strong an influence over the weather of the humid subtropical climate as it does in the summer. This difference appears especially in the two Northern Hemisphere humid subtropical areas, located in the southeastern parts of the United States and southern China. Winter temperatures in these two areas are greatly affected by blasts of cold air from the large continental land masses situated poleward of them. In Florida, however, temperatures are less affected by cold air masses from the continental interior than places in China on a similar latitude because it is mainly a peninsula, extending into the Atlantic Ocean, which at this latitude is relatively warm.

The Southern Hemisphere has three humid subtropical climatic regions: one situated on the east coast of the Union of South Africa, another that includes the pampas of Argentina, Paraguay, Uruguay, and Brazil, and a third on the northeastern coast of Australia and northern New Zealand. Distinct from Northern Hemisphere humid subtropical regions, all three have oceans, not large land masses, poleward of them. Since the polar air that reaches these Southern Hemisphere humid subtropical climates must first pass over water, their cold spells are less severe than those of comparable climatic areas in the Northern Hemisphere.

The cultural similarities between the United States and Australia are well known to people of both nations. Few Floridians are aware, however, that on the east coast of the Australian state of Queensland there is found a climate similar to that of Florida's east coast. Both states are officially designated the Sunshine State, and portions of each of their coasts are known as the Gold Coast. Situated just south of Brisbane, Australia's Gold Coast is served by Highway 1, the same number as the highway that serves Florida's Gold Coast. Along Australia's Gold Coast there are, as well, the towns of Miami and Palm Beach. In a lapse of geographical logic, an apartment complex on Australia's Gold Coast was named Tallahassee, after Florida's capital, which is located in the state's northern interior. Although there are similarities of climate between the two Gold Coasts, the sea off Australia's coast is far better for surfing, which is why it is also known as Surfers' Paradise.

Florida's Seasons

A source of frequent complaint among northern migrants to Florida is its lack of distinct seasons. It is true that the farther south one goes in the United States, the transition is less clear between one season and another, especially in temperature. Florida is not so close to the equator, however, that it experiences approximately the same temperature throughout the year.

Some who arrive from the North yearn for the brilliant display of fall colors that they remember from where they formerly lived. Many of Florida's deciduous trees shed their leaves throughout the year, not just in the fall. In the northern half of the state, there are a number of species that display fall colors, although the radiance of most does not equal that of northern trees. Many Florida trees that drop their leaves in the fall lose them more slowly than those of the North, which might be some compensation to those northerners who miss the bright autumnal colors. Although fall may be a disappointment to the transplanted northerner, spring is acclaimed by most. It is long, especially in South Florida, with weather that is mild and comparatively dry. A succession of trees, shrubs, and smaller flowering plants come into bloom for varying periods throughout this protracted period.

The offshore bars and keys from Miami Beach to Key West have the least difference between the coldest and warmest periods of the year. Barely 25°F separates the average maximum temperature of the warmest day of the year and the average minimum temperature of the coldest night of the year. The difference increases as one proceeds up the state, until the difference is over 55°F in the interior of North Florida. Coastal positions everywhere in the state always have less distinct seasonal variation in temperature than those in the nearby interior, since they are modified by winds off the water. To put Florida's less distinct seasons in perspective with those farther north, in Chicago, Cleveland, and New York City there is a difference of approximately 70°F between the average maximum temperature of the warmest day of the year and the average minimum temperature on the coldest night of the year. In Minneapolis, the difference is 84°F, in Atlanta, 58°F.

Although Florida's seasons are not as clearly differentiated from each other by temperature as are seasons throughout the northern United States, they do differ in other ways. In the southern half of the peninsula, normally there is a well-defined winter and spring dry season when the relative humidity is markedly lower than in the other two seasons. Throughout the state, thunderstorms set off the summer, since they are heavily concentrated in that season. Northerners who find Florida's climate monotonous compared with the places that they left might learn to use criteria other than temperature to differentiate one season from another. In the chapters that follow, a number of criteria besides those mentioned will be presented.

Airborne Allergens, Ozone, and Other Air Pollutants

Florida is not immune from airborne pollens that cause allergic reactions in humans (table 1.1). It even has ragweed, perhaps the nation's most infamous pollen and the leading cause of hay fever. However, Florida cities seldom appear on lists of the nation's cities with the highest pollen counts. Oak pollen seems to be the most common irritant, especially in north and central Florida. It is pine pollen, however, that regularly is blamed. Pine pollen certainly is more conspicuous, since it is larger and often coats automobiles in a yellow-green film. However, it is so heavy that it does not disperse very far. Oak pollen is smaller and lighter and drifts much farther. As a result of an especially dry winter and spring, Tampa was ranked first on the spring 2000 list of large U.S. cities with the highest pollen count, based on excessive amounts of oak, cedar, and grass pollens. On the same list, Orlando was third with approximately the same pollens.

Tropical South Florida probably has the most complex variety of pollen allergens. Here many exotic plants have been introduced, a number of which can produce pollen that is an irritant to a significant proportion of

Table 1.1. Common airborne allergens in Florida

	Jan	Feb	Mar	Apr	May	Jun	Jul	Aug	Sep	Oct	Nov	Dec
Pecan, oaks, cedar, pine, palms, etc.		x	x	x	x							
Grasses: Bermuda, Bahia, rye, fescue, etc.	x	x	x	x	x	x	x	x	x	x	x	x
Weeds: ragweed, plantain, nettle, etc.						x	x	x	x	x	x	

Source: University of Florida, Dept. of Otolaryngology, 2002.

the population. Furthermore, since it is tropical, there is no true pollen season for many plants. At any time of the year, some pollen that might cause an allergic reaction is in the air. The National Jewish Medical and Research Center, on its web page, has published a list of plants of the area that produce particularly irritating pollens, most of which are probably unknown to the general reader.

Florida does not suffer from the degree of air pollution that is experienced by many other states. In fact, it is only one of two states east of the Mississippi—the other being Vermont—that regularly meet all of the national ambient air quality standards established by the U.S. Environmental Protection Agency. The infamous smog days associated with cities in such states as California, Texas, Pennsylvania, New Jersey, and Ohio are rare in Florida. The year 2002 was one in which most states saw an increase in the number of smog days from the previous year. In Florida the number dropped from 14, already among the lower third in the nation, to 2 (USPIRG, 2002).

Florida has both the topography and climate to inhibit the buildup of pollutants in the atmosphere. Because it is flat, there are few valleys in which pollutants can be trapped during periods of temperature inversion. Also, because much of Florida is peninsular and no place in it is far from either the Atlantic Ocean or the Gulf of Mexico, breezes can sweep polluted air out to sea. The state's Department of Environmental Protection deserves some credit because it enforces emission standards.

Despite a physical environment that favors the dispersal of air pollutants and the government's rigid enforcement of pollution standards, Florida occasionally experiences air pollution problems. These occur especially during periods of drought, when high-pressure systems and their accompanying temperature inversions cover parts of the state. During droughts, wildfires may occur, creating enormous smoke plumes. Smoke from the state's coal-fired electric generating plants and paper mills also becomes trapped in the air, along with automobile emissions. Between 1998 and 2000, Florida experienced three severe droughts that were widespread, causing air quality to decline significantly. Since then precipitation patterns have become more normal, and air quality has improved to the point where, in most metropolitan areas it is even better than before the drought.

The U.S. Environmental Protection Agency requires all metropolitan areas with a population greater than 350,000 to calculate its Air Quality Index (AQI) daily. In Florida, 18 metropolitan areas participate, some because their size requires it, others because they volunteered. The index has five levels; a day may be good, moderate, unhealthy for sensitive groups, unhealthy, and very unhealthy. Florida's cities enjoy a remarkable high number of days in the year that are classified "good" (table 1.2), and all have shown considerable improvement over time, despite the fact that in 2001 the agency added a new pollutant to its index that had to be measured. Nonetheless, in each year there is considerable variation among them. Four stand out from the others as having markedly fewer days when air quality is good: Orlando, Pensacola, St. Petersburg, and Tampa.

The Tampa Bay area is currently the smog capital of Florida, but even here the number of days in which it appears is low. The fourth week of August in 2001 was one of those periods. During a prolonged dry period, which is unusual for August, ozone levels rose above those that scientists consider safe for people with respiratory problems. County officials began to encourage residents to reduce their amount of driving, as well as other activities that contribute to the high ozone levels. Those with respiratory problems were cautioned to stay indoors.

The Tampa Bay area has long experienced higher ozone levels than other metropolitan areas of the state (table 1.2). It has been the subject of investigations to ascertain the reasons why and what can be done to decrease the levels. Much of the problem rests with motor vehicle use, but the Tampa Bay area does not have a disproportionately higher per capita vehicular use than metropolitan areas elsewhere in the state. It does, however, have a higher concentration of coal-powered electric plants that expel noxious gases into the air (Pinellas County, 2001). Measures have

Table 1.2. Number of days designated good on the air quality index

City	1993	1994	1995	1996	1997	1998	1999	2000	2001	2002
Bradenton	203					274	259	248	330	345
Daytona Beach		310	309	312	285	277	192	295	340	350
Fernandina Beach						363	259	248	327	331
Fort Lauderdale	293	293	303	319	307	286	289	321	329	342
Fort Myers	325	321	322	331	309	291	295	292	343	359
Jacksonville	265	302	291	276	280	257	257	266	291	305
Kissimmee						274	277	252	351	358
Lakeland	293	310	294	307	288	265	264	257	324	337
Melbourne	259	213	311	318	298	273	274	277	339	350
Miami	287	305	293	300	303	279	281	301	319	330
Ocala	206					180	269	266	334	338
Orlando	269	213	267	294	284	252	247	252	283	300
Pensacola	284	295	271	248	252	254	220	224	289	292
Saint Petersburg		297	284	299	270	267	242	243	277	294
Sanford						267	266	269	335	348
Sarasota	262	296	255	311	261	264	268	243	318	340
Tampa	174	182	227	234	207	222	200	213	252	278
West Palm Beach	248	329	314	319	316	298	222	309	318	344

Source: Florida Dept. of Environmental Protection (1993–2002).
Note: Since 2001 a new pollutant (pm2.5) has been added to the air quality index. This markedly reduced the number of days classified as "good" in the northern part of the state but only slightly in the southern part.

been taken to reduce pollution from the power plants. One of the largest is being refitted to use natural gas, and efforts are under way to reduce coal pollutant emissions at other plants. Also, national motor vehicle emission standards on new vehicles are to be implemented in 2004 that will eventually reduce the level of ozone in the atmosphere.

Acid rain is not a major environmental issue in Florida compared with the Northeast, where it has become a subject of great concern. As previously mentioned, efforts are being made in Florida to reduce the introduction of noxious emissions into the atmosphere that raise the acidity of rain, and it is unlikely that acid rain will become a problem. Furthermore, storms that enter Florida do not bring as highly acidic rain as do those that reach the Northeast.

The Urban Heat Island

We have always known that the climate in cities is different from the climate of rural areas. Through countless movies we have come to identify London nights with intense fog, and most who swelter in cities during the summer long to escape to the countryside. The principal reason cities have different climates than even the area that immediately surrounds them is the difference in their surfaces (Henry, Portier, and Coyne, 1994).

Much of the surface of cities is either concrete, asphalt, or roofing material of various types. These artificial surfaces often absorb heat more easily than the natural vegetation of a rural area and retain it for longer periods. Furthermore, there is a much larger area in surfaces that absorb heat within a city than a rural area. Not only are there horizontal surfaces, but there are walls as well. Much of the surface of an urban area (roofs, roads, etc.) is impervious to rain, which runs off into sewers and is directed underground through conduits where it is released on the edge of town into bodies of water. Since there is so much less evaporation within cities than in rural areas, this reduces the opportunity for cooling.

Also, given the dense concentration of people in cities, their activities generate huge amounts of heat. Buildings and vehicles consume immense amounts of energy. In Florida this is particularly true during the summer. These and other factors mean that cities normally have higher temperatures than the less densely populated areas that surround them. They also have lower humidity, more fog and clouds, less solar radiation, lower wind speeds, more precipitation, and often more thunderstorms (Henry, Portier, and Coyne, 1994). The heat island effect is most operative in the winter and summer, periods in which interior climate control utilizes the most energy. Furthermore, minimum temperatures are more affected by them than maximum. This is because the lowest temperature of a 24-hour period is usually at night when surfaces are releasing, not absorbing, heat. In cities, the larger surface area absorbs more heat and therefore releases heat over a longer period of time. Consequently, average urban minimum temperatures, which usually occur during the night, tend to be higher in cities than in nearby rural areas.

The county within Florida with the largest population is Miami-Dade. It also has the highest number of active weather stations, scattered throughout in such a manner that its urban as well as its rural areas are covered. It is appropriate to examine the heat island effect by analyzing the temperature and precipitation data of these six stations (table 1.3). A 12-year period was chosen instead of the conventional 30 years because several stations would have passed from rural or suburban during the 30-year period, becoming suburban or urban. Hialeah and Miami International Airport are quite close to each other, and both are now completely surrounded by extensive urban development. Miami Beach is a climatic oddity and perhaps should not be included within the study. Its station is located in an urban setting but on the shoreline. However, it is not the urban environment that is largely responsible for its temperature but its proximity to the ocean. The station's temperatures are so modified by the ocean that it usually has the highest minimum temperature of any Miami-Dade County station throughout the year and the lowest maximum temperature. Perrine is a large suburb 12 miles south of the city center, Royal Palm Station is in Everglades National Park, and Tamiami 40-Mile Bend is on the extreme western side of the county, outside the park but in the Everglades.

Table 1.3 clearly shows that Greater Miami experiences a heat island effect, and it is especially evident from examining minimum temperature. When urban minimum temperatures are compared with those experienced in the suburbs and rural areas, they are found to be two to five degrees higher for all four seasons. The difference between the maximum temperature of lightly populated Miami-Dade County and its more densely populated portion is less apparent. In fact, except for the summer,

Table 1.3. Average annual and seasonal temperature and precipitation for six Miami-Dade County weather stations, 1990–2001

Maximum Temperature (in °F)

		Winter	Spring	Summer	Fall	Annual
Hialeah	Urban	79	89	91	86	87
Miami Beach	Urban[a]	76	80	88	83	76
Miami Int. Airport	Urban	78	83	90	85	84
Perrine	Suburban	77	83	90	85	84
Royal Palm Station	Rural	79	85	90	86	85
Tamiami 40 Mile Bend	Rural	79	86	92	87	86

Minimum Temperature (in °F)

		Winter	Spring	Summer	Fall	Annual
Hialeah	Urban	63	69	77	72	70
Miami Beach	Urban[a]	67	74	79	72	73
Miami Int. Airport	Urban	63	69	77	73	70
Perrine	Suburban	57	63	73	68	65
Royal Palm Station	Rural	58	62	73	69	69
Tamiami 40 Mile Bend	Rural	60	65	75	71	68

Precipitation (in inches)

		Winter	Spring	Summer	Fall	Annual
Hialeah	Urban	7.94	12.38	28.63	26.53	75.48
Miami Beach	Urban[a]	6.40	7.98	15.74	15.11	45.23
Miami Int. Airport	Urban	6.49	10.91	24.55	24.59	66.54
Perrine	Suburban	6.30	11.98	28.43	21.25	67.96
Royal Palm Station	Rural	4.65	10.46	23.23	18.28	56.62
Tamiami 40 Mile Bend	Rural	5.93	10.51	24.09	17.91	58.44

Source: Raw data from the National Weather Service, calculations by the author.
a. Strong oceanic influence.

the rural parts of the county are slightly warmer. It might be true that precipitation is often greater over large cities than the rural areas that surround them, but that does not seem to be true of Greater Miami. The pattern is irregular throughout the county, and it is not governed by degree of urbanity. It is evident, however, that Miami Beach's station has far less precipitation than the others. This can be explained by its proximity to the ocean and the lack of opportunity, compared with the other stations, for the conditions to produce convectional precipitation (thunderstorms).

Global Warming

Climate change, specifically the warming of the earth's atmosphere, has been a cause of recent concern among environmentally conscious Americans, but the earth has been experiencing climatic changes since its inception. For much of geological history, as the earth cooled, the atmosphere above it did so as well. However, the trend toward lower temperatures has not been constant. On any scale one wishes to choose, whether billions, millions, thousands, or hundreds of years, the average temperature of the earth has oscillated. The earth presently is in the interglacial period of an especially cold period that at its peak sent glaciers in North America as far south as the Ohio River. During these cold periods, so much water was locked up in ice that the levels of the oceans were much lower than today. Even within the interglacial period in which we live there have been periods of cold. For example, between the thirteenth and nineteenth centuries in the Northern Hemisphere, particularly in Western Europe, there was a period of cold that has come to be known as "the Little Ice Age" (Fagan, 2000). During the twentieth century, global temperature has been rising, especially since about 1980 (NOAA).

The first humans reached Florida about 10,000 years ago, at the close of the most recent global glacial period. They arrived at a time when the sea level was much lower than it is today, and as a consequence the peninsula was considerably wider, especially on its western side. The climate was both colder and drier, and as a result the natural vegetation and native fauna were markedly different from today's. The peninsula had fewer forests and more grassland. On the grassland grazed a number of animals that now are extinct, including the mammoth and the saber-toothed tiger.

A vivid example of how different the environment was then was discovered by underwater archaeologists in the 1980s. While exploring the bottom of Sarasota Bay, they found a 10,000-year-old Indian campsite beside a sinkhole that today is far below the surface of the Gulf of Mexico.

The Greenhouse Effect

Many scientists have come to believe that our increased use of energy, through the greenhouse effect, will lead to local climate change and global warming. They contend that the great increase in the use of fuels, particularly fossil, has released into the air many gases (primarily carbon dioxide, methane, nitrous oxide, and chlorofluorocarbons), which have created atmospheric conditions that approximate those in a greenhouse. Just as the sun's rays penetrate the glass of a greenhouse and warm the surface in its interior but the heat that radiates from that surface is trapped below the glass, the sun's heat warms the earth's surface but the aforementioned gases prevent the heat from escaping.

Although some still doubt that the world's climate is warming, the evidence continues to mount. Biologists have noted it through changes in the geographical distribution of both plants and animals (Schneider and Root, 2002). Plants and animals are spreading poleward, among other things. The National Climate Data Center recently announced that the 11 hottest years the world has experienced between 1880 and 2002 have occurred since 1987. If this evidence proves a global warming trend, and the temperature of the earth's atmosphere is lowered substantially, there will be severe environmental and economic consequences (U.S. Environmental Protection Agency, 1997). Higher temperatures are likely to bring more heat waves, the amount and distribution of precipitation will be altered, and one can expect more torrential rain episodes as well as prolonged droughts (Union of Concerned Scientists). A study of precipitation throughout the United States during the twentieth century, a period in which energy use expanded enormously, reports a steady increase in the number of torrential rain episodes and the share of torrential rain in the nation's total precipitation. The increase varies considerably by region (Karl and Knight, 1998). Under the stress of climate change, some flora and fauna would decline in importance and possibly become extinct. Others would flourish. If the direction were toward warming, glaciers would once again melt rapidly and the level of the sea would rise. Since a large share of the world's population lives close to the sea, the economic costs

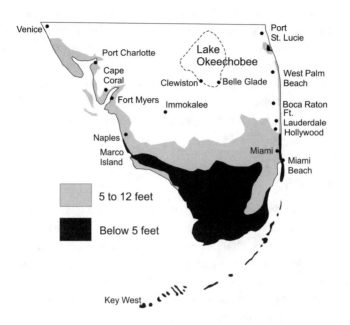

Fig. 1.11. Approximate area of South Florida that would be inundated if the seas rose five feet. *Source:* Titus and Richman, 2001.

of protecting this population from the encroachment of the sea will be enormous. Some have predicted a 20-inch rise in sea level by the end of the twenty-first century. Such a rise would have a tremendous effect on Florida's population, since most of its residents live along its shoreline. Although a sea level rise of five feet during the next century is inconceivable, figure 1.11 shows how low South Florida is by indicating how much land would be inundated.

These scenarios, however, are not certain. Today there is some evidence that some parts of the world are warming, but for most there is no clear trend in either direction (Soon, Idso, Idso, and Legates, 2003). A few have been cooling. However, if there truly were a rapid global warming, some scientists believe that it could not continue for long, because the warming itself would lead to a situation where the climate would turn cold. At present the warm Gulf Stream moves up the East Coast and at about the latitude of Maine turns eastward, where it continues toward Western Europe. The Gulf Stream modifies the air above it, and maritime Europe is considerably warmer than it would be if the Gulf Stream did not exist. However, global warming might melt so much water from the polar ice cap and Greenland's glaciers that the stream of freshwater released would flow with such intensity out of the Davis Strait between Greenland and Canada that when it reached the Gulf Stream it would divert it or even dissipate it, causing Europe to experience the same temperatures as frigid Newfoundland and Labrador, situated in the same latitudes (Lemley, 2002). The same phenomenon could affect warm currents elsewhere in the world, although it is not expected to be so dramatic in the southern hemisphere.

Climate Change

Mindful that many factors are involved in climatic change and that it is impossible to accurately disaggregate the contribution of each, it is appropriate here to examine changes over time in Florida's climate.

First, trends in the state's mean average temperature and precipitation are examined. These have been calculated since 1895 by averaging the temperature and precipitation of stations throughout the state that have been chosen in such a manner that all parts of the state are equally represented. Ignoring local and regional factors that might have caused the changes, if the average annual temperature of the state in the last quarter of the 1895–2001 period is compared with the first quarter, the more recent period was approximately 0.3°F warmer. The period 1990 to 2001 was one of exceptional warmth. When the warmest 27 years between 1895 and 2001 were identified (one-quarter of the total), six occurred between 1990 and 2001. That was slightly more than double the number that would have been expected if the same factors were operative throughout all 107 years. Florida's hottest year between 1895 and 2001 was 1990, and the second hottest was 1998. By contrast, no year since 1990 is among the 27 coldest years. Recently preliminary temperature data for 2002 has been released. That year the state experienced the twentieth warmest winter since 1895 (National Climate Data Center).

It is useful to examine the direction of change over time by season. Six of the top 27 hottest summers have occurred between 1990 and 2001, and 1998 was the hottest. Five of the 27 hottest springs, four of the hottest winters, and three of the hottest falls have been experienced since 1990. In contrast, no winter or summer between 1990 and 2001 was among the coldest 27. However, there were three in the spring and one in the fall. Clearly something has happened recently to cause so many unusually warm years, as well as summer and winter seasons, and so few that were unusually cool. It may result because some of the stations used to create the averages are located in places that have become increasingly more urban and are experiencing higher temperatures from the urban heat island effect. The contribution of global warming, however, no longer can be dismissed.

The difference in the state's precipitation averages between earlier and more recent years is less dramatic than it is for temperature. Nonetheless, the number of years between 1990 and 2001 that had average annual precipitation in the top 27 was slightly larger than normal (five), and somewhat below normal for the driest years. Summer in Florida is a good example of the fickleness of nature, since there were five summers between 1990 and 2001 that were among the wettest 27 in the 107-year period and four that were among the driest 27. The second driest summer on record was experienced in 1993, but 1995 was the fifth wettest. Five of the 12 falls between 1990 and 2001 were among the wettest. Since fall is the height of the hurricane season, and hurricanes are huge rain producers, this is not surprising. However, there were very few hurricanes during those 12 years.

An examination of the weather records of representative stations in different parts of Florida could further illuminate the direction and degree of climate change within the state. Although today the state has a dense network of weather stations, most have been in existence less than 50 years. Only 24 have maintained records longer. Ideally a station in a rural area, far from the modifying influence of the Gulf of Mexico and the Atlantic Ocean, with a complete set of observations over a long period would be the best choice. Unfortunately, many with observations of 70 years or more are situated in large metropolitan areas, and their climates have warmed over time because of urbanization. Others are coastal stations. Seven, however, met the criteria of being rural, far from the coast, and having almost complete records. Among them three were chosen, each representing one section of the state. Moore Haven, on the western shore of Lake Okeechobee, is the southern representative. Bartow represents the center, and Lake City, near the Georgia border, represents the north. The panhandle could not be included within the group, since there were no rural stations in its interior that had sufficiently complete records.

In table 1.4, annual and seasonal precipitation and temperature data for these stations were broken down into seven decades, beginning in

Table 1.4. Ten-year precipitation (in inches) and temperature (in degrees F) averages for three Florida stations

Moore Haven	1932–41	1942–51	1952–61	1962–71	1972–81	1982–91	1992–01
Ann. precip.	50.67	46.36	53.63	48.34	44.85	47.26	47.42
Ann. max. temp.	83.26	83.98	82.73	82.82	83.53	84.08	83.47
Ann. min. temp.	62.66	63.22	63.11	62.61	62.03	63.52	63.65
Winter precip.	2.23	1.53	2.41	2.35	1.75	2.93	2.54
Spring precip.	4.72	4.43	5.79	4.96	4.28	4.36	4.43
Summer precip.	7.62	7.55	6.87	6.36	7.19	6.11	6.58
Fall precip.	2.31	1.94	2.81	2.44	1.74	2.35	2.26
Winter max. temp.	77.03	77.97	76.00	75.07	76.30	76.70	76.47
Spring max. temp.	86.27	87.77	86.33	86.83	87.53	87.33	86.83
Summer max. temp.	90.20	90.63	90.00	90.40	90.67	91.10	90.83
Fall max. temp.	79.53	80.00	78.87	78.90	79.83	80.63	79.80
Winter min. temp.	54.14	54.74	53.63	52.54	52.05	54.48	54.44
Spring min. temp.	64.69	65.10	66.33	66.12	65.33	65.71	66.17
Summer min. temp.	71.81	71.81	72.55	72.52	71.66	72.49	72.84
Fall min. temp.	60.00	61.22	59.92	59.24	59.10	61.40	61.13

Bartow	1932–41	1942–51	1952–61	1962–71	1972–81	1982–91	1992–01
Ann. precip.	55.00	53.87	59.17	51.33	48.48	51.05	51.44
Ann. max. temp.	82.95	84.58	84.01	83.48	84.37	84.01	83.53
Ann. min. temp.	61.60	61.84	61.11	61.16	60.25	63.37	63.58
Winter recip.	2.91	2.37	3.50	3.09	2.61	3.07	2.85
Spring precip.	6.29	5.36	5.53	4.43	4.84	4.05	3.94
Summer precip.	7.25	7.97	7.99	7.41	6.81	7.24	7.91
Fall precip.	1.89	2.26	2.72	2.18	1.89	2.65	2.45
Winter max. temp.	75.33	77.60	76.13	75.00	76.53	76.47	76.13
Spring max. temp.	86.97	88.90	88.57	88.73	88.93	87.90	87.73

	1932–41	1942–51	1952–61	1962–71	1972–81	1982–91	1992–01
Summer max. temp.	91.17	91.73	92.10	91.50	91.80	91.63	91.27
Fall max. temp.	78.33	80.10	79.23	78.70	80.20	80.03	79.00
Winter min. temp.	52.51	52.62	51.47	51.13	50.06	54.11	54.09
Spring min. temp.	65.08	65.16	64.92	65.52	64.35	66.40	66.95
Summer min. temp.	71.95	71.86	71.48	71.39	70.63	73.07	73.47
Fall min. temp.	56.84	57.70	56.56	56.61	55.95	59.91	59.83
Lake City	1932–41	1942–51	1952–61	1962–71	1972–81	1982–91	1992–01
Ann. precip.	48.80	53.40	50.32	57.03	55.09	56.08	48.41
Ann. max. temp.	80.06	80.97	80.97	79.47	79.03	79.65	79.68
Ann. min. temp.	58.17	57.64	56.74	56.12	56.02	57.42	57.97
Winter precip.	2.86	2.97	2.95	1.52	3.84	3.91	3.04
Spring precip.	2.96	3.82	3.88	3.43	4.94	4.14	2.79
Summer precip.	7.36	6.67	6.20	7.66	6.78	7.16	6.62
Fall precip.	3.09	4.34	3.74	3.46	2.80	3.48	3.70
Winter max. temp.	68.00	70.17	68.70	65.87	65.17	67.23	67.10
Spring max. temp.	80.87	81.27	81.53	80.97	79.90	79.33	80.17
Summer max. temp.	90.83	91.13	91.90	90.57	90.43	90.97	91.00
Fall max. temp.	80.53	81.30	81.73	80.47	80.63	81.07	80.43
Winter min. temp.	44.79	45.20	43.64	42.06	41.86	44.03	44.95
Spring min. temp.	56.92	56.53	54.35	55.22	55.23	53.50	55.94
Summer min. temp.	71.38	69.82	69.51	69.27	69.28	70.36	70.86
Fall min. temp.	59.61	59.00	58.45	57.92	57.72	59.79	60.13

Source: Raw data from the National Weather Service; calculations by the author.

Table 1.5. Frequency of extreme weather at three Florida weather stations by 10-year intervals

Moore Haven	1932–41	1942–51	1952–61	1962–71	1972–81	1982–91	1992–01
Days 95°F or more	76	100	41	63	141	185	133
Days 32°F or less	21	13	19	25	27	17	14
Days 2" or more rain	36	45	40	38	32	31	35
Share of total rain							
2" or more	20	21	21	22	19	19	21
Months rain .50 below avg.	33	36	25	37	38	36	22
Months rain .50 above avg.	27	18	28	22	16	28	24
Bartow							
Days 95°F or more	230	304	315	221	221	171	179
Days 32°F or less	40	29	46	37	73	23	15
Days 2" or more rain	43	46	37	34	36	37	43
Share of total rain							
2" or more	23	25	17	18	20	20	22
Months rain .50 below avg.	31	33	22	27	29	35	31
Months rain .50 above avg.	28	24	34	18	17	22	24
Lake City							
Days 95°F or more	206	191	276	178	121	162	156
Days 32°F or less	118	136	212	216	252	154	147
Days 2" or more rain	42	42	38	44	40	52	46
Share of total rain							
2" or more	23	22	22	24	22	23	21
Months rain .50 below avg.	36	24	30	19	22	23	32
Months rain .50 above avg.	16	24	20	24	29	29	16

Source: Raw data from the National Weather Service; calculations by author.

1932. Trends were exceedingly difficult to discern. Those hoping that the data would reveal global warming should be especially disappointed, since there was virtually no difference in either maximum or minimum temperature between the earliest and the latest decade, and at the Lake City station the direction was toward cooler temperatures, both maximum and minimum. For annual precipitation, the direction was downward for all three stations. By season the results were more mixed, but it is as difficult to support global warming through an interpretation of them as it is for annual temperature. The best that can be said is that between 1932 and 2001 these stations have gone through periods of higher and lower than normal temperatures. The same can be said for precipitation.

Advocates of global warming also warn that as the atmosphere warms, the earth will experience more weather extremes. There will be more hot and cold periods. Torrential rain will become more frequent and will contribute more to the annual total. Droughts will be longer and more severe. In the case of Florida, none of this has occurred. An examination of the extreme weather by decade that has occurred at the three stations between 1932 and 2001 (table 1.5) reveals that in most cases it has been irregular, and no trend is discernible. The one notable exception is the remarkable growth in the number of days during the year that temperatures reached 95°F or higher at the Moore Haven station. This also took place at the Belle Glade station, 25 miles to the southeast. At first appearance it seems to have resulted from a regional change in climate. However, the station manager at Belle Glade suggests that it probably is because the instruments were relocated to more open areas. If this is true, this should be cautionary to those who try to interpret climate data solely by offering physical explanations.

2

Winter

When people of the northern United States begin to prepare for the winter, facing the prospect of spending much time in artificially heated environments, most Floridians have just begun to turn off their home and car air conditioners and are opening their windows to enjoy the recently arrived cool air. This air has begun to reach a temperature that northerners experience in early fall and late spring. For good reason it is the winter season that has earned Florida its reputation as a tourist state, although today visitors arrive in all seasons.

Even in the mid-nineteenth century, northern physicians would often recommend a lengthy winter recuperation in Florida for their affluent patients with a variety of ailments. Once railroads connected the state with the rest of the nation, their owners, in an effort to increase the number of passengers, built hotels along their lines and publicized throughout the North the pleasures of a Florida winter vacation (fig. 2.1). First St. Augustine became a fashionable spa. Then, as the railroads extended down the state, other resorts opened along both coasts and in the interior as well, particularly on the St. Johns River.

Using temperature to define the date when Florida winters begin presents a problem, since even in the depth of a North Florida winter the average maximum temperature is about the same as in New York or Chicago in mid-October or late April. Consequently, there are many residents of the southern part of the state who would vehemently deny that winter ever arrives. Though the difference between summer and winter is far less than in the North, there is a distinct cool season, even in the extreme south. If we use the first week in which the average daily maximum temperature is 75°F or lower as our criterion for defining the onset of winter, we see a progression of isotherms (lines connecting points of the same

Fig. 2.1. A sunny winter day on Daytona Beach in 1904. The Florida lifestyle had yet to evolve, and clothing worn by residents and visitors was more appropriate to the colder North. Note automobile in background, surely one of the first in the area. *Source:* Florida State Archives.

temperature) down the state from North Florida, where it reaches that level the first week in November, to the southern peninsula, where that average does not arrive until after the new year (fig. 2.2).

Temperature

Florida's winters, especially those of the southern half of the peninsula, owe their warmth primarily to latitude and proximity to the sea. Although in the winter the angle of the sun on the horizon in Florida at noon is much lower than it is in the summer, it is far higher at that time of year than it is in the North. Consequently, it does a better job of heating. Fur-

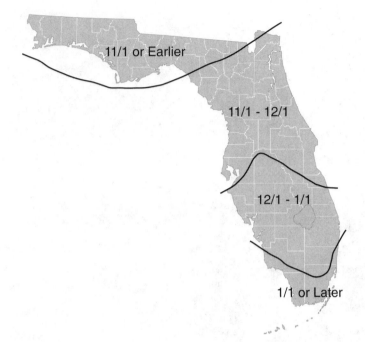

Fig. 2.2. Dates of the first week of winter, defined as the first week after July when the average maximum temperature falls to 75°F or lower (11/1 = November, first week).

thermore, it heats more strongly in South Florida than North Florida, since the angle of the sun on the horizon at noon is 6.5° higher in Key West in the extreme south than in, for example, Fernandina Beach near the Georgia border. During the winter, warm air masses from the Caribbean and the lower latitudes of the Atlantic Ocean also invade Florida, but the power of these masses to control temperatures diminishes as one proceeds up the peninsula. The northern part of the state more frequently receives cold drafts from the interior of the North American continent.

Since the easterly winds do not extend as far north in the winter as in the summer, the marine influence along both Florida coasts decreases rapidly as one proceeds north from the southern part of the state. On the Atlantic coast, between Stuart and Vero Beach, a distance of little more than 30 miles, the share of days between December and February when the temperature reaches at least 75°F falls from 61 percent to 49 percent (fig. 2.3). In part this rapid decrease in the percentage of winter days with

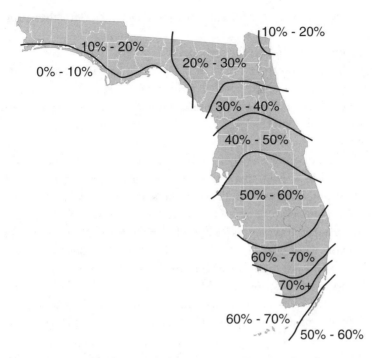

Fig. 2.3. Percentage of days between December and February when the maximum temperature exceeded 75°F.

maximum temperature at least 75°F is also because the relatively warm Gulf Stream at this point along the coast moves farther offshore. This drop in the percentage of warm winter days is equally conspicuous on the west coast, though it takes place slightly farther south than on the east coast; the drop occurs between Punta Gorda and Venice. It should be reemphasized that the maritime influence drops sharply from the state's coasts to the interior.

There are several reasons why, in the winter on the same latitude, there are slightly fewer days on the southwest coast when temperatures rise above 75°F than on the southeast coast. Winds off the Gulf of Mexico in the winter are a little cooler than those off the Atlantic Ocean, since the temperature of its water is a few degrees cooler than that of the Atlantic. Another reason is that the southwest coast in the winter usually receives cold air masses from the North before the southeast coast does. As these masses enter the peninsula and move toward the east coast, they often rise a few degrees in temperature as they pass over the relatively warm land mass.

Freshwater bodies on the peninsula can modify the air above them and affect the temperature of areas around them. There is a considerable lake effect around Lake Okeechobee, which is the largest freshwater body within one state in the nation. Smaller lake effects modify temperatures of places along other large lakes in the state such as George, Kissimmee, and Apopka.

During the winter one does not have to go very far inland to experience an increase in average maximum temperatures. In January, the Miami Beach weather station, which is at the shoreline, has an average daily maximum temperature of 74°F, whereas 8 miles away at Miami International Airport the average is 75°F, and 35 miles farther onto the peninsula, at Tamiami Trail 40 Mile Bend, it is 77°F. Since land loses its heat more rapidly than water at night, average minimum temperatures are lower by 4°F at the interior station of 40 Mile Bend than at Miami Beach. Temperature gradients between the coast and the interior, such as that in the Greater Miami area, are present throughout Florida during the winter. For example, Jacksonville Beach has a January average maximum temperature of 64°F, but at its airport, situated 18 miles from the coast, it is 65°F. At Tarpon Springs, on the Gulf of Mexico, the January average maximum temperature is 69°F, while in Plant City, 51 miles from that coast, on nearly the same degree of latitude, it is 74°F.

Since the 1970s, Miami has lost some of its appeal as a winter destination. With the decline in the city's importance as a tourist center, other towns north along both the Atlantic coast and the Gulf of Mexico, and even a few in the interior, have competed for a larger share of the winter tourist trade. The best example is Naples, which in recent years has greatly expanded its tourist facilities. The theme of warm winters with sunny skies frequently has been used by competing resort areas in their campaigns to attract guests. Actually, in the southern third of the peninsula there is little difference between coastal places on the same latitude in the percentage of days between December and February in which the high temperature reaches 75°F or more or when it is overcast.

Predicting Temperatures from Averages

A discussion of Florida temperatures would not be complete without mention of their predictability. Throughout the long hot period, about half the year, temperature averages are a reasonably accurate indication of what the temperature will be during a specific month or even on a certain day. This accuracy occurs because the high angle of the sun is the main influence on temperature. For example, Fort Lauderdale's average August maximum temperature is 90°F. In 53 years of its weather history, between 1950 and 2002, there were 1,571 August days when maximum temperatures were recorded. Of these days, none had a temperature of 10 percent or more above the monthly average. In fact, the highest daily maximum temperature recorded that month was 97°F, which was reached six times. The temperature fell 10 percent or more below the monthly average only five times. Since 1950 the lowest maximum temperature ever recorded at that station during August was 78°F. The variability of the August maximum in Pensacola, in the far north of the state, differs little from that of Fort Lauderdale. Between 1950 and 2002, the daily August maximum temperature was recorded 1,609 times. On only 13 days did it rise at least 10 percent above the monthly average, and on 34 days it was at least 10 percent below average. On August 31, 1986, following an extraordinarily early cold wave, the maximum temperature rose to only 68°F, well below the previous record low.

During the winter, temperatures vary far more widely between days of the month and years, especially in North Florida. Some winters are cold and others are mild, depending on the frequency of the arrival of cold blasts of air from the North. As a result, for predictive purposes winter temperature averages are not as useful as those of the summer.

Fort Lauderdale and Pensacola are used again as examples. The average maximum temperature of Fort Lauderdale in January is 76°F. Between 1950 and 2003, the daily maximum temperature was recorded on 1,649 days in that month, and on 157 it was at least 10 percent above the average. The highest temperature recorded during that period was 87°F (twice). There were 44 days when it fell at least 10 percent below the average. Since 1950, the lowest January daily maximum temperature recorded at the Fort Lauderdale station was 50°F (twice). Pensacola, which feels the brunt of invasions of cold air far more frequently than does Fort Lauderdale, has even wider temperature fluctuations from day to day and year to year. In that city the daily average temperature for January is 61°F. Of the 1,643 January days since 1950 for which we have records, 452 were at least 10 percent above that average and 422 were at least 10 percent below. The highest daily maximum temperature recorded for January in Pensacola since 1950 was 79°F (twice), and the lowest daily maximum was one bitter cold day when it never rose above 26°F. Variability from the average in maximum temperature during the two transitional seasons, spring and fall, is less than during the winter but more than during the summer.

Precipitation

The paucity of rainfall cannot be used to the advantage of one South Florida resort over another. During January, a typical winter month, all weather stations south of Orlando average no more than four days with precipitation of a tenth of an inch or more (fig. 2.4). South Florida gets only about 12 percent of its annual precipitation during the months of December, January, and February. During rare winters large amounts of rain do fall, usually brought by low-pressure systems from the Gulf of Mexico. In January and February 1983, rainfall south from the Kissimmee River valley was over three times the average for the period, much to the disgust of visitors. More will be said about this unseasonable event in chapter 3.

South Florida winters normally are dry because in that season the winds that blow out of the Azores-Bermuda high over the Atlantic are especially stable and inhibit the growth of cumulus and cumulonimbus clouds. Also, the land surface radiates far less heat during the winter, since it is not as intensely heated by the sun as in the summer. As a result, the convection and atmospheric instability required for cloud formation is inhibited. In addition, the winter battles of warm and cold air masses caused by the passage of midlatitude cyclones, which often rage over North Florida and bring that part of the state much rainfall, seldom extends into South Florida. Those fronts that do come through are weak and produce little rainfall (fig. 2.5).

Fronts can reach the state at any time, day or night. Consequently, the chance of precipitation occurring any time during the 24-hour day is about equal. For example, in Tallahassee from December through March,

6+

5 - 6

4 - 5

3 - 4

Fig. 2.4. Number of days in January on which at least a tenth of an inch of rain can be expected.

Less than 3

Fig. 2.5. Normally there is little rain in South Florida during the winter, and farmers must resort to irrigation. This field of celery in the mucklands near Belle Glade has an overhead irrigation system. Note the rich organic soils, a rarity in Florida. *Source:* Florida State Archives.

between 8 P.M. and 5 A.M., 46 percent of the daily rain falls. It is 44 per-cent for Orlando and 46 percent for Miami. For reasons that will be ex-plained later, this diurnal distribution differs from that of summer rain, which is heavily concentrated in the afternoon (Schwartz, 1978).

The absence of rain in South Florida during the winter also means that in that season the percentage of possible sunlight is high. During the win-ter in most of the southern half of the state, the share rises above 60 percent, exceeding 70 percent in Key West, which in both winter and summer is the driest place in the state (table D.4). The most overcast portion of Florida in the winter is in its north, where at that time of the year air masses of different temperature frequently meet. As the warm air rises over the cold air, stratus clouds often form, covering the sky for long periods, even days. In Pensacola during January, the chance of sunlight is only 48 percent.

North Florida Weather

For years a large number of Canadians have wintered along the Gulf coast from Panama City west to Pensacola Beach. Primarily a summer resort area, the coast in the winter has inexpensive accommodations compared with those in South Florida. In contrast to Canada, the weather along this coast may be mild, but it is considerably colder and wetter than coastal areas farther to the south, on both sides of the peninsula.

The emptiness of the tourist resorts along the panhandle coast during the winter is economic evidence that in that season Florida has two cli-mates, one peninsular, the other continental. Whereas the Gulf of Mexico and the Atlantic Ocean modify the temperatures of the peninsula, their influence on the temperatures of North Florida is much smaller. North Florida feels the effects of invasions of cold air masses from the interior of the continent far more strongly than does the peninsula.

It has become generally accepted that a line running roughly between St. Augustine on the east coast and the mouth of the Suwannee River on the west separates peninsular from continental Florida. Not only clima-tologists but also people who study soils recognize the line. Soil scientists divide the state into two soil temperature zones: the thermic zone to the north and the hyperthermic zone to the south. The line can be seen in figure 2.6, which shows the percentage of days between December and

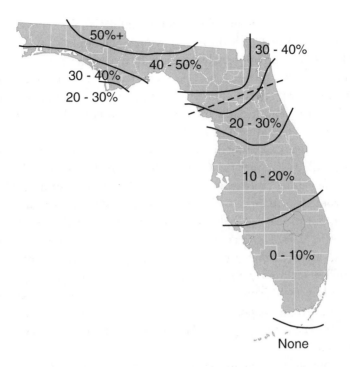

Fig. 2.6. Percentage of days from December through February on which the minimum temperature fell below 40°F. The dashed line crosses the state between St. Augustine and the Suwannee River, commonly thought of as the dividing line between Florida's peninsular climate and the more continental climate in the north.

February when minimum temperatures fall below 40°F. The two lines that define those places in which the percentage is between 30 percent and 40 percent are close together, signifying a steep temperature gradient at this point. They also closely parallel a line across the peninsula from St. Augustine to the mouth of the Suwannee River.

Since North Florida feels the full effects of cold fronts far more than the peninsula, and the arrival of these fronts is irregular, both its daily maximum and its daily minimum temperatures fluctuate far more from their averages than occurs elsewhere in the state. Winter average temperatures, as a result, contribute much less to an understanding of North Florida climate than they do to an understanding of climate elsewhere in the state.

Although it is impossible to predict accurately North Florida daily winter precipitation from its daily precipitation averages, accuracy rises when averages are used to predict the month's rainfall. Unlike peninsular Florida, which is normally dry during the winter, one can be confident North Florida will have an appreciable number of wet winter days.

Winter weather in North Florida is controlled by complex events that take place far from it. Air of different temperatures is continually arriving from distant regions, usually moved by storm systems drifting across the North American continent or the Gulf of Mexico. Fronts frequently pass through the region. During the winter, the source of North Florida's warm fronts normally is either the Gulf of Mexico or the Atlantic Ocean, the panhandle getting more from the Gulf and Northeast Florida getting the most from the Atlantic. Cold air masses usually develop in northern Canada, but the especially frigid ones may form over the Arctic or even Siberia (fig. 2.7). Florida's newspapers, as well as radio and television stations, often give the air masses behind the coldest fronts exotic names, presumably identifying their source region (e.g., Alberta Clipper or the Siberian Express). Typically during a winter month, two or three warm fronts and five or six cold fronts reach North Florida. Most cold fronts penetrate deep into the peninsula but weaken rapidly as they progress southward.

The conflict between air masses of different temperature is caused by the development of pressure systems, both low and high. One of the most important source areas for low-pressure systems that influence the weather of North Florida during the winter is south of the Aleutian Islands off Alaska, although a number of systems also develop in the Gulf of Mexico. Winter high-pressure systems that reach into Florida normally develop in northern Canada or over the northern Rockies of the United States.

Pressure systems that pass over the United States generally do so from west to east, steered by the winds of the westerly wind belt. Within this belt, at high altitude, there are rivers of wind that move at a much greater velocity than those below them. These narrow bands of rapidly moving air, known as jet streams, are storm tracks along which pressure systems frequently travel. Jet streams change their course relatively slowly, but especially in the winter they can do so abruptly, a challenge to those who predict the weather. At times a pressure system can be detached from a jet stream. Its path then may become erratic. At these times forecasting may become extremely difficult.

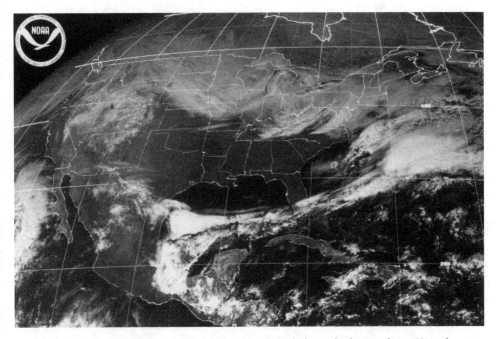

Fig. 2.7. A powerful low-pressure system passed through the southern United States in early January 1982. It exited and can be seen by the cloud cover over the North Atlantic. In its path a huge mass of bitter cold air from Canada was drawn into the South. The cold front, seen by the line of clouds that run from Texas through South Florida, kept moving southward. By January 12 the temperature had fallen to 14°F in Tallahassee, 23°F in Orlando, and 21°F in Belle Glade, on the south shore of Lake Okeechobee. Nearer the ocean, in Miami, the low was 33°F. Citrus and vegetables were severely damaged during this freeze. *Source:* NOAA.

The polar jet is the stream that most affects the winter weather of Florida, especially in the North. It usually enters the North American continent along Canada's west coast. During the summer the path of the jet stream commonly crosses the Great Lakes and then leaves through New England. As a result, at that time of the year, it usually plays a smaller role in shaping Florida's weather than in the winter. In the winter, however, after it enters North America, it frequently bends south, then turns east over Louisiana and continues along the Gulf of Mexico, passing over North Florida to the Atlantic Ocean. It is when the polar jet stream takes a southerly route that it can greatly influence the state's weather.

Low-pressure systems generally bring inclement weather to North Florida, since they attract air of different temperatures into them. When air masses of different temperatures meet, the warmer is forced aloft over the colder and is cooled, perhaps beyond the dew point. If the dew point is passed, clouds will form and precipitation may occur. During the winter, North Florida experiences long periods when clouds obscure the entire sky and there is a slow but steady rain. Although there may be other explanations for weather of this type, it usually indicates the presence of a stalled cold front over the region.

Winter high-pressure systems are associated with cold air masses. Their arrival in North Florida is often accompanied by a brief period of heavy winds, thunderstorms, and a rapid drop in temperature. Once the region is covered by a high-pressure system, wind slowly subsides, skies are normally cloudless, and humidity is low. During the day the sun burns brilliantly in the sky, though in the winter it is low on the horizon, even at noon, and has little power to heat. Although an invasion of cold air may bring tremendous hardship to winter vegetable farmers and citrus grove owners farther south on the peninsula, as well as those in the tourist industry, to many Floridians days dominated by these winter high-pressure systems are among the finest of the year. Low humidity, however, causes static electricity, much to the annoyance of those exiting from automobiles or turning on light switches in carpeted rooms.

During some winters, to some degree due to El Niño episodes, the polar jet stream dips deeply into the South more frequently than normal. In these years winters are especially cold. In other years the winter arrival of the jet stream is less frequent, sometimes the result of the influence of La Niña. These winters are warm, as moist air from the Gulf of Mexico often covers the region for long periods. During winter nights, when air from the Gulf of Mexico enters Florida's panhandle, fog becomes a common occurrence.

Fog

Fog is infrequent throughout most of Florida. In Key West it is virtually unknown. Fog develops an average of 6 times annually in Miami, 26 times in Orlando, but 50 times in Tallahassee (table D.1). Among Florida cities, Tallahassee has the highest frequency of fog. The number of foggy

Fig. 2.8. An early morning radiation fog on Interstate 95. Radiation fogs are frequent in North Florida during the colder months. They commonly form during the night and dissipate by midmorning. They are a frequent cause of traffic accidents. *Source:* NOAA.

days is still considerably lower than places along the Pacific Coast or in New England or in the southern Appalachian Mountains, where it rises above 80.

The fog most common in Florida that causes the greatest disruption of transportation results from a physical process known as advection. Advection fogs usually occur when warm maritime air masses move onto a cold land surface. If the warm air is chilled sufficiently by contact with the colder surface to permit water vapor within it to condense, and winds are light, fog will form. Fog, of course, is nothing more than a stratus cloud at the earth's surface.

In Florida, the most favorable conditions for fog development are in the winter, especially in the Big Bend area. When warm moist air from the Gulf of Mexico drifts inland over cooler ground and is chilled past the dew point, fog develops. Usually by midmorning these advection fogs are "burned off" from below by the sun, after it heats the land surface. In winter another variety of fog may occur, created by radiation loss (fig. 2.8). This fog is more localized than that formed through advection. It usually forms on calm nights when air directly above a cool surface is cooled below the dew point. An unusual Florida weather event, but one of extraordinary beauty, is the steam fog. Like a radiation fog, steam fog is often local. It forms when cold polar or arctic air masses pass over water that is much warmer. The cold air is heated at its bottom by the warmer water, and evaporation takes place. Visually the event looks much like what occurs when water is brought to a boil in a pot and steam rises. Over bodies of water, the ascent of the "steam" is slower and reaches only a few feet. The sight can be dramatic in a North Florida cypress swamp on a cold, clear morning.

Frosts, Freezes, and Snow

Severe cold can assault Florida if the polar jet stream dips deeply into the lower South. Circumstances that may lead to a particularly powerful invasion of cold air occur when an intense low-pressure system is followed by a strong high-pressure system. Winds spiraling counterclockwise into the low-pressure system may meet and flow in the same direction as the winds that spiral clockwise out of the high-pressure system. The spiraling winds of the two pressure systems may come together and convey a mass of cold air toward Florida that could cause temperatures to drop below freezing as far south as Miami. That such weather events are unusual on the peninsula is illustrated by figure 2.9, showing the total number of hours between November 1937 and March 1967 when the temperature was 32°F or below. The number of hours drops by 2,000 very quickly as one moves south on the peninsula. The transition from the colder North Florida and the peninsula may also be seen from figure 2.6, which shows the percentage of winter days with minimum temperatures below 40°F.

Snow is not unknown to Florida, and since 1886 there have been more than 80 months in which at least a trace has been reported somewhere in the state (Bradley, 1973; Ludlum, 1958). In 18 of those months, the fall was sufficient to be measured (fig. 2.10). The state's most widespread heavy snowfall was on February 13, 1899. This cold wave was of such ferocity that it became known as the Great Arctic Outbreak. During that stupendous invasion of frigid Canadian arctic air, the lowest recorded temperature in 12 states was surpassed, including that for Florida. Even today, the 1899 low survives as the lowest temperature ever recorded in five of these states, including Florida. The temperature in Tallahassee reached –2°F. Snow up to three inches deep was reported by a number of panhandle communities. As far south as Fort Myers, snow flurries were

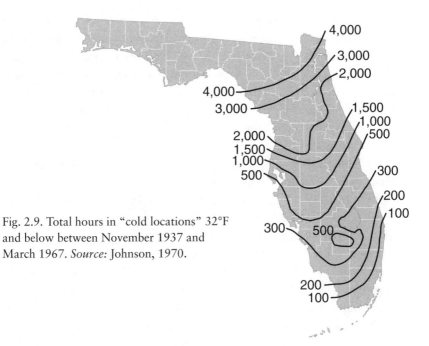

Fig. 2.9. Total hours in "cold locations" 32°F and below between November 1937 and March 1967. *Source:* Johnson, 1970.

Fig. 2.10. View of the Capitol in Tallahassee during the winter of 1958, following an unusually heavy snowfall. Snow of this depth has been experienced in Tallahassee only occasionally. *Source:* Florida State Archives.

witnessed. Miami, however, has reported snow flurries only once, on January 19, 1977, the date of South Florida's most severe freeze of the twentieth century. Prior to that date, snow had never been reported south of Fort Myers. On that date snow fell on Miami and was seen in Homestead, a town 22 miles south of the city's center (Schwartz, 1977). Understandably, this unusual event caused considerable excitement among residents of Miami-Dade County, even though the snow melted on contact with the ground.

Available statistics suggest that snow is likely to occur somewhere in Florida annually, but only about twice each decade does enough fall anywhere in the state so that it can be measured. The deepest snowfall ever measured in Florida, four inches, occurred in the panhandle town of Milton on March 6, 1954.

Cold weather may bring economic chaos to the state's citrus and winter vegetable industries, especially if the temperature falls below freezing. In the southern half of the peninsula, freezes are rare. In some years, near the coast, temperatures below 32°F may never occur (Attaway, 1997; Weeks, 1977). Their frequency at any place is determined by factors such as latitude, local relief, proximity to water bodies, and type of soil (Bradley, 1975). The farther north in the state, other things being equal, the more frequent a freeze. Local relief plays a role because cold air is denser than warm air, and in a period of calm the cold air will settle in low places. In the Florida Highlands, where there is considerable local relief, orange grove owners prefer to plant on the hills, not in the valleys. Proximity to water lowers the probability of frost, well illustrated along South Florida's coasts, especially the east coast. East coast locations are modified by prevailing winds directly off the Atlantic Ocean. The large size of Lake Okeechobee makes it particularly effective in reducing the chance of freezes along its western perimeter, but the lake effect does not extend far beyond it. The state's richest agricultural area, the mucklands, situated on the south side of the lake, does not benefit from the lake's effect on air temperature nearly as much as areas along the western shore. Between November 1937 and March 1967, there were 500 hours with temperatures below 32°F in the mucklands, but along the west side of the lake there were 200 hours fewer (Johnson, 1954, 1970). It might be added that on the Pompano Sand Ridge, another agricultural area on the same latitude as the mucklands but near the Atlantic coast, the number of hours of below freezing temperature during the 30-year study period was merely

100. The Pompano Sand Ridge is modified by the ocean. It also has better air drainage than the mucklands and has soils that do not radiate cold as easily.

In Florida, as elsewhere, when temperatures fall below 32°F there may be either a frost or a freeze. Essentially they are the same, but a freeze is of longer duration, covers a larger area, and may have lower temperatures. Both frosts and freezes are caused either by advection or radiation, or combinations of the two.

Advection freezes take place when frigid air is brought to the state from a great distance, usually Canada or even Siberia. Although common in North Florida, they are far less frequent in the southern half of the state. The infrequency of their arrival in South Florida is the reason for the citrus and winter vegetable industry being located there. When an advection freeze does reach the citrus and vegetable growing areas, it may cause widespread damage to crops. A severe advection freeze spares no ground, high or low.

In 1977, between January 18 and January 21, Florida was invaded by a particularly cold mass of air, and a severe advection freeze was experienced throughout the state. Its severity was such that it has been ranked as one of the top ten weather events in the state during the twentieth century. As mentioned, snow was reported in Miami-Dade County, where the temperature dropped into the middle twenties. Although few weather stations established record lows during the invasion, the damage was caused by the unusually long period that the freezing temperatures persisted. The U.S. Department of Agriculture reported that 35 percent of the state's citrus crop was lost, 95–100 percent of the vegetables, 50–75 percent of commercial flowers, and 40 percent of the sugarcane. The state's tropical fish industry was nearly wiped out. Estimated losses in 2003 values were approximately $6 billion.

The radiation frost or freeze occurs when the earth's surface and its vegetation cool through radiation until temperatures fall below freezing. This may happen on cool, clear nights when relative humidity is low and winds are calm. Through conduction the air above may then drop below freezing. Radiation freezes are much more restricted geographically than advection freezes. Within a small area there may be places where frost is present and places that have escaped frost. Radiation freezes are most common in low places, since the colder, denser air may sink from higher elevations. The composition of the soil also plays a role in frost frequency.

Moist sandy soils are less prone to frosts or freezes of the radiation type than the dark muck soils. This gives the vegetable-growing area of the Pompano Sand Ridge an advantage over the Everglades mucklands, where the soils are highly organic and dark.

To citrus growers, the most devastating sequence of events is an early freeze in November or December followed by a month or more of warm weather and then another freeze in February. The warm weather between freezes will awaken the trees from their cold weather–induced dormancy and make them extremely vulnerable to a second hard freeze. In its worst form, this sequence occurred during the 1894–95 citrus season, when a bad freeze that reached the citrus belt on the morning of December 29, 1894, was followed by mild weather until February 7, 1895, when a second blast of cold air hit the belt, devastating the weakened trees (Attaway, 1997). Freezes in 1983 and 1985 were similar, although a whole year separated the freeze of 1983, which reached the citrus belt on December 25, and that of 1985, which arrived on January 21. These two periods of cold waves are regarded as being the freezes of their respective centuries, and their impact upon the citrus industry deserves elaboration.

The freezes of 1894–95 came after almost steady growth in the industry following the Civil War. Before that war, in 1835, there had been a severe freeze in North Florida that destroyed most of the small acreage in groves, then located mainly in the lower St. Johns River valley to the south of Jacksonville. This freeze was a contributing factor in the relocation of the citrus belt farther down the peninsula. By 1894 the major concentration of groves was in Orange and Lake Counties, but there also were large plantings farther north, in Volusia and Marion Counties, and in Polk County to the south.

As the Florida citrus belt expanded, growers quickly recognized the importance of knowing about impending periods of cold. Shortly after the Civil War, Congress authorized the U.S. Army Signal Service to provide weather information to the public. At that time the U.S. Weather Bureau (predecessor to today's National Weather Service) was created. Bureau forecasts of up to 36 hours were relayed through press associations, telegraph companies, newspapers, and railroads. Storm warnings were wired directly to regional weather stations, which in turn passed the information on to be disseminated by press, wire, or post. Railroads and telegraph companies carried the information free to towns along their routes, where cold-weather flags were flown from public buildings. Trains did so by

Fig. 2.11. Citrus trees are capable of producing fruit for decades and are a major capital investment. Florida's first grove owners began to take measures to protect them from frost during the nineteenth century and continue to do so today. This early-twentieth-century owner chose to protect trees with canvas tents, an effort that probably proved ineffectual. *Source:* Florida State Archives.

using the locomotive whistle and putting placards depicting cold-weather flags on the sides of the cars. On December 28, 1894, cold-wave placards were attached to the cars of trains moving through the peninsula. Temperatures plunged that night. By 7 A.M. it was 24°F at Fort Myers, with much colder temperatures farther north. Even with the warnings, few grove owners were able to take steps to protect their trees (fig. 2.11). Those who did resorted mainly to burning cordwood and pitch or piling earth around the trunks of their trees.

Immediately following the freeze, the thawed oranges were quickly harvested and sent north to market. More oranges were shipped north in the two weeks following the freeze than in any earlier two-week period in Florida's history. Upon reaching the market, however, the damaged Florida oranges quickly spoiled. As a result, boards of health in a number of northern cities placed temporary bans on the state's fruit.

Most orange trees survived the freeze, especially those that were mature, but almost all the lemon trees were killed, and to this day that segment of the state's citrus industry has never fully recovered. The new year brought warm weather to Florida, and grove owners were confident that the December 1894 freeze was only a relatively small economic setback. Then, without warning, on February 7, 1895, a violent cold front began to pass through the state, accompanied by heavy winds. In the northern portion of the citrus belt, the temperature fell 61.5°F in 20 hours and temperatures dipped into the low teens. Citrus growers reported that in their groves, over the roar of the gale, one could hear sharp cracking sounds as the trunks of citrus trees split open from the pressure of the frozen sap. The destruction of the groves was appalling, and the economic hardship that followed affected the entire region. As grove owners were forced to cut back on their expenses, factories and stores closed, several banks became insolvent, and there was massive unemployment. Many people left the area, some to settle in South Florida, which was beginning to feel the prosperity brought by the arrival of the railroad.

Following the 1895 freeze, growers were especially bitter toward the U.S. Weather Bureau, which they felt had given them inadequate warning at the time of the December freeze and no warning preceding that of February. Most infuriating was the fact that the Jacksonville station had been aware of the rapidly changing February weather, but bureaucratic procedure had made it impossible for a warning to be issued. Public outcry over the inefficiency of the warning system was so loud that President Grover Cleveland asked for the resignation of the chief of the U.S. Weather Bureau.

The December 1894 freeze had killed only young trees but weakened the mature ones. That of February 1895 had killed 90 percent of all the trees north of a line between Tampa and Melbourne. Three decades of investment had been wiped out in a single night, and fruit shipments dropped from 5.1 million boxes in the 1893–94 season to 147,000 in 1895–96. It would be 15 years before citrus production reached the level of the 1893–94 season. Some considered the freeze a blessing in disguise because it forced Central Florida farmers to diversify their agricultural activities.

Almost a century elapsed between the nineteenth century's freeze and that of the twentieth, but despite enormous advancement in weather observation, communication, and citrus cultivation, there were similarities between the two. Groves in 1983, however, were in a considerably poorer state than in 1894. Even before the freeze of 1983, the citrus belt had suffered from less severe freezes in 1981 and 1982. Annual production was running about 25 percent lower than during the 1970s.

The freeze in 1983 arrived on Christmas Day, but during the days preceding that holiday, Florida newspapers were running front-page stories of an intense cold wave that had descended over the northern part of the nation. In Florida during the winter, cold weather elsewhere in the nation usually is given lavish attention in its newspapers, in part to convince visitors that they were wise to have chosen to come and perhaps to induce them to stay longer. On Christmas Eve, several items appeared in the newspapers about the intense cold in the North, but it was not predicted that a cold wave would reach the state. The Christmas Day forecast for the Tampa Bay area, issued the previous day, was for highs in the 60s and 70s and lows in the upper 40s. Central Floridians were surprised to awaken on Christmas morning to temperatures in the low 20s. The following morning, in many places, temperatures were even lower. Meteorologists were caught by surprise because they believed that winds from the south, off the Gulf of Mexico, were sufficient to keep the cold wave out of Central Florida. What happened was the sudden and unexpected spilling of cold air over the state, similar to a dam giving way.

Despite a variety of defenses against freezes, citrus growers and vegetable farmers suffered severely. Among grove owners, those in the northern part of the belt were especially hard hit. Estimates were made of destruction or damage to 230,000 acres of citrus trees. Fortunately, frozen oranges, if harvested immediately, can be processed into orange juice concentrate without a decline in quality. Many growers, consequently, did not suffer severe financial loss that season.

The freezes of 1983 and 1985 were by far the most costly of the twentieth century to the state's citrus industry. The National Weather Service was able to give ample warning for the 1985 freeze. There were people, however, who later said that because the service the previous week had issued a warning of a freeze in the citrus belt, one that did not materialize, some farmers did not take the new warning seriously. The 1985 cold wave, which came to be known as the Polar Express, sent temperatures in Tallahassee on January 21 to 6°F. The temperature was 19°F on that date in Orlando, 20°F in Lakeland, 21°F in Tampa, and 34°F in Miami. The night of January 22 was also severely cold, with temperatures similar to those of the previous night. In Miami it was even colder than the night before, and temperatures fell below freezing.

Following the 1985 freeze, grove acreage declined 26 percent from that of 1982. The harvest of the 1984–85 season was only half that of the 1979–80 season, when Florida had the biggest citrus harvest in its history. Most grove owners in the northern portion of the citrus belt, many who were only small-scale growers without the financial resources to replant, turned to other activities. Nonetheless, even in 1989 much land in that part of the state remained covered by dead orange trees. The state's citrus acreage has largely recovered, but most replanting has taken place farther south, in areas less subject to freezes. In addition, there is greater interest in planting more freeze-resistant species of citrus or those whose fruit ripens early in the season before the risk of a freeze is great. Until Florida's production was restored to normal, the United States was forced to import large quantities of orange juice from Brazil to meet national demand.

Since Florida supplies fresh vegetables to northern markets during the winter, when most of the rest of the nation is too cold for their cultivation, the frequency of freezes is of great concern to farmers. The farther south on the peninsula a crop is planted, the less the chance of freeze damage. Even on the same latitude, however, there can be considerable difference in the risk. For example, vegetable growing areas in Palm Beach County a few miles from the Atlantic Ocean experience appreciably fewer freezes than those on the same latitude 30 miles in the interior, around Belle Glade. This difference is due in part to the modifying influence of the winds off the Atlantic Ocean but also to differences in the heat absorption ability of soils in the two places and to better air drainage on the sand ridge near the coast than on the lower lands in the Everglades.

Local environmental conditions make a big difference in the frequency of freezes in all parts of the state. As a result, there are found, scattered throughout Florida, small farming areas that enjoy a reputation for being frostproof compared with those nearby. Some of these places are near lakes, which provide a local maritime influence. Others are higher than surrounding areas, and the cold, dense air drains from them to lower elevations. In Polk County, the founders of one community named it Frostproof. The name proved to be no guarantee against frost to its farmers who, when they established citrus groves there, found that their chances of avoiding freezing temperatures were no better than those of nearby communities.

Citrus growers, whose trees take years to mature and may produce fruit for many decades, make great efforts to protect their groves from freezes. Citrus is able to withstand a light freeze, but if temperatures drop below 26°F, there is loss of fruit, and if subjected to cold below 22°F for more than four hours, the entire tree may be destroyed. Growers will spend large sums to prevent freezes from damaging their trees. Heaters may be employed to raise the temperature of the still air and cause it to circulate, while huge fans have been installed in some groves to be used to keep air below freezing from settling on the ground. Young trees may be insulated to prevent the sap from freezing. Damage to fruit also can be lessened during times of temperatures below freezing by misting them with water and permitting a layer of ice to form. The film of ice, due to certain laws of physics, keeps the temperature of the interior of the orange from reaching the critical low temperature at which damage will occur.

Until recently, vegetable growers did little to prevent damage in the event of a freeze, since their investment is in annual plants that can be quickly replanted and brought to maturity. In 1997 a hard freeze in the vegetable-growing areas of the Everglades destroyed $200 million worth of crops, and another $75 million of crops was lost in 2001. In every decade farmers experience "hard freezes," and they bitterly accept the loss as part of the cost of farming.

In the past decade, some vegetable farmers have made efforts to reduce freeze damage. Where water is available, some growers have flooded their fields in advance of an approaching freeze, relying on the water to keep the air close to it above freezing. Strawberry growers in the Tampa Bay area, in advance of a freeze, sometimes spray the plants with water in the hopes that the ice that will form will insulate the plant from even lower air temperatures. In the late 1980s, farmers began to purchase rolls of thin film that can be placed over entire fields at times of impending freeze conditions. Heat radiating from the ground, trapped under the film, may be sufficient to save the plants from freezing. Until recent environmental regulations prevented it, some farmers would burn material that released much smoke (for example, used tires) to ward off a freeze. These smudge fires released particles into the air that would reduce the rate of radiation cooling. Unfortunately, often during the day, if the winds were light, the particles would linger in the air and impede warming of the ground by solar radiation.

Research has been undertaken to analyze the relationship between ENSO and freezes as well as other adverse weather to help Florida farmers to anticipate weather conditions during the growing season (O'Brien, 1999). Among other observations, made by researchers from Florida State University, the University of Florida, and the University of Miami, it was identified that during Florida's winter growing season when ENSO is in its El Niño phase there is considerably more rainfall than in years of La Niña. The excess during El Niño years can adversely affect yields of winter-harvested vegetables. In La Niña years, since they are warmer than normal, winter crops insensitive to day length are likely to develop about 5 to 10 percent faster than when ENSO is in an El Niño or Neutral phase. The research of Hansen and Jones, professors in the College of Agriculture of the University of Florida, supported the findings published in the aforementioned study. They found that in El Niño winters, yields of most Florida winter vegetables were lower and prices were higher than in the two other ENSO phases. The yield response resulted from increased rainfall in El Niño winters, as well as lower daily maximum temperatures and less solar radiation (Hansen and Jones, 1999).

January of 2003 was unusually cold throughout Florida, especially on the peninsula. Twenty weather stations evenly distributed throughout the state that had complete or nearly complete records since 1950 were chosen by the author to ascertain their January minimum temperature. That month in 2003 was at least the fourth coldest at sixteen stations during the 53-year period. Four stations reported it in the upper two. Yet during the month, because there were no major freezes, the state's agriculture sustained little damage.

The Florida Climate Center has published a report that suggests that there is a relationship between intense Florida freezes (but not freezes in general) and phases of ENSO (Florida Climate Center, 2000). It was concluded that in ENSO's El Niño phase, highly destructive freezes on the peninsula are less frequent than in either the La Niña or Neutral phase, especially the latter. By the center's calculation, between 1893 and 1999 there were 24 El Niño years, and during those El Niño years only one highly destructive freeze occurred. There were an equal number of La Niña years during the same period, but they only produced six freezes that were costly to farmers. However, during the 58 years in which ENSO was in the Neutral phase, there were 15 freezes that caused severe crop damage.

Florida in January 2003 was in the El Niño phase of ENSO. In this phase the eastward-moving polar jet stream, which frequently carries pressure systems across the continent, generally stays farther to the north than during years when ENSO is in its Neutral and La Niña phases. Also, the more southerly subtropical jet stream that flows eastward across the continent is quite stable and acts to "block" the invasion of bitter cold Arctic air masses. However, it does not prevent milder cold air masses from entering the state. In La Niña years, compared to the Neutral ENSO phase, the polar jet stream also is more stable. Although this configuration of the polar jet permits more high-impact cold air masses to reach Florida than in the El Niño phase, they still are rare.

In Neutral years, the polar jet stream tends to meander across the continent, sometimes in high latitudes, sometimes much lower. It also can follow a more circuitous path than in the two other ENSO phases, entering the continent on the west coast in Washington or British Columbia, moving over the center of the continent and dipping down into the southeast, sometimes even passing over North Florida. When this occurs the state is especially vulnerable to high impact freezes. In the year 1981 ENSO was in its Neutral phase. For the twenty weather stations examined, January of that year was the coldest since 1950. It also was one of the most costly to Florida farmers, in both frozen citrus and frozen vegetables. On the thirteenth the temperature fell to 8°F in Tallahassee, 28°F in Fort Myers, and 32°F in Miami. The two most destructive freezes in Florida, that of December 1894 (followed closely by another in January 1895) and that of December 1983 also happened while ENSO was in its Neutral phase.

3

Spring

Spring is Florida's most pleasant season. As elsewhere throughout the nation, it is transitional between winter and summer. Florida's cold season, of course, is far less severe than that of the northern parts of the nation. For example, in Chicago and New York, between the middle of May and the middle of June spring is generally considered at its finest, with average daily maximum temperatures between 70°F and 80°F. In Miami, average daily maximum temperatures never drop below 70°F year-round. Undeniably they are high in the summer, but by mid-November they fall below 80°F. They stay between that temperature and 70°F until late March, when once again they rise above 80°F. In Orlando average daily maximum temperatures range between 70°F and 80°F from the first week in November until the last week in March.

Temperature

To establish a comfort index for Florida, the number of days in which the average maximum temperature fell within the range of 70°F and 85°F was calculated for its weather stations. The range is arbitrary, but it serves to show variation not only within Florida but also between Florida cities and others throughout the nation. In both New York and Chicago, days between the third week in May and the last week in September fall within that range (133 days in Chicago, 140 days in New York). In Florida, the eastern seaboard from Key West to Daytona Beach and the Tampa Bay area have the most number of days during the year in that range, all having over 200. Miami Beach is the state's weather station with the most days in the comfort range, 269. The northern part of the state has the

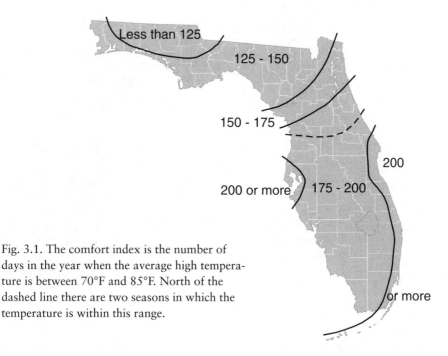

Fig. 3.1. The comfort index is the number of days in the year when the average high temperature is between 70°F and 85°F. North of the dashed line there are two seasons in which the temperature is within this range.

fewest number of days in this comfort range, and in the western panhandle the number falls below 125 (fig. 3.1).

In North Florida, during both winter and summer, the average daily maximum temperature drops out of the comfort range. In Tallahassee, for example, temperatures are normally in this range from the first week in March until the second week in May and from the fourth week in September through the third week in November. A short distance south of Orlando the average daily maximum temperature never falls below 70°F. Here the only period in which average maximum temperature leaves the comfort range is in the summer.

The beginning of spring in Florida, like the other seasons of the year, must be defined differently than in the northern United States. Although admittedly subjective, it is defined here as beginning during the first week in which the average maximum temperature rises above 75°F. Northerners would regard the week in which average maximum temperatures reached that level as belonging to late, not early, spring. Yet, if we defined Florida's spring as beginning with a lower temperature, say, 70°F, it would

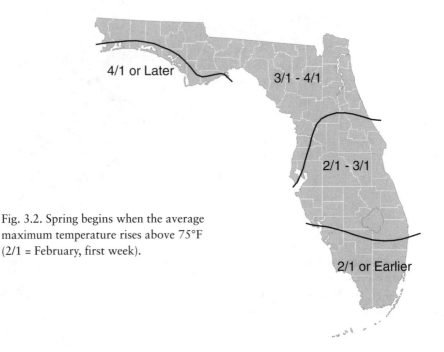

4/1 or Later

3/1 - 4/1

2/1 - 3/1

Fig. 3.2. Spring begins when the average maximum temperature rises above 75°F (2/1 = February, first week).

2/1 or Earlier

never begin in South Florida, since average daily maximum temperatures do not drop that low.

Using 75°F as its beginning, spring commences at the southern end of the peninsula in late January and reaches the panhandle by the beginning of April. Admittedly, few residents of Miami would accept that spring begins in late January. Yet, by identifying a precise temperature when spring begins, it does serve to illustrate the speed with which mild temperatures migrate up the state. Figure 3.2 is only a crude representation of the northern movement of spring within the state, however, since the season's arrival is retarded at places near the sea by the marine effect. Though few residents of Greater Miami would recognize such subtle climatic differences within their city, at Miami International Airport, eight miles from the coast, by the third week in January the average daily maximum temperature has begun to reach 75°F. Cooled by sea breezes, Miami Beach does not begin to attain that level until the first week of March. The arrival of average maximum temperatures of 75°F to the city of Key West, located on an island 100 miles southwest of Miami, is delayed until the third week in February.

Throughout Florida in the spring, the range in temperature between the warmest and coldest periods of the 24-hour day is often greater than in the summer. By the middle of April in the southern part of the state and the middle of May in the northern part, daily high temperatures often reach above 90°F, temperatures typical of the state's summer season. During the night, the land rapidly loses the heat it gained during the day. By early morning, temperatures may fall below 60°F, unheard of during the summer.

Places near the shore, especially those on the east coast that are under the influence of the prevailing winds from the Atlantic Ocean, do not enjoy low night temperatures in the spring as frequently as those in the interior. Daytime temperatures at maritime locations in this season, however, seldom rise as high as places on a similar latitude in the interior. During the fall, for most of the same reasons as in the spring, throughout Florida there is an appreciably greater range in diurnal (daily) temperatures than in the summer.

Precipitation

It has been noted that Florida in spring is generally dry. Throughout most of the state, rain totaling a tenth of an inch or more falls fewer than six days in April. Along the northern border, where winter frontal storms persist into the spring, this amount of precipitation falls six or more days in April (fig. 3.3). In effect, during the spring, the winter dry period of the southern half of the peninsula reaches far into the northern half of the state.

The explanation for comparatively low rainfall over Florida in the spring is the weakness in that season of the two most important mechanisms by which precipitation reaches the state. By spring, the polar jet stream seldom passes into the Deep South. Frontal precipitation, the product of low-pressure storms that often are steered by the jet stream, falls on Florida less frequently than during the winter. The other reason is that the stable air flowing from the high-pressure cell over the Atlantic Ocean that brings dry conditions to South Florida during the winter continues during the spring and then even reaches into North Florida. This stable air, whose stability is enhanced on passing over the still relatively cool surface of Florida, inhibits convectional and convergent rainfall, the state's principal source of summer precipitation.

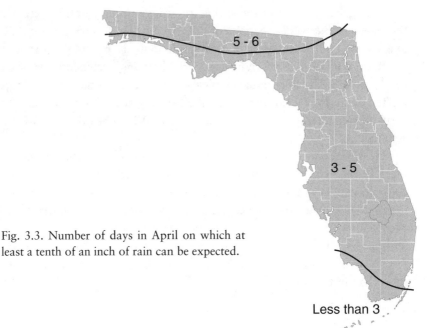

Fig. 3.3. Number of days in April on which at least a tenth of an inch of rain can be expected.

Low rainfall means that in the spring the air has less water vapor in it than in other seasons, and its humidity is lower (table D.6). Relative humidity is measured by the calculation of the amount of water vapor present in the air as a share of the total water vapor that the air could hold before it becomes saturated. In the spring at 1 P.M. throughout the state, relative humidity ranges from 46 to 56 percent (except in Key West, which has high daytime relative humidity throughout the year). In the summer the range is between 60 percent and 64 percent. At night, however, in all seasons at most stations it is above 80 percent. It should be added that even in spring relative humidity during the day is well above that of the nation's dry Southwest, where it is below 20 percent.

Precipitation Variation

Although Florida is situated in one of the wettest parts of the nation, it experiences great variation in its total annual precipitation from one year to the next. The variation between years is the same as that of the eastern portion of the nation's Great Plains, a region periodically ravaged by intense drought, as in the 1930s, but on occasion by floods as well. Though droughts may not be as disruptive in Florida as on the Great Plains, they do occur, as do floods.

Within Florida there is considerable geographical variation in the dependability of annual precipitation. It is most reliable, that is, one can expect the least variation from one year to the next, from Orlando north through the St. Johns River valley to Jacksonville. It is least reliable along the east coast from Key West to Vero Beach and along the west coast from the Tampa Bay area to Pensacola.

It is impossible to predict the amount of daily rainfall from precipitation averages. There is far too great a variation from one year to the next. Even when predicting from averages the amount of rainfall that will fall during a season of the year, one must exercise considerable caution, especially for the transitional seasons of spring and fall, and winter as well in South Florida.

The precipitation records of Tampa during the entire twentieth century illustrate the problems of using averages to predict amounts of rainfall for seasons. The average rainfall was calculated for the four seasons. The number of years when rainfall was 50 percent higher and lower than normal for each season was then determined. The season of greatest variability was fall, followed closely by spring. In the fall, 24 percent of the months were 50 percent above the seasonal average, while 38 percent were below. Summer experienced the smallest variation: 13 percent above and 12 percent below the seasonal average for the century.

The pattern of precipitation variability from the average differs somewhat between North Florida and South Florida. In North Florida yearly rainfall in fall, more than any other season, clearly has the greatest variation from its average, followed by spring. In South Florida, which normally has a winter drought, but one that in some years is broken by large quantities of rain, winter is the season that has the greatest precipitation variability from its average, followed by spring.

Spring and fall are seasons of low rainfall predictability because they are periods of climatic transition between a warm and wet summer and a cooler and, in the case of South but not North Florida, drier winter. During the height of both spring and fall, the state's weather normally is dry.

In some years conditions may arise when the dry period is both long and intense, while in other years it may not occur at all. April is the least predictable month, followed by November and October. In South Florida, but not North Florida, January also has yearly precipitation that varies greatly from its average. In all of Florida, July, August, and June (in that order) have the most predictable rainfall.

Spring in South Florida is the transitional period between the cool and dry winter and the hot and wet summers, when precipitation is of convergent and convectional origin. In North Florida the change is from winters when rain is produced from midlatitude cyclones to summers when it is usually convergent or convectional in origin. In South Florida, however, there are years when winter dry conditions may continue well into spring or when summer rains come early. In North Florida, midlatitude cyclonic storms may bring frontal rainfall late in spring, greatly reducing the length of the transitional dry period and in some years even eliminating it. Conversely, a persistence of the stable Azores-Bermuda high pressure system or one that is west of Florida may extend the dry season into June or even later.

The lack of dependability of rain in the fall is almost entirely because of the occasional arrival of tropical disturbances, which include low-pressure waves, storms, and hurricanes. These disturbances are capable of producing enormous amounts of rainfall in a short period of time. Some years they are numerous, but in others only a few arrive. Like spring, fall in Florida is normally dry. The dry period begins in North Florida and gradually moves down the peninsula.

The influence of these tropical disturbances on the amount of fall precipitation is enormous. Those weather stations with the least dependable rainfall during that season are found along coasts hit frequently by storms. Weather stations in Florida with the most reliably predictable rainfall are located where there is a very low probability of the arrival of these storms.

The predictability of precipitation occurring at a certain time of day also varies by season (Schwartz and Bosart, 1979). On summer days, if there is rain, and in most places throughout the state there is a very good chance of it, it normally occurs between 2 P.M. and 8 P.M. The chances are remote, except near the coast, that it will rain during the night. In other times of the year, since the rain is produced by weather systems that come from far away and reach the state at any hour, the chance of rain is approximately the same at any time during the 24-hour day.

Superstorm of 1993

Spring is normally the most benign of the state's four seasons, but violent weather is not unusual. One episode deserves to be singled out: the Superstorm of March 1993, sometimes called "the storm of the century." This storm wrought havoc from south of Tampa through the Big Bend area and continued north through New England. From Georgia, the blizzard that accompanied it set records for that date. Almost the entire eastern half of the nation was hit, road traffic was paralyzed, and virtually every airport along the eastern seaboard from Georgia to Maine had to be closed for a time.

The storm began as a low-pressure system in the Rockies. It was picked up by a powerful jet stream that carried it into the Gulf of Mexico. There it met a strong cold front coming down from the north. The meeting of such a cold front and an intense low-pressure system can set the stage for a powerful storm. In fact, the situation that was developing was similar to that which occurred in October 1991 in the ocean off New England when the famous "Perfect Storm" formed. Meteorologists predicted that the meeting of the two systems over the Gulf would cause a severe storm, one going so far as to say it might be the storm of the century. However, the consensus was that the storm would turn north before it hit Florida, and enter through Mississippi or Alabama. Instead, it began to turn north over Florida, entering the state in the Big Bend, then proceeding northward along the Atlantic Coastal Plain until it left the continent in New Brunswick two days later. The pressure fell below 28.42 inches in places along its path. The author, who has maintained a weather station in Tallahassee since 1965, recorded 28.79 inches, a personal record.

Snow fell in North Florida, and several towns released unofficial estimates of falls of as much as 5 inches. A number of stations from Miami to the northern border reported record low temperatures for the day. Florida's weather violence, however, was largely caused by strong winds. Gusts of near hurricane velocity were recorded at a number of locations, primarily along the Gulf coast, and several tornadoes touched down in Central Florida. The storm surge along the Gulf from south of Tampa to Apalachicola was between 6 and 12 feet, in places causing severe beach erosion. The damage to recreational boats moored along the coast reached into the millions of dollars. At least 2 million Floridians lost electric power for various periods. Total damage was approximately $200 million in Florida and about $2 billion throughout the nation. There were 44 deaths in Florida and an estimated 10 from boats offshore. Six members of a family of 10, who were attending a family reunion on Dekle Beach, near Cedar Key, were drowned while fleeing their home, which was about to be swept into the sea. The nation suffered 270 fatalities, not counting the estimated 50 people lost at sea. By comparison, 80 deaths were attributed to hurricanes Andrew and Hugo together.

As a result of more sophisticated technology, including, among other things, more satellites with higher resolution images, computers of larger capacity, and better forecasting models, meteorologists today believe their predictive accuracy has doubled since 1993. In that year they believed that they could predict the weather two to three days in advance with a high degree of competence. By 2003 they were confident that they could do so about five days in advance.

Drought

For a state that receives on an average day about 150 billion gallons of rainwater as well as 25 billion gallons from rivers leaving Georgia and Alabama (Fernald and Patton, 1984; Benson and Gardner, 1974), a discussion of drought in Florida appears to be of little relevance. It must be remembered, however, that on an average day over 100 billion gallons of water evaporate from the state's surface or are transpired into the atmosphere by plants. That leaves 75 billion gallons to enter the ground or move along its surface. This is the amount that potentially is available for human consumption. The balance between the water available for use within the state and what it needs is sufficiently delicate that when the rains fail for a protracted period, water shortages may develop (Jordan, 1984).

Drought is a difficult concept for scientists to define. Basically it is a prolonged period when there is a precipitation deficiency. Using this definition, during most years Florida would experience two seasons of drought, the spring and the fall. During these seasons, precipitation is usually low throughout the entire state. On the peninsula during the winter, precipitation is also normally infrequent. Of course, even in those seasons in which precipitation is infrequent, copious amounts of rain can fall, especially during the autumn, which is the hurricane season. Weaker low-pressure systems, however, can arrive in all seasons, bringing heavy rain. The spring dry period usually ends in May, a little earlier in South

Florida, and summer convectional showers rapidly increase in frequency. When these showers fail to arrive, concerns about water supplies begin to increase. As with other weather conditions, the El Niño Southern Oscillation may affect its length and magnitude through its influence over the paths of the jet streams that pass through North America.

Various measures of drought have been developed for different purposes. The best known is the Palmer Drought Severity Index, which attempts to calculate drought by considering both precipitation and temperature. Use of this index seems inappropriate for the purposes of understanding weather, and use of the actual amount that fell is more appropriate. This study has calculated the difference from the average monthly precipitation for the 21 stations between 1900 and 2002 and for an additional 12 for which there are data from 1940 to 2002. These stations are well distributed throughout the state. Although the definition is highly subjective, a station is said to have entered a state of drought when precipitation has been 40 percent or less than normal during at least four of the previous six months. A drought is said to end when that number falls below three.

Precipitation reflects the geographic distribution of pressure systems and winds. Water vapor in the air only has one way to condense into liquid and that is through cooling. The ground can act as a cooling agent, but the dew that results constitutes only a small fraction of the liquid that is condensed from water vapor. Virtually all is derived from air lifted aloft and cooled to the point where its water vapor condenses. In chapter 1, the various means by which massive amounts of air can be raised to higher elevations were described. When weather controls are such that lifting is impeded, the amount of precipitation that occurs declines.

Droughts develop within Florida when the state is dominated for long periods by huge high-pressure air masses, whose stability greatly inhibits the upward movement of air. These air masses usually come from the east, the west, or the north. That from the east is the best known. Named the Azores-Bermuda high, and centered between the Atlantic Ocean islands for which it is named, it waxes in size as it moves north in the summer and wanes in size as it moves south in the winter. In no year, however, is this migration the same. When it is slow to retreat northward, Florida may experience drought well into the summer. High-pressure systems that originate west and north of Florida also may stall over or near the state and reduce the opportunities for precipitation. Some of these high-pressure systems have been so huge that they produced drought over a large portion of the nation. For example, the high-pressure systems over the center of the nation that produced the prolonged "Dust Bowl" drought of the 1930s also brought drought to Florida, but not nearly of that magnitude.

Weather reports on television today are far more sophisticated than in the past, and they use more complex visual aids. In fact, many who now report the weather have college degrees in meteorology. In August 2002, while in the Panama City area, the author heard a television meteorologist challenge her audience in approximately these words: "We continue to be dominated by a high-pressure system, and the inversion layer is low again today. The chances are slim that cumulonimbus thunderheads will develop. Our long dry period continues, and it will be another day of high temperatures." Hopefully her audience comprehended that statement. If so, why we usually have a long spring dry period, especially in North Florida, and without the arrival of hurricanes in the fall, is understandable.

It has been suggested that the extensive land drainage south of Lake Okeechobee might be increasing the frequency of drought in South Florida (Pardue and Freeling, 1982). The argument is put forward that in its natural state about 75 percent of the area south of Lake Okeechobee was wetlands. Drainage for agricultural and urban use has reduced that figure to roughly 50 percent, so that today there should be less evaporation over the area and a decrease in the normal buildup of cumulus and cumulonimbus clouds, the source of most of South Florida's precipitation. Recently this hypothesis has been tested. Meteorologists designed a model to compare the amount of summer rainfall that would have fallen on South Florida in 1973 and 1993 if it had remained in its natural state and what actually fell in those years (Pielke et al., 1999). The model predicted that in 1973, if it had remained in its natural state, precipitation would have been 9 percent greater. By 1993 land development had advanced so rapidly throughout the wetlands that, had it remained in its natural state, precipitation would have been 11 percent more. How accurate these figures are still may be questioned, since the model of the original landscape that the data were compared with may not be accurate.

The threat of drought in Florida must be taken seriously, particularly on the southern portion of the peninsula. Today one-third of the state's rapidly growing population live along the southeast coast and one-quarter live on its southwest coast. Both coasts draw their water from shallow aquifers that are increasingly inadequate to meet both the urban and agricultural demand for water. Water today is being diverted from lakes and rivers to replenish aquifers, and more recently desalination plants have been built to process salt water. One that was being built in Tampa in 2002 will be the largest in the Western Hemisphere and is expected to significantly reduce the city's dependence on groundwater. North Florida is lightly populated and has ample fresh water that it can draw from the Floridan Aquifer, one of the nation's largest and said to contain as much freshwater as the entire Great Lakes. It also has rivers and streams of considerable volume. Although it has been opposed by environmentalists and is unlikely to be built, a proposal was made to carry water by pipeline from the Suwannee River in North Florida to meet the needs of people in the southern part of the state.

An examination of weather records since 1900 reveals that in every decade there has been at least one severe and widespread drought somewhere within Florida. Those that began in 1906, 1927, 1945, 1950, 1955, 1961, 1968, 1980, 1984, and 1998 were the most severe. The majority, to varying degrees, had an impact on the southern half of Florida (U.S. Department of Commerce 1978; Waller, 1985). Using the criterion developed by the author to determine the beginning and end of a drought, an examination of 19 Florida droughts reveals that most began between May and August as a result of the failure of the summer rains. Part of that failure may be attributed to an absence of torrential rain, which usually comes to Florida in the form of tropical depressions of varying intensity. Although torrential rain is not as effective in replenishing underground water supplies as rain of lesser intensity, in normal years it contributes a significant share of the annual precipitation. For unexplained reasons, 11 of the 19 droughts ended in the months of January and February.

There is no "normal" length of a Florida drought. Many are quite short, lasting approximately six months. Several have lasted over a year, notably that which began in the fall of 1980 and ended in the fall of 1981. Most severe droughts are followed by periods of normal rain, but there have been exceptions, particularly during 1967 and 1968 and more recently between 1998 and 2002.

Between 1998 and 2002, using the criteria here employed to define the length of a Florida drought, there were three. A contributing factor to the intensity of Florida's drought was that a strong La Niña episode had developed over the equatorial Pacific, reducing the likelihood of midlatitude low-pressure systems passing close enough to Florida to produce rain. The first drought began along the Big Bend coast in the fall of 1998 and then expanded to reach Tallahassee and Tampa (fig. 3.4). It ended during the winter of 1999. Only two stations in the state during the following six months experienced drought conditions. However, in early 2000, another drought began to form over the state. The National Oceanic and Atmospheric Administration (NOAA) stated that 2000 was the driest year on record in Florida. It also was the driest July on record for the southern Great Plains and the driest May to October in the southeastern states. The upper Midwest, however, experienced the warmest winter on record, and for New England July was the coolest. This severe drought first affected the western portion of Central Florida, and then spread toward the east, south, and north, bringing drought to stations as far west as Pensacola, east to Jacksonville, and south to West Palm Beach and Naples. There was a very short hiatus when most of the stations experienced normal precipitation, but in the fall of 2001 drought once again descended over a large portion of the state. It lingered the longest in Tallahassee, fading away only during the summer of 2002.

An unusual variable may have contributed to the drought that occurred in South Florida during 1982. In the spring of that year, a volcano in southern Mexico erupted and sent huge quantities of highly acidic particles into the air. Within four months of its eruption, satellite photography revealed that these particles had circled the earth at a high altitude and had spread through at least 20 degrees of latitude. Some theorize that these particles reduced the amount of heat transmitted from the sun that reached the ground, strengthening the high-pressure cell that was already limiting rainfall. Whether true or not, a drought in Florida cannot be explained without considering events far from it, even on the sun itself. A positive correlation exists between sunspot activity on the sun's surface and periods of drought, although it is far from proven whether there is a cause-and-effect relationship.

Seeding clouds to produce rain was undertaken on a large scale in South Florida during the drought of 1970–71. It began in April 1971, when clouds had become sufficiently large and numerous to be good potential sources of precipitation. Silver iodide crystals were spread in the clouds to trigger the coalescence of water droplets, which it was hoped would increase in size sufficiently to precipitate from the cloud. Between

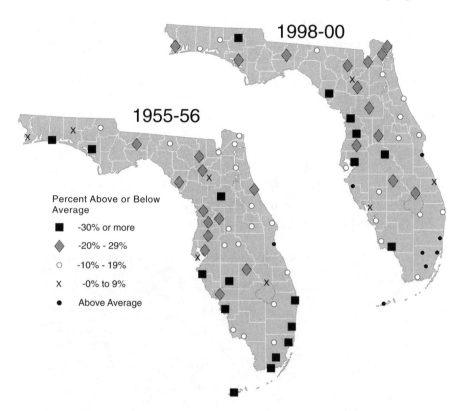

Fig. 3.4. Three closely spaced droughts occurred between 1998 and 2002. The one between 2001 and 2002 was the worst on record in Florida, extending from North Florida to Key West.

April 4 and May 26, a total of 196 seeding passes were made in a test area. The reported conclusions from the experiment were that over the test area between 5 and 10 percent of the rainfall during the period could be attributed to the seeding and that no cloud-seeding method can break a drought but may lessen its severity. During the 1980–82 drought, in August 1981, seeding was again attempted, but with such poor results that it was quickly discontinued. The quest for a means of inducing precipitation from clouds continues, but success remains illusive.

One aspect of drought in South Florida that is the source of great anxiety for its residents is fire. In the Everglades, fire set by lightning is an annual natural occurrence during the dry season, since at that time much of the vegetation has died and is highly inflammable. Regrettably, arson is also a cause of these fires, with accompanying wanton destruction of vegetation and wildlife.

During the drought of 1970–71, volunteer crews had to be mobilized to prevent fires from reaching the populated areas of Dade County. In April 1989, smoke from fires in the Everglades became so dense over Miami that it was regarded as a health hazard. Several city government buildings near the fire had to be evacuated. In periods of drought in the mucklands, a swampy area of highly organic soils south of Lake Okeechobee that has been drained for agriculture, the soil may even catch fire. Once ignited, these fires are difficult to extinguish and may smolder for years. Wildfires became a major state issue during the droughts that began

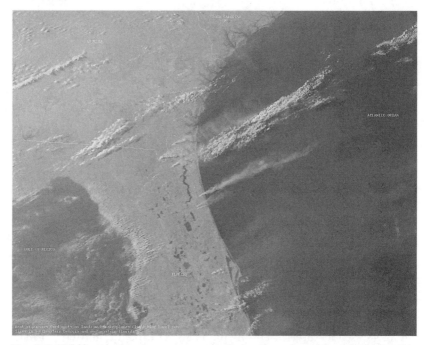

Fig. 3.5. Wildfires become more common during droughts and are highly visible from satellites. In the spring of 1998, the drought became most intense in northeastern Florida. In Flagler County, more than 30 homes were destroyed or severely damaged by fire; in Seminole County, the number was slightly lower. A significant share of fires were intentionally set. Thin plumes of smoke can be seen drifting eastward from fires in various parts of the state, especially near the St. Johns River of northeastern Florida. The larger and thicker bands are clouds. *Source:* NOAA.

Fig. 3.6. Wildfire in the Everglades can be especially damaging when they occur over the highly organic soils of the mucklands, south of Lake Okeechobee. These rich soils, which support intense cultivation, are highly inflammable, and once they begin to burn it is difficult to extinguish the fires. *Source:* Florida State Archives.

in 1998 and continued until 2002. They were most frequent in Central Florida and along the east coast from St. Lucie County north to the Georgia state line (figs. 3.5 and 3.6). At times sections of the interstate highways in several counties had to be closed, and for a brief period the wildfires covered so large an area of Flagler County that disaster managers entertained the idea of evacuating most of the population. Fortunately, it was not necessary. A statistical correlation has been identified between ENSO and the number of acres that have been burned in Florida by wildfire (Brenner, 1999). During the La Niña phase of ENSO, as a consequence of it creating conditions that reduce the chances of rain over the state, the area burnt is greater than during episodes when the oscillation is neutral or in the El Niño phase (Jones et al., 1999).

The Tampa Bay area was at the center of the epic drought that began in 1998. It is instructive to examine the themes of the hundreds of articles published by the *St. Petersburg Times* related to it. The most common theme was the introduction of water-use restrictions, the possible increase in water rates, and the public response to these issues. Although there was frequent mention of various businesses that were adversely affected by the drought, of clergy who offered rain prayers, and of lawns and golf courses turning brown, there was no suggestion that an economic crisis was at hand. The region's agriculture, which depends on irrigation, experienced relatively few problems. Probably the most dramatic references to the drought were stories of the wildfires. Some were so large that traffic on major highways and the interstates had to be diverted. There were a few articles that actually identified a positive side to the drought, since it exposed lake and riverbeds, making it possible for sediment removal. By spring 2002, after the drought had begun to abate, the water table rose to a level near normal.

Floods

South Florida's variable precipitation was well illustrated in 1983. Following the long drought of 1980–82, the area was subjected to one of the wettest winters and springs in its weather history. A succession of low-pressure systems from the Gulf of Mexico as well as strong cold fronts from the North passed over the southern part of the peninsula, destabilizing the air above it. Rain began to fall in January 1983 and continued well into March. Precipitation throughout that period was over three times what normally would be expected. Miami International Airport received 16.25 inches of rain, surpassing the previous record of 13.78 inches, set in 1966. (The 1983 record was broken in 1986.) During the three-month period, 17.33 inches fell at the airport, over 10 inches in March alone. Lake Okeechobee, which fell during the drought of 1981 to the lowest level ever recorded, almost surpassed its record high in 1983.

What Florida was experiencing in 1982–83, at least in part, was the effects of one of the strongest El Niño episodes that had ever been recorded (Glantz, 1996). Not only was it especially strong, but it differed greatly from the typical El Niño, leading some meteorologists to declare that no longer could we say there was a typical one. Before a discussion of the relationship between ENSO and the excessive rains in Florida in the winter of 1983, it must be reiterated that unusual weather can take place at any time, and local and regional atmospheric conditions can override those produced during an ENSO episode. The weather could be opposite what would be expected during an ENSO phase. The popular press, in its search for facile explanations, has frequently turned to ENSO episodes as the reason for extreme weather while ignoring other factors.

The powerful rainstorms that assaulted Florida and California during the winter of 1983 were costly in property loss and even caused some loss of life. Crop production in both states was severely impacted. A prolonged drought in the Midwest reduced the yield of corn and soybeans. Despite economic losses brought about by floods and drought, it was estimated that the warm winter in the eastern United States reduced the nation's fuel costs by half a billion dollars, more than compensating for property losses (Glantz, 1996).

The South Florida Water Management District, to avert an overflow from Lake Okeechobee into farmland that surrounds it, pumped billions of gallons of water into its conservation areas. When these holding areas could accept no more, water was diverted into Everglades National Park and canals that led to the coast. Environmentalists complained loudly about the flooding of the Everglades and the coastal estuaries. Normally at this time of year, when water levels are low in the Everglades, wildlife reproduces. The flooded Everglades in 1983 provided a poor environment for nesting. A lack of forage brought great suffering to the deer population. Along the coastal estuaries, where brackish water was diluted by the arrival of enormous quantities of freshwater, marine life died, especially shellfish.

Late winter and spring floods may also occur in the northern part of the state. They are usually the result of heavy precipitation over the region associated with stalled fronts. The catchment basins of most North Florida rivers extend deep into Georgia and Alabama. Here, and in North Florida as well, local relief is much greater than on the peninsula, and the soils are less permeable. If there is a large amount of rain during a short period, it cannot all be absorbed into the ground to be released later slowly from springs into the rivers and streams. Instead, much rain is carried quickly along the earth's surface to the sea. At these times river valleys, which are much narrower and deeper than those on the peninsula, may be overwhelmed by rainwater.

One of the most costly floods the state has ever experienced not associated with a tropical low-pressure system occurred in 1998 in the Big Bend area of North Florida between March 10 and March 30. Like the South Florida floods during the winter of 1983, those in North Florida in 1998 were experienced during another El Niño episode of at least equal strength (LeComte, 1999; Changnon, 2000). However, unlike in South Florida, precipitation in North Florida had been close to normal before the great rainstorm. A front passed through during the night of March 10 that dropped approximately 5 inches of rain throughout the region. The valleys of the rivers between the Apalachicola and the Suwannee were flooded. Over 100 federal, state, county, and city roads were closed by water. Several thousand homes and businesses suffered damage. The devastation was so intense that eight counties were declared federal disaster areas. Property damage was later estimated to have reached into the tens of millions of dollars. Miraculously there were neither fatalities nor injuries.

Tornadoes and Waterspouts

Spring and summer are the seasons in which truly destructive tornadoes are most frequently sighted in Florida, and spring is the season when the most powerful usually strike. Conventional wisdom suggests that powerful tornadoes would occur during the fall hurricane season, since tornadoes often are formed within hurricanes. However, 61 percent of tornadoes whose maximum velocity was estimated at 158 miles per hour or higher (F3 on the Fujita strength scale) were sighted in the spring, and only 9 percent at the height of the hurricane season (August through November). Perhaps, given the strength of winds during a hurricane, it becomes difficult to identify within it a tornado. Tornadoes are seen most frequently between 11 A.M. and 4 P.M., the warmest period during the day. The hours when they are least likely to be sighted are between 6 P.M. and 9 A.M. To what degree the difficulty of seeing tornadoes at night contributes to the low share of tornadoes during these hours cannot be established.

Florida has the dubious distinction of having more tornadoes per 10,000 square miles than any state in the nation, even Oklahoma (Grazulis, 1993). Most Florida tornadoes, however, are much lower in intensity than those on the Great Plains or, for that matter, in most other states where they are commonly experienced. National tornado records from 1950 through 1995 indicate that 2.7 percent of Oklahoma's tornadoes were within the two highest categories, compared with only 0.7 percent for Florida. Nonetheless, tornadoes in Florida have caused considerable loss of life and damage in the hundreds of millions of dollars.

Tornadoes are small atmospheric pressure systems with incredibly low pressure in their centers that are produced from thunderstorms. They are closely associated with four general weather conditions: (1) along the squall line ahead of an advancing spring cold front from the North, (2) along the squall lines in areas where masses of warm air converge, (3) from isolated local summer thunderstorms, and (4) within a hurricane. Tornadoes usually are very short lived and at times are so violent that scientists until recently were unable to learn very much about their origin and structure. Now, with Doppler radar and other instruments, observers are penetrating the heart of these storms and know much more of their genesis and are able to predict them with greater accuracy.

What triggers a tornado is still not altogether clear. They are born inside clouds in which there is great turbulence, usually cumulonimbus. Winds of various speeds and velocities come in contact, and when conditions are right, a rapidly spinning eddy of air is formed. Meteorologists now can identify atmospheric conditions in which the chances of tornadoes are high, and the National Weather Service issues watches if it believes the population should be alerted. Warnings are issued when a tornado is actually sighted.

Tornadoes typically have a path about 500 feet wide, travel 6 miles along the ground, and last less than 15 minutes. Most in Florida are not that wide, do not travel as far, and do not remain on the ground as long. They may skip along, but it is difficult to establish whether a tornado truly is skipping when it reappears or if it is another tornado. Based on historical information, Florida can expect about 45 tornadoes each year and two resulting deaths.

In Florida, measured in frequency of tornadoes for every 10,000 square miles, the coast between Tampa Bay and Fort Myers has a particularly high incidence, as do the western panhandle and parts of the Atlantic coast (fig. 3.7). No doubt many of the tornadoes sighted along the coast originated as waterspouts that had come ashore and were then considered tornadoes (fig. 3.8). The high frequency of tornadoes between Fort Myers and the Tampa Bay area is primarily because of squall lines that develop over the Gulf and produce thunderstorms, often so large and so turbulent that meteorologists designate them as "supercells" (Hagemeyer, 1997). Tornadoes in North Florida, usually events of late winter or spring, are

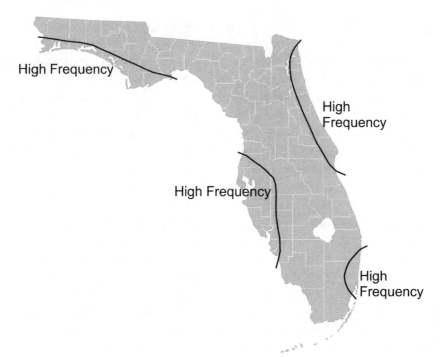

High Frequency

High Frequency

High Frequency

High Frequency

Fig. 3.7. Areas in Florida in which tornadoes are frequent.

less frequent and are associated with the squall lines that sometimes accompany cold fronts when they invade the region. They generally are more powerful than those that develop later in the year from air convergence over the center of the state.

The highest incidence of tornado deaths and injury in Florida has occurred between Tampa and Daytona Beach. Here, most tornadoes that have caused multiple deaths along their paths originated in huge supercells that formed over the Gulf of Mexico and came ashore in the Tampa Bay area. Shortly after sunrise on April 4, 1966, a squall line associated with one of these supercells formed so quickly that forecasters, who lacked the equipment available today, were taken by surprise. A tornado descended from the squall line and struck Pinellas Point. The line then proceeded east, and more tornadoes struck Tampa, particularly in the Carrollwood–Forest Hills area. Later northwest Lakeland was hit by them, as were Winter Haven, Auburndale, and the east coast town of Cocoa. At Cape Kennedy, winds gusted to 70 miles per hour, and an unoc-

Fig. 3.8. A giant waterspout in the mature stage with a diameter of about 90 feet at its base. Photographed from an airplane over the Keys. *Source*: NOAA.

cupied Polaris missile tower was blown over. During the passage across the state there were 12 fatalities, more than 400 injuries, and an estimated $30 million in property damage (almost $150 million in 2002 dollars).

Florida's worst tornado outbreak began on the evening of February 22, 1998, when a supercell came ashore from the Gulf of Mexico in the Tampa Bay area, and exited in the early morning of the February 23 on the east coast. It produced a number of tornadoes, at least one in the most powerful category. During that night, 42 people were killed by the tornadoes. More than 800 homes were destroyed, 700 were left temporarily uninhabitable, and more than 3,500 were damaged to some extent. There also was much property damage to public and commercial buildings. Damage from the tornado was estimated at $60 million. Although thunderstorms were the proximate origin of the tornadoes, some believed that the ENSO phenomenon was indirectly involved, since it is associated with violent weather. Between May 1997 and June 1998, the world experienced one of the strongest El Niños ever recorded. The degree to which this El Niño contributed to the tornado outbreak cannot be determined, but it may be presumed it was a contributing factor.

Powerful North Florida tornadoes also occur in the spring and can be as destructive as those that strike central Florida. On March 31, 1962, in Santa Rosa County in the northwestern panhandle, tornadoes killed 17 and injured approximately 100. Most of the deaths and destruction from those tornadoes occurred in Milton. The squall line continued to spawn more tornadoes as it passed into Alabama and then Georgia, causing further fatalities and property damage. On April 19, 1988, one or more tornadoes (the number is not known) struck the North Florida town of Madison. Along the 10-mile path of destruction, 4 people were killed and 11 injured. There was over $4 million in property damage, principally on the campus of North Florida Junior College.

The type of dwelling most easily damaged by the winds of tornadoes is the mobile home, whose thin outer wall makes it extraordinarily vulnerable to penetration by flying objects. In addition, unless anchored to the ground by tie-downs, it can easily be toppled by heavy winds. Data are available for the number of deaths in the United States by tornadoes that were incurred while the victim was in a mobile home. Between 1985 and 1995, those who died in mobile homes constituted 28 percent of all fatalities. In several counties in Central Florida, including Polk, a part of the state particularly vulnerable to violent tornadoes, 30 percent of the homes are mobile. To reduce the danger of living within them, the Florida legislature has put into law aspects of mobile home construction as well as the manner in which they are anchored to the ground.

Hail frequently falls during squall-line tornadoes or when conditions are ripe for their development. The violent circulation within squall lines provides one of the best environments in which hail may form. Approximately half of all Florida hailstorms occur in May and June, a period when North Florida crops are especially vulnerable. No part of the state is immune from these storms. Hail the size of baseballs and a few as large as softballs fell between Lakeland and Lake Wales on the afternoon of March 30, 1996. The roofs and windows of 600 homes were damaged, as were approximately 3,000 vehicles. The local fire department reported that during the peak of the storm, which lasted only 15 minutes, hail in places covered the ground to a depth of almost six inches. Estimated property damage was $26 million.

An unusual weather event took place in Fort Pierce at 7 P.M. on December 13, 1973. A 10-inch chunk of ice fell out of a clear sky (Pielke, 1975). It passed through the roof of a home onto the floor of its den, narrowly missing an occupant. At first the event was attributed to natural causes. The distraught resident fortuitously had recovered the piece of ice and placed it in a freezer. Chemical analysis of the ice revealed that it probably had fallen from a commercial airplane that had taken off earlier from a northern airfield covered with snow.

Waterspouts, normally less violent than tornadoes, are frequently seen along Florida's coasts during the summer (Everling, 1987; Golden, 1971, 1973, 1974). There are two types of waterspouts: those associated with fair weather and those that accompany storms. The most common, the fair-weather variety, develop over water of relatively high temperature and are associated with the vertical development of cumulus but not cumulonimbus (thunderhead) clouds. They are most often sighted around noon, when solar heating is greatest. The life of these waterspouts is generally shorter than that of tornadoes, their paths usually are not so long, and their winds are weaker. They commonly develop over shallow water that has been intensely heated by the sun. Excellent breeding grounds for waterspouts are found in the Keys, Biscayne Bay, and the bays of Tampa and Pensacola.

The stronger type of waterspout, the storm-associated variety, fortunately is less common than the fair-weather type. It is spawned from squall lines along fronts and thus is close in origin to a true tornado. Although wind velocity normally is not so great as in a tornado, the arrival of a storm-associated waterspout should not be taken lightly. On June 7, 1968, one touched down at Dinner Key Yacht Club on Biscayne Bay, doing approximately $750,000 damage (2002 dollars) to boats. Only one person was injured, which was regarded as something of a miracle, since over 100 people were on their boats in the marina at the time the waterspout arrived. A 50-foot cabin cruiser was lifted out of the water and carried over 200 feet. Another illustration of the strength of this waterspout was that it lifted a 5-ton, 35 by 14 foot houseboat, then transported it at a level from between 6 and 10 feet above the surface of the bay for a distance of 100 feet, where it was impaled on an 8-foot wooden piling. In May 1969, another waterspout in the Keys lifted an entire concrete foundation and carried it several yards. In June 1989, waterspouts of the squall-line variety came ashore at Eastpoint in the panhandle. Three people lost their lives, and there was much property damage. Approximately half the dwellings heavily damaged were mobile homes.

Doppler radar stations now cover the nation and are linked to both the Internet and television stations. With an ability to detect motion directly, radar can identify movement within the interior of a thunderhead up to 150 miles away, offering viewers a visual display of weather activity in their local area. Funnel clouds can be detected even before they descend from the thunderheads. Since local National Weather Service offices today are better able to monitor atmospheric activities, some are authorized to issue warnings when a tornado has been sighted or is indicated on radar.

Preparing for Tornadoes

Inhabitants of areas where the danger of tornado development is great are urged to exercise certain safety precautions, which are listed below:

Develop a Home Tornado Plan

- Pick a place where family members can gather if a tornado is headed your way: your basement, a center hallway, bathroom, or closet on the lowest floor. Keep this place uncluttered.
- If you are in a high-rise building, you may not have enough time to go to the lowest floor. Pick a place in a hallway in the center of the building.

Assemble a Disaster Supplies Kit

- First aid kit and essential medications.
- Canned food and a manual can opener.
- At least three gallons of water per person.
- Protective clothing, bedding, or sleeping bags.
- Battery-powered radio, flashlight, and extra batteries.

- Special items for infant, elderly, or disabled family members.
- Written instructions on how to turn off electricity, gas, and water if authorities advise you to do so. (Remember, you'll need a professional to turn natural gas service back on.)

Stay Tuned for Storm Warnings

- Listen to your local radio and TV stations for updated storm information.
- Know what tornado *watches* and *warnings* mean. A tornado watch means a tornado is possible in your area. A tornado warning means a tornado has been sighted and may be headed for your area. Go to safety immediately.
- Tornado watches and warnings are issued by county or parish.

When a Tornado Warning Is Issued

- If you are inside, go to the safe place you picked to protect yourself from glass and other flying objects. The tornado may be approaching your area.
- If you are outside, hurry to the basement of a nearby sturdy building or lie flat in a ditch or low-lying area.
- If you are in a car or mobile home, get out immediately and head for safety.

After the Tornado Passes

- Watch out for fallen power lines and stay out of the damaged area.
- Listen to the radio for information and instructions.
- Use a flashlight to inspect your home for damage.
- Do not use candles at any time.

www.redcross.org/services/disaster

4

Summer

For most people who live throughout the year in Florida, its hot, humid summers are endured, not enjoyed, in much the same way that most residents of the northern United States confront their cold, dark winters. The arrival of summer to the state instilled more than a sense of resignation among its nineteenth-century occupants. It was the season in which malaria and other tropical diseases were common, sicknesses for which there was little known defense or cure. Although northern physicians of the period often recommended convalescence in Florida for their patients during the winter, they would urge them to leave upon the arrival of warm weather.

Temperature

May is the month when Florida begins to be enveloped in summer heat. The sun at noon is high in the sky and heats the ground with great efficiency. Cold fronts are few, and the temperature of the air behind them is far warmer than that behind fronts that arrive earlier in the year.

In spring, the temperature of Florida's land surface increases more rapidly than that of the water that surrounds the peninsula. Consequently, the interior of the state is the first to begin to warm up. The week when average maximum daily temperatures reach 88°F is used here to define the beginning of summer. The first place in the state to reach this temperature in early May is the interior of the peninsula between Sumter and Hardee Counties (fig. 4.1). The average daily maximum temperature of 88°F or more is reached throughout most of Florida in May, except along the Atlantic and panhandle coasts. Onshore winds keep the maximum

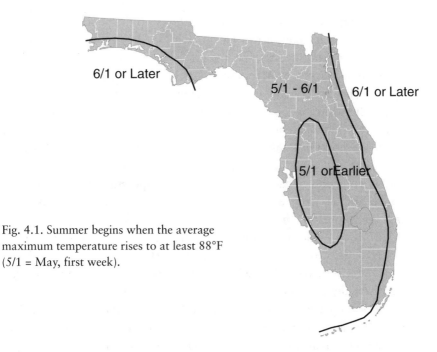

Fig. 4.1. Summer begins when the average maximum temperature rises to at least 88°F (5/1 = May, first week).

temperature below 88°F on these coasts until at least the first week in June.

During the summer there is little geographical variation in average daily maximum temperatures throughout the state, although the east wind from the Atlantic Ocean, augmented by the sea breezes, keeps maximum temperatures a few degrees lower along the east coast than elsewhere. The number of days with high temperatures is considerably fewer along the southeastern and panhandle coasts and the Keys than elsewhere in the state. These Florida coastlines share with those of California, the Atlantic from the Outer Banks of North Carolina north to New England, and the Lower Great Lakes a strong temperature-modifying effect from onshore winds. The maritime effect, however, penetrates only a short distance into the interior (Williams, 1974).

Onshore winds from the Atlantic Ocean reach farther north during summer than winter and are the dominant regional-scale summer winds as far north as Daytona Beach between June and September (table D.3). They are also frequently felt in Jacksonville in the summer. Lacking the benefit of a powerful onshore wind like that from the Atlantic Ocean, the

Gulf of Mexico cannot modify temperatures on the peninsula so far inland. As a result, that part of Florida with the longest hot season is the interior of the southwestern portion of the peninsula.

In recent years, Fort Myers often has been singled out in the press as being the hottest city in Florida. While this is true, the distinction occurs during the winter when it is not excessively hot. Although it lies in that part of Florida where it heats up early and where the heat remains well into the fall, in the summer it is no hotter than other interior peninsular cities such as Orlando, Ocala, and Gainesville. They all have comparable percentages of days in the year when temperatures rise above 90°F. Naples and Sarasota, whose weather stations are nearer the coast, also have approximately the same share of warm days.

Florida's summer temperatures are high, but they rarely reach above 100°F, as they do in southern Arizona and the Rio Grande valley of Texas. Nor are there as many days when temperatures reach 90°F or higher (fig. 4.2). Actually, in Phoenix, Arizona, the average July daily maximum is 104°F, and it frequently will rise above 115°F. In Orlando it is 92°F, Miami, 89°F, and Tampa, 90°F. Temperatures above 100°F are a rarity in Florida. The main reason for Florida having summer maximum temperatures lower than the Arizona desert on a comparable latitude is that it experiences the modifying effect of the Gulf of Mexico and the Atlantic Ocean, whereas Arizona has a much more continental position.

Of course, Florida's relative humidity is far higher than that in Arizona. For example, at 1 P.M. in Orlando during July, the average humidity is 59 percent; in coastal cities like Miami and Tampa, it is about four percentage points higher (table D.6, appendix). In Phoenix in July, the average humidity is slightly over 20 percent. Another reason for lower maximum temperatures in Florida during the summer is that clouds obscure the sun for long periods, reducing its power to heat the ground (table D.5). Typically throughout most of Florida during the summer, the sun is not visible from the ground for 30 percent of the daylight hours. The share is slightly less in Key West, situated in the driest part of the state (table D.4). By contrast, in Phoenix it is only 8 percent.

Throughout Florida during the summer, the daily maximum temperatures vary little. In most places, the temperature rises until it reaches slightly above 90°F in the afternoon. Unlike places farther north, cool air masses do not bring relief from high temperatures. In fact, by the time cold fronts reach Florida from the North between June and early Septem-

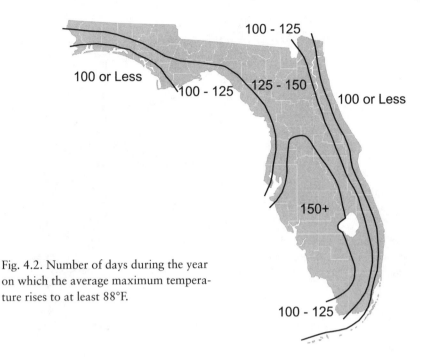

Fig. 4.2. Number of days during the year on which the average maximum temperature rises to at least 88°F.

ber, their air temperature has become so elevated that they bring very little modification.

Heat waves in Florida are unusual, usually occurring during a drought, a period of low humidity and mostly clear skies. Often they are the result of the presence of stalled high-pressure cells over the southeastern United States that have brought stable atmospheric conditions to a part or sometimes all of the state, greatly decreasing the chances of rain. In shape like a gigantic but invisible dome, once one of these cells descends over the state, it often becomes very difficult to dislodge. In early June 1985, a particularly severe heat wave developed over Florida as a result of a stalled high-pressure system over the Gulf of Mexico. Ocala reported 106°F, Lakeland reported 105°F, and even Hollywood, on the southeastern edge of the peninsula, experienced 100°F. Temperatures above 100°F, unusual in the northern part of the state, are almost unknown in its extreme south. Florida's highest temperature, 109°F, was recorded in Monticello on June 29, 1931. The highest recorded temperature of 39 other states exceeds that temperature.

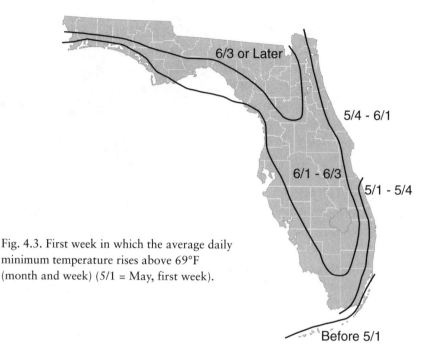

Fig. 4.3. First week in which the average daily minimum temperature rises above 69°F (month and week) (5/1 = May, first week).

Map labels: 6/3 or Later; 5/4 - 6/1; 6/1 - 6/3; 5/1 - 5/4; Before 5/1

During the summer, night provides little relief from the heat. As spring progresses, average daily minimum temperatures, which occur late at night, mount steadily and peak during the summer. In fact, the date when the daily minimum temperature first rises above 69°F is a good indication of when the hot and wet season has arrived (fig. 4.3). Minimum temperatures first reach above that level in the Keys in late March. By late May, stations up the eastern seaboard as far as Stuart have begun to experience average daily minimum temperatures of 70°F or higher. These temperatures reach the interior of the peninsula in early June and continue north until they arrive in the interior of the Big Bend area and the panhandle at the end of the month. Once they reach 70°F, they stay at or above that level for months, since cool masses of air from Canada, which arrive regularly during the winter and intermittently in other seasons, are so modified by the time they reach Florida in the summer that they bring little temperature relief. They do, however, briefly reduce the humidity.

The high temperatures of both Florida's land surface and the surface of the water surrounding the peninsula make the summer night temperatures so high. The surface of Florida becomes extremely hot during a summer day, but loses much of that heat at night. Nonetheless, in the summer the temperature of the surface of the ground never falls so low that the ground cools the air above it to the point where it can be thought of as chilled. During the entire summer the surface water of the Gulf of Mexico and Atlantic Ocean remains close to 80°F throughout the 24-hour day. The average daily summer minimum temperature at coastal weather stations clearly reflects the high nighttime surface temperature of the water. In Key West the highest the average daily minimum temperature reaches in the summer is 80°F, which it does on 24 days. Farther north, especially in the state's interior, it is markedly lower but far from cool. For example in Orlando, located 55 miles from the Atlantic Ocean, the highest average daily minimum temperature is 74°F, achieved on 11 days. In Tallahassee, 25 miles from the Gulf of Mexico, it is 72°F, realized on 33 days.

Humidity

The statement "It's not the heat but the humidity," commonly heard during the summer throughout the eastern half of the nation, has particular significance to Florida. By June, the waters of the Gulf of Mexico and the Atlantic Ocean have been heated sufficiently to make them excellent source regions for hot and humid air masses that blanket the state. For at least the next four months Floridians must resign themselves to enervating weather.

Although in Florida high humidity is associated with all seasons, it is in the summer that it creates the most discomfort. For this reason it is appropriate here to examine this element of climate more carefully. During the summer, 15 cubic yards of Florida air at noon normally contain the equivalent of a cup (8 ounces) of water. The measure of humidity of most concern to a Florida resident, however, is not the absolute amount but the relative amount of moisture in the air, that is, the amount of water vapor in the air relative to the amount that would be in it if it were saturated. The higher the temperature of the air, the more water vapor it is able to hold. Since the air in Florida during the day is high in temperature, that usually means a large quantity.

The air over Florida in the summer becomes so humid that conditions are similar to those during the rainy season in the Amazon or Congo basins. Of course, the Amazon and Congo basins have much longer rainy seasons and high temperatures all year. Too few Florida weather stations report relative humidity for a map to show its distribution throughout the state. There is so little variation from one place to another, however, that a general figure may be used for all. At 1 P.M. on a typical summer day, when the temperature is 90°F, the relative humidity will be between 60 and 65 percent everywhere in the state. That is, the air contains between 60 percent and 65 percent of the water vapor needed for it to be saturated. Cool air cannot hold as much water vapor as warm, so when temperatures drop at night, the relative humidity will rise if the same amount of water vapor remains in the air as during the day. By midnight, relative humidity typically will approach 90 percent.

High humidity inhibits evaporation of sweat from the skin, thus lowering the body's ability to cool itself, and increases the oppression of the heat. It is not surprising that so many Floridians spend as much of this season indoors as they can, in an air-conditioned environment, whether at home, at work, or in a large shopping mall. Molds thrive in humid environments. If homes are not artificially dehumidified by air conditioners, mildew will damage walls, shoes, and clothing.

The relationship between heat and humidity is of such importance to human comfort that an index has been devised that takes both into consideration. By looking at the relationship of these two climatic factors, the temperature-humidity index can determine the sensible as opposed to the actual temperature. For example, when the actual temperature is 90°F and the relative humidity is 60 percent, a normal midday situation during the summer throughout the state, the sensible temperature is 100°F. Throughout Florida, noon sensible temperatures, unless the sun is obscured by clouds, will hover around that level until at least October and even longer in the southern part of the state. Though infrequent, on occasion a low-pressure system crossing the nation will dip deeply into the southern United States during the summer or come ashore from the Gulf of Mexico. At these times, because of the cloud cover commonly associated with their passing, for a day or two there may be temporary relief from the summer heat, at least in the northern part of Florida. If clouds obscure the sun all day, or even most of a summer day, the maximum temperature may not rise above 80°F. Though relief from the heat is welcomed, since temperatures are lower, relative humidity will increase and may cause discomfort.

It might be added that summer sensible temperatures in Phoenix, Arizona, a popular retirement area, are slightly higher than those in the retirement areas of Florida. Although humidity is much lower in Phoenix than in Florida, maximum temperatures are far higher. In July they may reach over 115°F; in Florida they seldom reach 98°F.

Most longtime residents of Florida adjust to its hot and humid summers, and the sensible temperature may not appear as high to them as to the visitor. People who spend a great deal of time outdoors in the summer ought to drink large quantities of fluids to prevent dehydration. Other recommendations are to wear loose, lightweight clothing that is light in color and will better reflect the sun's rays than darker clothing, and to limit consumption of high protein food because it takes more metabolic heat to digest than other types and increases water loss. Unrelated to either temperature or humidity but potentially an even greater danger associated with summer outdoor activity is excessive exposure to the sun. The incidence of skin cancer is higher among residents who do not protect their bodies against its rays than those who do. Those who enjoy the state's beaches ought to be especially cautious.

Land and Sea Breezes

Land and sea breezes are two closely related local winds that blow throughout the year on both of Florida's coasts but are strongest in summer (Williams, 1974; Burpee, 1979). The sea breeze is especially esteemed by those who live near the sea, because it is cooler than the air it replaces. The mechanism for both breezes was explained in chapter 1. Sea breezes form in the morning and are strongest by early afternoon. Then, when the sun begins its descent to the horizon and its ability to heat diminishes, the surface of the land begins to cool until it is the same temperature as the nearby water body. At this time, unless the area is affected by a regional-scale wind system, there is a period of calm. People who go to the beach on a summer afternoon often witness thunderstorms that develop landward of them but never reach the coast. The sea breeze is able to prevent many storms from ever reaching the shore.

Sailors who depend on the wind are acutely aware of the period of calm between the onshore sea breeze and the offshore land breeze, since they must rely on wind to return to port. The land breeze, usually not as strong as the sea breeze, develops in the evening, although in South Florida during the summer it forms much later, even in the early morning hours. It forms because during the night land temperatures fall below those of the water. At that time a low-pressure system begins to develop over the water, and air moves to it from the land.

Sea breezes are present along the entire Florida coast but are weakest on the small islands that make up the Keys. In the summer, when these breezes are strongest, they blow at 8 to 15 miles per hour and reach 10 to 20 miles into the interior. Their ceiling is seldom greater than 1,000 feet. During the summer, on the east coast, with the extra push of the prevailing easterly winds, sea breezes are felt farther in the interior than on the west coast, where they usually must blow against these regional-scale winds. There are times, however, when strong winds from the west can push the west coast sea breeze to the east coast.

Sea breezes bring relief to communities near the coast, sometimes lowering the temperature as much as 10°F in a short time. Their effect, however, diminishes quickly in the interior. For example, in July the average maximum temperature on Miami Beach is 87°F; at Miami International Airport, eight miles in the interior, it is 89°F; and 35 miles farther onto the peninsula, at 40 Mile Bend on the Tamiami Trail, it is 92°F. At night, however, the land cools faster than the water, so the July average minimum temperature at 40 Mile Bend is considerably lower than Miami Beach (5°F), and at Miami International Airport it is 2°F lower than on Miami Beach. Similar differences in maximum temperatures can be found elsewhere in the state. For example, in July Jacksonville Beach has an average maximum temperature 3°F lower than that of the city's airport, approximately 15 miles in the interior. The average July maximum temperature at the West Palm Beach airport, 3 miles from the ocean, is 3°F lower than that of nearby Loxahatchee, 14 miles from the ocean.

Florida's cities seem to blaze with heat in the summer because pavement, roofs, and walls absorb the sun's rays. Cars and air conditioners release large amounts of heat. Higher temperatures within a city compared with lighter populated areas nearby have intrigued scientists for centuries. The term *urban heat island* has been coined to describe the phenomenon.

Cooling and Heating Degree-Days

A large share of Florida's annual energy consumption is for air-conditioning, considered a necessity in most months, especially in South Florida. An index has been devised by heating engineers for the estimation of energy demands for heating and cooling (U.S. Department of Commerce, 2002). Called heating and cooling degree-days, it is based on the concept that neither heating nor cooling would be required in a building if the outside temperature were 65°F. The number of degrees the mean temperature for the day falls below 65°F are called heating degree-days. The number of degrees that the mean temperature for the day is above 65°F are called cooling degree-days. For example, if the mean temperature of a station were 60°F on December 3, it would have 5 heating degree-days on that date. If the average temperature on July 10 were 90°F, the number of cooling degree-days would be 25.

The National Weather Service has calculated the average cooling and heating degree-days for all Florida weather stations with sufficient data. Twelve representative stations were selected for the size of the community in which they were located and their geographic location. The state's cooling season extends far beyond the summer months, and even in North Florida in January there are days in which the mean temperature rises above 65°F (table F). Among the cities selected, the one with the highest number of cooling degree-days is Key West, with 4,798; the city with the lowest is Tallahassee, with 2,518. It is just the reverse for heating degree-days, the northern part of the state having the largest number. Tallahassee had 1,705, closely followed by Jacksonville and Pensacola. Key West had the least, 100.

When the average number of heating and cooling degree-days for the entire year are added together, most stations have about 4,000. The southeastern part of the state has the largest number of degree-days, and many stations have over 4,200. For Key West the number is 4,898. The lowest numbers accumulate in stations along the Atlantic coast from Vero Beach to the Georgia border, most having around 3,800 each year.

For those entertaining the idea of moving to Florida and wishing to know the cost of maintaining a comfortable temperature in their homes, Florida's total number of degree-days is roughly the same as for places between Atlanta and Norfolk, Virginia. Of course, a far higher percentage of Florida's degree-days are of the cooling variety than places between Atlanta and Norfolk. Even within the state there is great variation from south to north in the percentage of heating degree-days. South of Lake Okeechobee the share is 10 percent or less, and in Key West it falls to 2 percent. Throughout most of the panhandle of North Florida, it is over 40 percent. The Florida homeowner should not grumble too loudly about the cost of maintaining a comfortable home temperature. While a typical Florida community may have 3,000 cooling and 1,000 heating degree-days, throughout the Lower Great Lakes area there are between 6,000 and 7,000 heating and 750 to 1,200 cooling degree-days.

Precipitation

Summer is the dominant precipitation season in Florida, more so in the southern part than in the north. If we define the state's rainy season as May through September, in South Florida over 70 percent of the annual rainfall occurs during this period. In North Florida, which receives rain from passing winter storms more frequently than does the southern part of the state, it falls below 60 percent. In Pensacola it does not even reach half the annual total.

In addition to being the wettest season of the year, rainfall during summer is more reliable than in any other season. Although predicting summer rain from precipitation averages is not as accurate as predicting summer temperatures from their averages, nonetheless it is far more accurate than using averages to predict rainfall in other seasons.

The air above peninsular Florida is usually stable in winter, but as summer approaches it becomes increasingly unstable, some years earlier than others. By summer, air warmed by the increasingly warm water of the Atlantic and the Gulf, and laden with water vapor, begins to be carried onto the land. Once that highly humid air reaches land, the most common way in which water vapor condenses from the air that reaches the state at this time of the year is through convection or convergence (Blanchard and Lopez, 1985; Burpee, 1979). Either way, moist air is forced aloft, clouds form throughout the morning, and frequently by the middle of the afternoon rainstorms develop. This rainfall pattern begins in southeastern Florida in early May, extends up the peninsula during the rest of the month, and reaches the coastal portion of the Big Bend or the Jacksonville area only in early June (fig. 4.4). There is, of course, considerable varia-

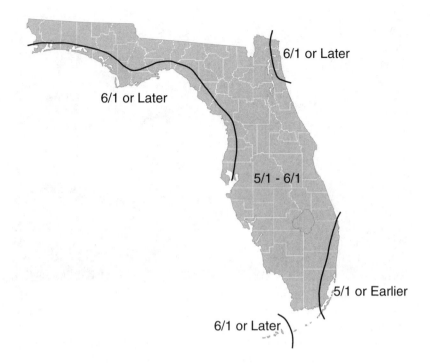

6/1 or Later

6/1 or Later

5/1 - 6/1

5/1 or Earlier

6/1 or Later

Fig. 4.4. The beginning of the summer rainy season (6/1 = June, first week).

tion each year in the beginning of the state's rainy season and in its diffusion throughout the state.

Although described in chapter 1, convectional and convergent precipitation are such important elements of summer weather that it is useful to repeat their definitions. Convection takes place when a parcel of air near the ground is warmed by conduction from the ground to a higher temperature than the air that surrounds it. This heated air expands and is carried aloft in search of air of comparable pressure. As it rises, the parcel of air is cooled, perhaps to the dew point. At that time cumulus clouds begin to form that may mature into the larger cumulonimbus clouds (figs. 4.5 and 4.6). There then may be a torrential rainstorm or at the least a shower. Convective rain is usually very localized. Given the high angle of the sun over Florida during the summer, conditions are excellent for this form of rainfall.

Fig. 4.5. Cumulus clouds form above an island in the Dry Tortugas chain to the west of Key West. The ground became sufficiently warm for air to be lifted aloft high enough for water vapor within it to condense and form clouds. However, the air above the cooler water that surrounds the island was not heated sufficiently for it to rise to a level where clouds could be formed. *Source:* NOAA.

Convergence also involves large quantities of air that are forced to rise, but the way the elevation occurs is different from that of convection. Air masses of similar temperature meet, and their convergence results in general uplifting through crowding. To repeat the analogy used in chapter 1, if a toothpaste tube is squeezed from the bottom by thumb and forefinger, the toothpaste will rise from the top. During the summer Florida has ideal conditions for air masses of approximately the same temperature to converge. As the peninsula heats up during the day, a low-pressure system develops in its interior. Sea breezes then move in from the Atlantic Ocean and Gulf of Mexico (Pielke et al., 1991). When they meet, they become crowded and are forced up, often high enough for their temperature to reach the dew point, when clouds will form. Whereas convection produces relatively small local cells of cumulus and cumulonimbus clouds and scattered rainstorms, through convergence immense cells of storm clouds form and heavy rain may fall over a large area.

Within easterly waves, tropical depressions, and hurricanes, there also is air convergence, and through uplifting, moisture condenses and rain

Fig. 4.6. Satellite view of the Florida peninsula looking south. Lake Okeechobee is clearly visible in the middle of the peninsula and Lake Apopka on the lower right. Along the Atlantic Coast (*left*) there is little cloud cover, an indication of the sea breeze that often keeps clouds from reaching the coast. The ocean, Lake Okeechobee, and Lake Apopka have little cloud cover. During the day the land heats up, the warm air rises, and clouds often form. Water on a clear summer day is cooler than land, so it does not experience the degree of convectional heating over it as does land. As a result, fewer clouds form over bodies of water. *Source:* Florida State Archives.

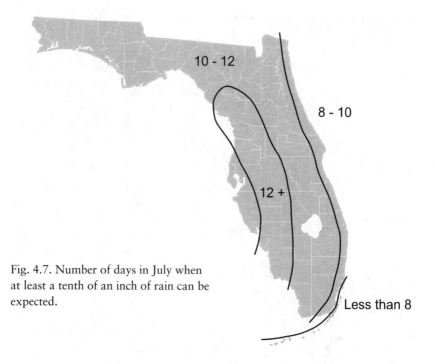

10 - 12

8 - 10

12 +

Fig. 4.7. Number of days in July when
at least a tenth of an inch of rain can be
expected.

Less than 8

may fall, often in very large quantities. Easterly waves are common occurrences throughout the Caribbean and Gulf of Mexico during the summer,
and it is not unusual that two or three may be in the area at the same time.
Not all will affect the weather of Florida, but many do. Tropical depressions and hurricanes are less frequent and might not appear at all some
years. When they do arrive over the state, they are capable of producing
enormous quantities of rainfall. They are most common from August
through September, but since they are infrequent, these months have great
variability in their total precipitation from one year to the next.

A map of the distribution of the number of days in July in which half an
inch of rain or more may be expected is a good indication of the frequency
and intensity of convectional and convergent rainfall activity throughout
the state. In that month, within a narrow area a short distance from the
Gulf of Mexico from Citrus to Collier Counties, on at least 12 days there
may be expected rainfall of a tenth of an inch or more. Many of these
storms are of such intensity that they produce at least half an inch of
precipitation (fig. 4.7).

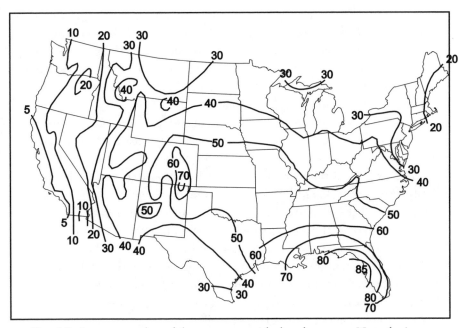

Fig. 4.8. Average number of days per year with thunderstorms. Note the importance of the Gulf of Mexico in the formation of thunderstorms. *Source:* NOAA.

Throughout most of Florida, the frequency and intensity of rainstorms usually peaks sometime in July or August. An important exception occurs along the east coast from West Palm Beach through the Keys. In July this part of the state is normally covered by the Azores-Bermuda high-pressure cell, whose presence reduces the intensity of the rainfall during storms but not its frequency. By the end of the month, the cell's influence declines and the amount of rainfall produced by storms increases. In South Florida, rainstorms continue with great frequency into November, but they usually begin to abate in North Florida by September.

Thunderstorms

Virtually all summer rainstorms are accompanied by thunder and lightning. No other part of the nation has more thunderstorm activity than Florida. In the western half of the peninsula in a typical year, there are over 80 days with thunder and lightning (fig. 4.8). The number is lowest in the Keys and in Jacksonville, where it is approximately 65 (table D.2).

Central Florida's frequency of summer thunderstorms equals that of the world's maximum thunderstorm areas: the Lake Victoria region of equatorial East Africa and the middle of the Amazon basin. The East African and Amazon areas, however, maintain the frequency throughout most of the year, whereas the number in Florida drops sharply in the fall and does not become high again until late spring.

Florida's thunderstorms are of such frequency and often of such magnitude that their origin and development deserve at least an elementary explanation (Byers and Rodebush, 1948; Pardue and Freeling, 1982; Woods, 1985). All thunderstorms evolve by stages (fig. 4.9). They normally begin to develop during hot and humid mornings when the ground begins to heat the air above it. The warmed air rises to elevations where the water vapor within it condenses and cumulus clouds begin to form. Fed by a continuous supply of moist air, these cumulus clouds can develop into huge cumulonimbus clouds. As cumulus clouds mature into cumulonimbus, strong updrafts of air keep the water droplets and ice crystals within them aloft. These updrafts may reach 100 miles per hour. They can present grave danger to airplanes, and pilots endeavor to avoid areas of thunderstorms. From the ground a cumulonimbus cloud will appear black, since it is so laden with water droplets and ice crystals that little light from the sun passes through it. Viewed from above, however, they are white.

Within the cloud, water droplets and ice crystals are rapidly coalescing and becoming larger. Finally their weight becomes too great for the updrafts to support, and they fall from the cloud. As precipitation falls out of the cloud, a drag occurs, causing a downdraft. At this time the cool, dry air surrounding the cloud begins to enter it, intensifying the downdraft. When the downdraft leaves the bottom of the cloud, cool winds, lightning, intense precipitation, and at times even hail are experienced. The temperature at the ground may drop 20°F in a few minutes. Hail has been the cause of millions of dollars of crop loss to vegetable farmers and grove owners, as well as property damage on farms and in cities.

Powerful downdrafts, called downbursts, as well as cross-currents of air known as wind shear during thunderstorms over airports when planes are taking off or landing have been the cause of several commercial airline crashes. Instruments employing Doppler radar have been developed to detect both winds and are now widely deployed among the nation's air-

Fig. 4.9. Cumulonimbus cloud over Avon Park, Florida. Within these clouds, in their mature state, there is a powerful vertical flow of air that commonly rises many thousands of feet. Once the water vapor has condensed, clouds can quickly discharge enormous amounts of rain (and sometimes hail). The air movement within them generates huge amounts of static electricity, followed by many lightning discharges with accompanying thunder. *Source:* NOAA.

ports. This new technology has greatly reduced the risk of both landings and takeoffs when there are thunderstorms in the area.

The thunderstorm begins to dissipate when downdrafts become stronger than updrafts. Without the updrafts, the cloud loses its supply of moisture and begins to evaporate. Rain becomes less intense and eventually ceases. Normally from inception to dissipation the life span of a mature cell of cumulonimbus clouds is one to two hours.

In most of Florida, conditions are excellent for the development of several types of thunderstorms. The smallest in scale is the local thunderstorm, born over ground that has been heated by the sun sufficiently for convectional circulation to begin. This local convectional cell may produce cumulus and later cumulonimbus clouds and finally a heavy local thunderstorm. Proof that heat from the surface of the earth is necessary for these cumulus clouds to develop can often be seen from the window of an airplane or from satellite photography. Although by noon much of the state may be covered by cumulus clouds, over the relatively cool surfaces of Lake Okeechobee, Lake Monroe, the St. Johns River, and other large freshwater bodies, where convectional circulation is weak, there will be few or even none (fig. 4.6).

A second type of thunderstorm, larger in size, also common in Florida occurs during the summer through the convergence of air masses from the Gulf of Mexico and the Atlantic Ocean over the hot interior of the peninsula. When the two masses meet, huge quantities of moisture-laden air are driven aloft, forming cumulonimbus clouds. Thunderstorms usually follow, often along long squall lines. Tornadoes sometimes develop within these squall lines. This type of thunderstorm is particularly common in the southern half of the peninsula, except over the Keys. The land surface in the Keys is too small for convergence to occur on the large scale it does on the peninsula.

A third way in which violent thunderstorms are born occurs when fronts advance, particularly those with cold air masses behind them, and there is enormous air turbulence. In Florida these thunderstorms develop more frequently in winter and spring than in summer and are most common in the northern part of the state. While canoeing in spring on a North Florida river, the author was overtaken by a line of thunderstorms accompanying a late spring cold front. Within 15 minutes, the temperature dropped more than 20°F and the storm's downdraft blew off the thatched roof of the shelter where he sought cover and felled a nearby live oak tree. Hail pelted the area, and a mile downstream lightning split open a cypress tree over three feet in diameter.

During the summer, thunderstorms are generally midafternoon events. They come with such regularity that they sometimes are referred to as Florida's monsoons, though they differ greatly in origin from the true monsoons of India. Between June and September in Orlando, 60 percent of the daily precipitation falls between 2 P.M. and 7 P.M. For the same period in Tallahassee the share is 48 percent, and in Miami, 36 percent (Schwartz and Bosart, 1979). Less summer rain falls in the afternoon in Miami than at the other two stations because of its maritime position. Generally throughout the state the intensity of daytime rainfall concentration decreases near its coasts. In part this fall occurs because the sea breeze convergence zone, which brings rain to the interior of the state during the day, later, even during the evening, is pushed toward the coasts by regional-scale winds. In addition, air is often less stable over water at night than during the day, the reverse of air over land.

In both Tallahassee and Orlando only 19 percent of the daily summer precipitation falls between 8 P.M. and 6 A.M. The share is markedly higher in Miami because of its coastal position. There, 28 percent of the daily rainfall occurs between those hours. A regular summer nocturnal display witnessed by people who live along Florida's coasts is the play of lightning offshore among huge cumulonimbus clouds that develop after sunset.

Lightning

Lightning is the most lethal component of the thunderstorm (Hodanish et al., 1997; Lericos, Fuelberg, and Watson, 2002). On average throughout the nation, 96 deaths occur annually from this powerful electronic discharge, 10 in Florida. The process is not fully understood. During the violent circulation of air within the cumulonimbus cloud, friction causes negative and positive electrical charges to develop in different places within it. Since air is a poor conductor of electricity, before lightning will occur, the difference between the charges must grow immense, often millions of volts. When it does, one charge leaps to the other, which may be on the ground (which is negatively charged) but more likely is in another place within the cloud or in a cloud nearby. This giant spark is intensely hot, far hotter than the surface of the sun. It causes a sudden and explosive expansion of air around it, followed by an equally rapid contraction when it has passed. This sudden expansion and contraction produce sound and are the explanation for thunder.

Since lightning and thunder occur at the same time, and we know sound travels at roughly 1,000 feet per second, we can calculate our distance from the bolt by measuring the time between seeing the lightning and hearing the thunder. If five seconds elapse between a sighted lightning flash and the arrival of its sound, the distance of the lightning from the viewer would be one mile. A flash of lightning followed immediately by a loud clap of thunder indicates the discharge was nearby. Rolling thunder is due in part to hearing sound produced from that part of the lightning bolt nearest to us before the sound arrives that emanated from the same bolt farther away. Also, it may be caused by the sound waves reflecting off clouds.

Martin A. Uman, a researcher at the Lightning Research Laboratory of the University of Florida, estimated that an average resident of the state can expect each year to be within half a mile of 10 to 15 lightning bolts that reach the ground (Uman, 1987). He also calculated that a given square mile of South Florida could be expected to receive about 25 bolts annually. The Southeast Regional Climate Center provides additional interesting statistics. Between 1959 and 1993, 32 percent of all Florida injuries and deaths from lightning occurred in open fields and playgrounds, 14 percent in the water or on boats, 9 percent under trees, 5 percent on heavy equipment, 4 percent on golf courses, and 3 percent on telephones. In most years Florida has the largest number of deaths from lightning of any state. Between 1959 and 2001 in Florida, there were 401 lightning-related deaths and approximately 1,000 injuries. Eighty-eight percent of victims were killed in the months June through September.

Although 4 percent of all lightning deaths were associated with golfing, there have been some tragedies associated with other sports. In 1949, a bolt hit a baseball diamond in the North Florida community of Baker, killing the first and second basemen and the shortstop and injuring 50 spectators. In 1970, during a football practice at St. Petersburg's Gibbs High School, a bolt struck a huddle, killing two players and injuring 20 others, including a coach. In 1975, football practice was disrupted at Christopher Columbus High School in Miami by a lightning bolt that killed one player and injured 14 players and 3 coaches.

Lightning may disrupt electrical power transmission and set grass and forest fires. During the thunderstorm season of 1988, the National Weather Service in Miami employed the services of a private research firm to study the location of lightning strokes in South Florida. The firm placed five computerized lightning detectors in the area. When a stroke reached the ground, it registered on their computers. When the difference in time for the discharge signal to get to each computer was measured, its location was accurately identified. One spectacular display of lightning detected by this apparatus is worth recounting: On May 27, 1988, a line of thunderstorms passed over northeast Broward County, and the system recorded roughly 2,500 lightning strokes within three hours. On August 27, 2002, a similar squall line passed over Tallahassee, and the National

Weather Service reported 1,556 cloud-to-ground strokes between 6 P.M. and midnight.

Periodically, lightning has caused great disruption at the Kennedy Space Center on Cape Canaveral, delaying launchings and causing destruction (fig. 4.10). The Apollo 12 launch on November 14, 1969, was struck by lightning 30 seconds after lift-off, momentarily opening circuit breakers on board (Williams, 1985). Fortunately, in a few seconds normal conditions were restored, and the mission proceeded. On March 26, 1987, when the National Aeronautics and Space Administration (NASA) sent an unmanned Atlas-Centaur rocket aloft, lightning struck its nose cone, disabling the electric guidance system. The $160 million rocket had to be destroyed 51 seconds into its flight. Danger from lightning is taken so seriously at NASA that today it has some of the most sophisticated monitoring systems of this phenomenon of any place in the world. In experiments reminiscent of those made by Benjamin Franklin in the eighteenth century, NASA researchers have been sending three-foot rockets pulling 2,100-foot wires toward thunderheads. These wires, connected to instruments on the ground, pull lightning charges out of the clouds for analysis.

Hodanish and others (1997) completed a 10-year study of lightning in Florida that recorded over 25 million flashes. They ascertained that during the winter the greatest flash density was over the panhandle and resulted from midlatitude storms. Flashes were more evenly distributed throughout the state during the spring. Flash density is highest in the summer, and in central Florida it exceeds 26 flashes per square mile. The high density is the result of the convergence of air masses from the Gulf and the Atlantic. September and October experience the lowest number of flashes.

If lightning strikes a power line, it can set off an intense surge of electricity that will damage sensitive electrical equipment. Protectors can be installed to guard against such surges. Lightning surges can also pass through phone lines, injuring users.

Though justifiably noted as a destructive force, lightning indirectly benefits living organisms. In its passage through air, it fixes both nitrogen and oxygen to form nitric oxide gas. Dissolved in rainwater, this gas falls to the earth as nitrate, where it becomes available to plants.

Despite the fact that Florida has the nation's highest lightning fatality rates, the chance of being struck by a bolt is remote. Nonetheless, people

Fig. 4.10. The night of August 30, 1983, on Cape Canaveral at the Kennedy Space Center as preparations were being made to launch a shuttle mission. Lightning is a common occurrence along the Florida coasts on summer nights. Given the high degree of inflammability of the rocket fuel and the cost of the shuttle and the rocket to launch it, NASA monitors weather activity at all times but especially during launchings. *Source:* NASA.

caught outdoors during a thunderstorm should observe some simple precautions. The best advice, of course, is to seek shelter in a large building, but failing that an automobile will do. If a car is struck by lightning, the discharge usually passes along its surface and that of the tires before it reaches the ground. If there is no possibility of seeking safe shelter in a building or car, several simple rules should be observed.

Before Lightning Strikes

- Keep an eye on the sky. Look for darkening skies, flashes of light, or increasing wind. Listen for the sound of thunder.
- If you can hear thunder, you are close enough to the storm to be struck by lightning. Go to safe shelter immediately.
- Listen to NOAA Weather Radio, commercial radio, or television for the latest weather forecasts.

When a Storm Approaches

- Find shelter in a building or car. Keep car windows closed and avoid convertibles.
- Telephone lines and metal poles can conduct electricity. Unplug appliances. Avoid using the telephone or any electrical appliances.
- Avoid taking a bath or shower or running water for any other purpose.
- Turn off the air conditioner and other expensive electrical equipment such as computer and TV, or invest in a power surge protector.
- Draw blinds and shades over windows. If the wind blows objects through your windows, the shades will prevent glass from shattering into your home.

If Caught Outside

- If you are in the woods, take shelter under the shorter trees.
- If you are boating or swimming, get to land and find shelter immediately.

- Go to a low-lying, open place away from trees, poles, or metal objects. Make sure the place you pick is not subject to flooding.
- Be a very small target! Squat low to the ground. Place your hands on your knees with your head between them. Make yourself the smallest target possible.
- Do not lie flat on the ground; this will make you a larger target.

www.redcross.org/services/disaster

Torrential Rain

Florida lies within a broad region along the Gulf and Atlantic coastal plains of the southeastern United States and experiences frequent episodes of torrential rain, defined here as three or more inches in one day (Florida Climate Center, 2001). Rain of this magnitude contributes approximately 10 percent of the total precipitation that falls on the state, more in some parts of it, less in others. In the Panhandle and the Gold Coast (the southeastern peninsula), torrential rain makes the heaviest contribution, while in the interior of the peninsula it contributes the least. For example, in Apalachicola and Pensacola on the Gulf, torrential rain typically contributes approximately 17 percent of annual precipitation, while in Avon Park and Lakeland, located in the interior of Central Florida, it is between 6 and 8 percent.

Thirty-year weather data were used for figure 4.11, which shows the share that torrential rain contributes to a place's total precipitation. During drought years, a few torrential rains can contribute a much larger percentage. Using Tallahassee as an example, one torrential rain produced 18 percent of the total precipitation in 2000, a year when the city's rainfall was 31 percent below normal. In 2002 annual precipitation was close to normal, but three torrential rainstorms—in March, November, and December—produced 30 percent of that year's total precipitation. During 1970, Miami's total precipitation was 23 percent below normal, and three torrential rains produced 21 percent of that rain. Comparable figures can be produced for most weather stations in Florida, especially along the coast. During those years it is remarkable that the vegetation can survive because for long periods there is virtually no rainfall. Florida vegetation has adapted to irregular rainfall, but some of the exotic plants that have been brought in are not so hardy.

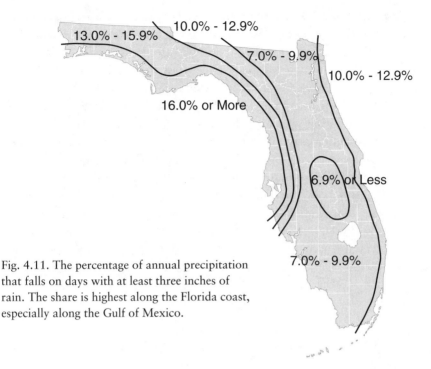

Fig. 4.11. The percentage of annual precipitation that falls on days with at least three inches of rain. The share is highest along the Florida coast, especially along the Gulf of Mexico.

Torrential rain may cause much property and agricultural damage and kill livestock. Florida is especially vulnerable to flooding because it is both low and flat. Although the sandy soils of the peninsula are capable of absorbing water rapidly, absorption is limited because the water table is normally very close to the surface. Most of the state's densely populated areas are situated on the shore of either the Atlantic Ocean or the Gulf of Mexico and are especially vulnerable to rainstorms. Not only are such storms more frequent than in the interior of the state, but a large share of the urban area is covered by pavement and roofs, which concentrate run-off into low areas. Most of Florida's cities today have adequate storm drainage systems to meet the demand of a sudden intense downpour, but flooding does occur, sometimes on a major scale.

Torrential rain in Florida primarily results from the passing of low-pressure systems through or close to it. The best-known low-pressure system is the tropical hurricane, which is capable of producing truly enormous amounts of precipitation over a short period of time. These and the weaker but much more frequent tropical depressions, waves, and storms also produce heavy rainfall. These storms originate in the Atlantic, the Caribbean, the Gulf of Mexico, and on rare occasions the Pacific (after first passing through Mexico). They most frequently occur from May through November, but they may be experienced during any of the other months. Although even in North Florida the dominant period of torrential rain is during warm weather, midlatitude low-pressure systems that pass through or close to this part of Florida occasionally have brought huge amounts of rain over a short period in cooler seasons.

As mentioned in chapter 3, the valleys of North Florida rivers are more subject to flooding than those of the peninsula. The soils of their watershed are more impervious to water absorption than those on the peninsula. Also, since relief is hillier in North Florida, the river valleys are deeper and narrower, confining the excess flow to a smaller area. These two factors, during a torrential rain, lead to rivers quickly rising.

5

Fall

Most Floridians await the arrival of fall with the same anticipation that is common among northerners who long for the first warm days of spring. After a season of heat and humidity that can last up to five months, the first break in the high temperatures comes as a great relief.

Temperature

Unfortunately, the arrival of the first cool mass of air from the North is not easy to predict. In some years people may conclude they never will escape the grip of summer's heat, while in other years a cool air mass arrives early. The first two consecutive days when the minimum temperature drops below 60°F is used here as the definition of the arrival of the first draft of cool air from the North (fig. 5.1). This date varies widely from one year to the next. To illustrate how wide the variation is, the date on which the average minimum temperature fell below 60°F for two consecutive days was calculated for Tallahassee, Orlando, and Miami for each year from 1972 through 2001. Air this cool arrives first in Tallahassee, and as the cold fronts that reach the state become stronger, cool air penetrates deeper down the peninsula. During this period of observation, half of the cool spells in Tallahassee began between September 28 and October 6, in Orlando half fell between October 18 and October 29, and in Miami, half fell between November 1 and November 17. The period when half the cool spells first arrived was over a week longer in Miami than in Tallahassee, evidence that cold air masses are less liable to penetrate deeply down the peninsula than to reach the northern part of the state.

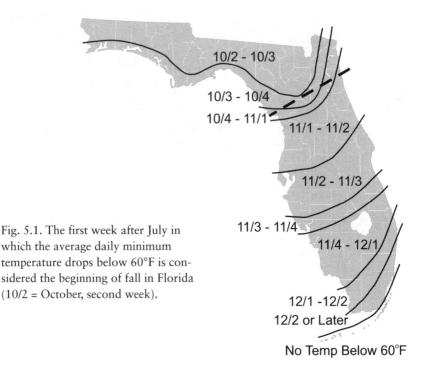

Fig. 5.1. The first week after July in which the average daily minimum temperature drops below 60°F is considered the beginning of fall in Florida (10/2 = October, second week).

The span of days between the earliest and latest time of arrival of the first cool spell is longer in Miami than in either Orlando or Tallahassee. Between 1972 and 2001, the earliest arrived in Miami on October 21, 1989, and the latest on January 5, 1986. In Tallahassee the difference was much less: August 31, 1992, was the earliest and October 19, 1985, the latest. For those who predict the severity of a winter by the date of the arrival of cool air, there is little support from the data. The first cold front may be early, with cold air behind it, but it can be followed as readily by weeks of warm weather as by more cold waves. On the other extreme, the first cold wave may be late and barely bring temperatures down to 59°F, but it can be followed quickly by fronts with bitterly cold air behind them.

Fall is defined here as the first week in which the average daily minimum temperatures drop below 60°F. Typically temperatures first reach this level in the interior of the panhandle in early October, then gradually proceed southward. The natural dividing line between continental and peninsular Florida, which runs from St. Augustine to the mouth of the

Suwannee River, appears clearly in figure 5.1 using this criterion for fall. Immediately to the north of the line, average daily minimum temperatures drop below 60°F considerably earlier than just to the south. For example, although only 30 miles separate Gainesville and Ocala, average daily minimum temperatures drop below 60°F in Gainesville the third week in October but do not reach Ocala until the first week in November. Using this criterion for fall, it never arrives in the Keys.

During November, the Canadian breeding ground of cold air masses becomes sufficiently frigid, and the continental pressure systems that deliver them become strong enough, to push cold air deep onto the peninsula. While it takes two weeks for our definition of fall to move from Gainesville to Ocala, it only takes two more weeks for the average weekly minimum temperature to progress down the peninsula from Ocala almost to Lake Okeechobee, 120 miles farther south.

As in other seasons, the marine effect brought about by air entering the peninsula from the large water bodies on either side retards temperature change along Florida's coasts. This effect is stronger on the Atlantic coast, which gets the full force of the prevailing easterly winds off the ocean, than on the west side of the state, which receives them after they have first passed over the peninsula. On Miami Beach, the effects of the prevailing onshore winds are so great that throughout the year its daily average minimum temperature never drops below 60°F, although on 38 days the average drops below that level at Miami International Airport, only 8 miles to the west.

Precipitation

Aside from the drop in temperature to more moderate levels, another pleasure of fall weather in Florida is that it is normally drier than summer. Like spring, it separates the hot summer from the mild winter. The angle of the sun at its zenith is less each day, and its ability to heat the ground is declining. Without the intense heating of the ground, as experienced in the summer, convectional rainstorms cease to be so frequent. Nor is there as strong a convergence of moist air masses from the Gulf of Mexico and the Atlantic Ocean over the interior of the peninsula as in the summer. Also as the Azores-Bermuda high-pressure system migrates south in the fall, it brings atmospheric stability to the part of the state it covers, reduc-

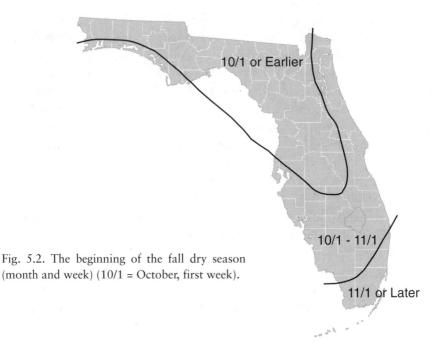

Fig. 5.2. The beginning of the fall dry season (month and week) (10/1 = October, first week).

ing the likelihood of rain. The stability, however, may be interrupted by the arrival of tropical storms. In North Florida during the fall, few continental low-pressure systems pass near enough to bring frontal precipitation.

Throughout most of the state, the dry period begins during the last week in September or the first week in October, although it is retarded along the eastern seaboard, where the rainy season lingers into late October and in a few places even until the middle of November (fig. 5.2). In October along the state's Atlantic coast, seven to ten days normally have at least a tenth of an inch of rainfall. The number of days with rain of this intensity drops steadily toward the north and west, until in the panhandle during that month there are less than four days with precipitation of that amount or more (fig. 5.3).

The north of the state has only a short dry period. By the middle of November it begins to experience frontal precipitation from continental storm systems that have begun to dip into the nation's South. Throughout

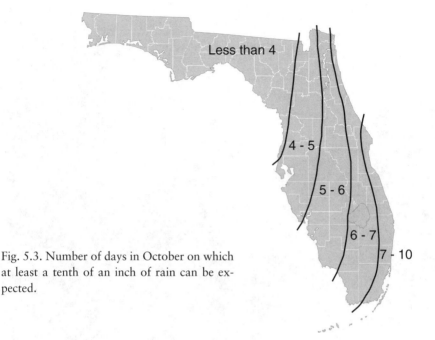

Fig. 5.3. Number of days in October on which at least a tenth of an inch of rain can be expected.

the fall and winter, these storm systems seldom bring rain to South Florida, which is normally dry during the cool months.

Although a dry season begins in fall throughout Florida, heavy rains may occur in association with tropical cyclones. Fall is the season in which hurricanes and weaker tropical low-pressure storm systems are most frequent, though they may come as early as June. Until 1979, when Hurricane Claudette dumped 42 inches of rain on Alvin, Texas, the highest amount of rainfall that had ever fallen in 24 hours in the United States was in Yankeetown, on Florida's Big Bend coast. On September 5, 1950, a hurricane drowned the town in 38.7 inches of rainfall. The state's second-highest 24-hour period of rain was associated with a weak tropical low-pressure system that drenched the North Florida town of Trenton with 30 inches of rain in October 1941. Similar storms, both in November, have brought heavy rains to Key West and Fernandina Beach, and each community has had a 24-hour rainfall exceeding 20 inches.

Fortunately, rainfall of such magnitude is rare in Florida. It is not un-

Fig. 5.4. Governor Farris Bryant inspecting downtown Live Oak after the flood of September 12, 1964. The passage of Hurricane Dora caused 18 inches of rain to fall on the town in two days. *Source:* Florida State Archives.

usual anywhere in the state, however, for a tropical disturbance of some type to produce eight inches or more of rain in a two- or three-day period, or for three inches of rain to fall in a two-hour period (fig. 5.4). In fact, during the past 30 years, approximately three-quarters of all Florida weather stations reported at least one day in which eight inches of rain fell, and 12 percent experienced such torrential storms four or more times. Almost half of all these heavy rains occurred in September and October and were associated with tropical depressions. Rain of this magnitude may occur throughout most of the year, but it is rare during the height of the winter.

Most Florida cities are laid out on flat surfaces, making the rapid removal of water difficult. In addition, like cities everywhere, Florida cities have a large share of their surface covered by roofs and pavement, impermeable to water. Heavy rain often disrupts traffic, and the city water supply may become contaminated as neighborhoods are flooded, causing sewers to back up and septic tanks to overflow. When rains in Florida cease, flood waters normally recede rapidly, since much of the state is covered by sand and underlain by limestone, both of which are highly permeable.

Hurricanes

Hurricanes have brought greater loss of life and destruction to Florida than any other weather event, and no other state has suffered more frequently from them (Barnes, 1998; Williams and Duedall, 2002). Though the number can only be estimated, it is believed that in this century over 3,000 Floridians lost their lives during these intense tropical storms, almost 2,000 in one hurricane alone. Property damage, when converted to the present value of the dollar, exceeds $50 billion (table B.2). This figure includes severe damage to vegetable crops and citrus groves (Attaway, 1999).

A hurricane has been described as a heat engine. Its central core is warmer than the atmosphere that surrounds it. The storm is fueled by energy released when huge quantities of water vapor condense as air spirals up through the storm's eye. The warmer the ocean where these storms develop, the more powerful they may become. The word *hurricane* is of Mayan Indian origin and is specifically used to describe mature tropical cyclones that develop north of the equator in the Atlantic Ocean. Similar storms also form in the lower latitudes of the Pacific Ocean on either side of the equator. West of 180° longitude in the Northern Hemisphere they are known as typhoons; east of that longitude, in the same hemisphere, they are called hurricanes. In the Southern Hemisphere, where they periodically invade northern Australia, they have the curious name "willy-willies." They are found in the Indian Ocean as well, where they are simply called cyclones.

Scientists now have a reasonably accurate idea of how tropical cyclones evolve. In the case of hurricanes, conditions for their birth develop in spring, when water temperatures in the Atlantic Ocean begin to rise. Conception commonly occurs over that ocean between 20° N and 5° N, the belt of the westward-moving trade winds. This zone is bounded on its poleward side by the Azores-Bermuda high-pressure cell and on the equatorward side by a low-pressure belt known as the intertropical convergence zone (Elsner and Kara, 1999).

A hurricane may develop in several ways. One of the most common is from weak troughs of low pressure that often form in the lower latitudes over the Atlantic Ocean and begin to drift toward the west. Known as easterly waves, as they move from east to west, they are identifiable on satellite imagery as masses of cumulus clouds. On any given day in summer there may be several in the Atlantic and Caribbean. Most die, but a few mature into tropical depressions with centers into which winds spiral. These have well-defined cloud patterns, shaped by that counterclockwise airflow. Many easterly waves originate in the vicinity of the Cape Verde Islands, off the North African coast. Once a tropical low-pressure system reaches the tropical depression stage, the likelihood of it growing into a hurricane increases, but even at this stage few mature any further.

The Cape Verde breeding ground for easterly waves was well known even in the last century. Further evidence, however, was provided in the middle of July 1984 when a milky haze descended over South Florida. The haze was attributed to dust from the Sahara Desert, whose western shore is 600 miles from the Cape Verde Islands. This dust had been swept into an easterly wave, which had then crossed the ocean to reach the Western Hemisphere. It was not the first time this long-distance transfer from the Sahara Desert had taken place. But dust blows in from the Great Plains far more frequently, particularly in North Florida.

In the stage when the hurricane is still only a depression, an intense circulation of air has already developed, and massive amounts of water vapor are being condensed as air spirals up the depression's center. Banks of cumulus and, increasingly, cumulonimbus clouds form. The storm will increase in intensity as long as more air exits from the top of the center than comes in from the bottom. When wind speeds within the depression reach 39 miles per hour, the meteorologists change its classification to a tropical storm, and it is given a name. If the wind speed in a tropical storm exceeds 74 miles per hour, it is reclassified to a true hurricane. Tropical cyclones die when they are deprived of warm, moist tropical air, which happens if they move over colder water in higher latitudes. They also expire rapidly when they come ashore, in part because they lose their source of energy, which is relatively warm water, and also because of the greater frictional drag from moving over land than over water. Although a tropical cyclone quickly loses its hurricane force winds when it comes ashore, it often retains its physical structure and can release huge amounts of precipitation over the nation's interior, causing flash floods.

Since 1970, hurricanes have been classified on a scale from one to five, based on wind velocity, central pressure, and the height of the storm surge (Saffir/Simpson Scale). The storm surge is an unusual rise in the water level along a coast as a result of the storm, and it will be described in more detail later. It also should be noted that storm surges could be produced by storms other than hurricanes. A storm surge was responsible for the death of ten people at Dekle and Keaton beaches along Florida's Big Bend coast during the Superstorm of 1993, which was not a hurricane. Minimal hurricanes are ranked one; those with extraordinary wind velocities and low pressure are given a classification of five. Of the 164 hurricanes that made landfall between 1900 and 2002 in the United States, 36 percent were category one, 23 percent category two, 30 percent category three, 10 percent category four, and 1 percent category five. Florida is particularly prone to violent hurricanes. Whereas it has experienced 29 percent of the nation's category one hurricanes, 38 percent of those of category three or higher have made landfall within the state.

Elsner and Kara (1999) have made a detailed study of hurricane landfalls in the United States. Between 1851 and 1999, 253 hurricanes crossed into one or more of the 48 coterminous states. The states with shorelines along the Gulf of Mexico and the Atlantic Ocean south of North Carolina are the most vulnerable to these storms. Florida, with its extreme southern location and long coastline, most frequently finds itself in the path of these intense storms. In fact, 44 percent of all hurricanes that reached the United States between 1886 and 2002 during their progress passed into Florida. Of the 115 hurricanes that entered Florida from the sea during that period, 41 percent struck the panhandle, 27 percent the southwest coast, 25 percent the southeast coast, and 7 percent the northeast coast (fig. 5.5). Since these coasts are of varying lengths, a more accurate way to determine the chances of a hurricane entering a specific place in Florida is to calculate how frequently they enter a specific coastal county (fig. 5.6).

These powerful tropical storms may reach over 400 miles in diameter, and maximum wind velocities have been estimated to exceed 200 miles per hour, although sustained winds usually are closer to 100 miles per hour. Hurricane-force winds seldom extend more than 50 miles from the center of the storm, but in the most powerful they may reach out several hundred miles. Hurricanes generally produce tremendous amounts of

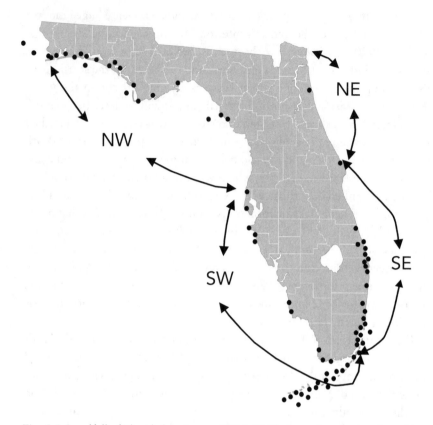

Fig. 5.5. Landfall of Florida hurricanes, 1900–2002. Several came close but either reverted to tropical storm status or moved into neighboring Alabama.

rainfall, and it is not unusual that during their passage 10 to 20 inches will fall over a wide area. Tornadoes often are spawned by the hurricane, adding to the storm's destructive force. The usual life of a tropical storm in the hurricane stage is from 3 to 12 days.

Satellite photography has offered dramatic views of the development of these tropical storms and their movement over water and land. The most noticeable feature of the hurricane is the eye in its center. Within the eye is the storm's lowest air pressure. The eye wall, formed from cumulonimbus clouds, surrounds the eye. Here are located the storm's strongest winds and heaviest precipitation. Eyes reach heights of more than 50,000 feet and vary in width from as little as 5 miles to more than 40. The eye

Fig. 5.6. Number of years between hurricane landfalls along the coastline of a Florida county, based on landfalls since 1900. *Source:* Elsner and Kara, 1999.

moves at an average speed of 10–15 miles per hour, but when it enters higher latitudes where the water is cooler, the storm's energy declines. At that time it often gains forward speed while the speed of the wind entering it decreases.

The few tropical storms that reach hurricane intensity in May and June usually originate in the Gulf of Mexico. July storms that mature into hurricanes develop mainly off the northern coast of the Greater Antilles and Bahamas. In August and September, the height of the hurricane season, they frequently reach full hurricane status several hundred miles east of the Lesser Antilles. By October, a disproportionate number of storms attain hurricane status off Mexico's Yucatan peninsula.

Florida Hurricanes

Between 1900 and 2002, 68 hurricanes entered Florida or passed within 50 miles of it (table B.1). During that period there also were hundreds of tropical storms of less severity. Fully 70 percent of the 68 hurricanes reached Florida between the first week in September and the third week in October. The earliest hurricane, a category one that originated in the Caribbean, came ashore on the panhandle coast on June 9, 1966. The latest, also originating in the Caribbean, struck near Sarasota on December 2, 1925. Like the earliest arrival, it also was weak, with winds barely at hurricane strength. Since the strength of a hurricane is, to a degree, dependent upon the temperature of the water it passes over, powerful storms are seldom generated during the early months of the hurricane season.

Between 1900 and 2000, of the eight hurricanes whose eyes either made landfall in Florida or came extremely close before August, five were in the lowest two categories at their height, two were in the third category, and one in the fourth. None was in the fifth. Of the 36 hurricanes whose eyes reached or came close to the state in August and September, only 10 were in the first two categories at their height, 17 in the third and fourth categories, and 9 in the fifth. Between November and December the four hurricanes were evenly distributed among the first four categories. None attained category 5.

Many variables interact to create the right physical environment for a hurricane to be born and the path it will follow. Although meteorologists now have a clear idea of how these violent storms are created, the research to predict their birth, their evolution, and their paths is still in a formative state. To deal with so many variables, researchers must utilize computers of enormous power. It is interesting to note that in 2002 the major use of three of the world's ten most powerful computers was to analyze the weather. The rest primarily were employed to simulate nuclear explosions and for other military purposes.

Although the use to predict the behavior of future Florida hurricanes is marginal, analyzing the behavior of those that arrived during the twentieth century may have some utility. Their frequency has varied by decade.

The decades when they were most frequent were between 1920 and 1949. The decades when they were least frequent were the 1970s and 1980s. The decade of the 1990s produced an average number of hurricanes (seven). Actually, in 54 years of the twentieth century, Florida experienced no hurricanes. The period from 1980 through 1984 was the longest in which no hurricanes were experienced, but that interval was almost equaled between 1988 and 1991. There have also been years when hurricanes were especially common. In 1933, three made landfall and one was a near miss. The near miss passed through the Florida Straits, its eye almost reaching Key West on September 1. Three days later, another came ashore at Jupiter on the southeast coast. Jupiter had already experienced a hurricane on July 30, and on October 5 another hurricane came ashore in the Keys. There have been a number of other examples of two hurricanes reaching Florida during a 30-day period, but none where four hurricanes buffeted the state in one hurricane season.

The paths of twentieth-century Florida hurricanes also are worthy of analysis. The northwest, southwest, and southeast coasts sustain far more hits than the northeast coast (fig. 5.5). The Keys are especially vulnerable because they are not only on a well-traveled path of hurricanes that formed in the Atlantic but one that Caribbean hurricanes frequently follow. The northwest coast is most frequently assaulted by Caribbean-born hurricanes, but occasionally it will be struck by one that has passed into the Gulf of Mexico from the Atlantic by crossing the islands of the Antilles or even the Florida peninsula. The northeast has been spared because it is off the regular path of hurricanes. Some truly violent ones have passed offshore, including Hugo and Floyd, but have continued northward, reaching land in Georgia, the Carolinas, or even farther north.

Meteorologists today are incorporating the El Niño Southern Oscillation phenomenon into their study of the behavior of hurricanes. It has been observed that, during the El Niño phase, upper-level winds over the Atlantic basin become unfavorable for tropical cyclone development, and compared with the Neutral phases, and even more so the La Niña, fewer develop (O'Brien, 1999). Tartaglione (2002) supported the conclusion that there was a distinct difference in the frequency of hurricanes making landfall between the La Niña and El Niño phases, but she took issue with the generality that during neutral phases the frequency was between the other two. Florida was an exception. Although it applied to the eastern seaboard from Georgia northward, in Florida the frequency of hurricanes making landfall during the Neutral phase was no different than during the La Niña phase.

Since 1980, only one powerful hurricane has struck a highly populated area: Andrew, which entered Miami-Dade County in August 1992. As a consequence, today most Floridians who live in coastal counties have never experienced the destruction that a truly strong hurricane can create. This fact is of great concern to state and local officials who are responsible for disaster preparedness. Newcomers sometimes dismiss the hurricane experiences of older residents as exaggerations. These storms can be dangerous, and one is well advised to heed official announcements issued during their passage.

Despite being highly traceable through satellite imagery, because hurricanes are steered by upper-air currents and pressure systems far distant from them, their path remains difficult to predict far in advance. Today meteorologists usually can predict 24 hours in advance of their arrival that a hurricane will make landfall somewhere along a 200-mile coastline. Their accuracy improves to a specified 100-mile coastline 12 hours before landfall. Predictions on landfall made more than 24 hours before arrival become increasingly less accurate.

Since the paths of hurricanes are so difficult to determine, meteorologists have been reticent in warning the public of an approaching hurricane too far in advance. The National Weather Service began to issue three-day warnings in 1964, but for the 2003 hurricane season, for the first time, it will begin to issue warnings five days in advance. This change has been made possible through improved technology and better predictive models. Meteorologists believe that their new forecasts will be at least as accurate as the three-day kind that were issued fifteen years ago. It should be noted, however, that the five-day forecast, like the earlier one, will not be very specific as to where the hurricane will strike. What it is expected to do is make it possible for residents to begin to make storm preparations earlier than before.

The violence of these storms and their need to be closely monitored motivated the U.S. government to establish an office whose entire responsibilities involve hurricanes. The National Hurricane Center in Miami reports the location of hurricanes and predicts their paths. Its work is greatly facilitated by weather satellites, which today are usually the first to identify weather aberrations that might evolve into hurricanes. The center's staff also works with other public officials on problems of evacuation.

Efforts have been made to modify the power of a hurricane. Bizarre proposals were rejected, such as exploding powerful bombs within them. However, in the past 20 years, the National Oceanic and Atmospheric Administration has supported a number of efforts to weaken hurricanes. None, however, has succeeded (Kahn, 2002). One suggestion was to coat the water below the path of a hurricane with a thin layer of oil to slow evaporation. Another suggestion was to bombard tornadoes with microwaves from space. The latest effort is to release from an airplane tons of absorbent polymer powder to dissolve clouds.

To be in the direct path of a hurricane's eye is an unsettling experience. The storm is most intense as the wall of the eye passes over. Suddenly, after the wall has passed and the eye is directly overhead, winds can decline in strength to those of an average day. If it is daylight, the sun might appear in a sky that is only partially cloudy. Many who have been in an eye comment on the strange sensation of being surrounded by the roar of the wind coming from its wall yet not feel it. It may take as little as a few minutes or as long as several hours for an eye to pass, depending on its size and forward speed. Once it passes, the full force of the storm resumes as quickly as it ceased but usually from another direction. The structure of hurricanes is so well known today that few are deceived by the comparatively balmy period during the passage of the eye. In the past, however, some were emboldened to emerge from shelters and resume outdoor activities in the belief the storm had subsided, only to be caught outside when the hurricane winds resumed.

Labor Day Hurricane

A particularly vivid account of being in the eye of a hurricane was given by J. E. Duane, a cooperative observer on Long Key for what was then known as the U.S. Weather Bureau (Ludlum, 1982). Duane survived the Labor Day Hurricane of September 2, 1935, one of the two most powerful hurricanes ever recorded in Florida (the other was Andrew in 1992). Like that of many powerful hurricanes, the eye had a small diameter, roughly 10 miles. Within it the air pressure was incredibly low. As it passed over Long Key, it produced what for a time became the lowest sea-level adjusted barometric reading ever recorded in the Western Hemisphere (26.35 inches). That record was broken in 1988 by Hurricane Gilbert, which struck islands in the Caribbean and the Yucatan peninsula of Mexico. Even today it stands as the record for the United States. No accurate measurement was ever made of the strength of its winds as the eye passed over the Keys, since the anemometers that recorded wind velocity were blown away. Nonetheless, from the damage done it was calculated that wind gusts must have reached well over 200 miles per hour. Wave wash marks on trees provided evidence that the wall of water that struck Long Key when the eye arrived was at least 20 feet above mean sea level. Duane wrote of being in the eye:

> 9:20 P.M.—Barometer now reads 27.22 inches, wind has abated. We now hear other noises than the wind and know the center of the storm is over us. We head for the last and only cottage that I think can stand the blow due to arrive shortly. A section hand reports that a man, his wife, and four children are in an unsafe place a half-mile down the track. Aid is given them and now all hands, 20 in number, are in this cottage waiting patiently for what is to come. During this lull the sky is clear to northward—stars shining brightly; and a very light breeze continues throughout lull; no flat calm. About the middle of the lull, which lasted 55 minutes, the sea began to lift up, it seemed, and rise very fast; this from the ocean side of camp. I put my flashlight out on sea and could see walls of water which seemed many feet high. I had to race fast to regain entrance of cottage, but water caught me waist deep, although writer was only about 60 feet from doorway of cottage. Water lifted cottage from its foundations and it floated.
>
> 10:10 P.M.—Barometer now 27.02 inches; wind beginning to blow.
>
> 10:15 P.M.—The first blast from SSW, full force. House now breaking up—wind seemed stronger than any time during storm. I glanced at barometer, which read 26.98 inches, dropped it in water and was blown outside into sea; got hung up in broken fronds of coconut tree and hung on for dear life. I was then struck by some object and knocked unconscious.
>
> September 3: 2:25 A.M.—I became conscious in tree and found I was lodged about 20 feet above ground. (Ludlum, 1982)

Duane was fortunate to have survived the hurricane. More than 400 residents of the Keys lost their lives. Deaths were especially heavy among 700

Fig. 5.7. The rescue train sent to evacuate residents of the Keys during the Labor Day hurricane of 1935 stalled outside of Islamorada, where wind and waves quickly swept the cars off the tracks. Several hundred lost their lives. *Source:* Florida State Archives.

World War I veterans, part of the Bonus Army that had marched on Washington earlier in the year from all over the nation in search of economic benefits. Some of this army of the unemployed had been sent to work on public road projects in the Keys. Warnings of an approaching hurricane had reached their camps on Upper Matecumbe Key, and a train from Miami was requested. Unfortunately, through poor communications between the camp officials and those of the railroad, the train left too late (Drye, 2002). Although it reached Islamorada and had begun to pick up veterans and other Keys inhabitants, water rose above the tracks, putting out the steam engine's fire and stalling it near the town's station. It was here that wind and waves swept all the cars off the tracks, drowning many of the passengers (fig. 5.7). Most Keys inhabitants sought shelter in wooden homes and barracks that quickly began to break up under the winds. Many had to find shelter elsewhere, a number choosing the nearby railroad embankment. Here the death toll was high, both from drowning and being blasted to death from the sand and debris driven by the powerful winds. Bodies were found naked, without skin, clad only in belts and shoes. They had been stripped and skinned by the sand-laden winds.

The loss of so many lives created a furor throughout the state, and a search was initiated to identify who was to blame (Drye, 2002). Ernest Hemingway, who came from his home in Key West to help in the cleanup, wrote a vitriolic piece for a national magazine condemning the federal government for sending the veterans to the Keys without adequate emergency plans in the event of a hurricane. There were those, however, who believed that the guilt for the lack of disaster preparedness rested more with Florida's state and local governments. The lethal nature of these storms certainly should not have been any surprise to government officials. Before 1935, Florida had experienced four twentieth-century hurricanes in which loss of life had exceeded 100.

One of the most destructive hurricanes ever to strike the state was that which passed directly over Miami on September 18, 1926. It proceeded across the peninsula, exiting at Fort Myers, but after crossing the Gulf of Mexico it reentered near Pensacola on September 20. More than 6,000 were injured and 372 were killed. Property damage was estimated at $112 million, well over $1 billion in today's terms. In Miami, more than 120 people were killed and 5,000 homes were destroyed. At least 150 ships were driven onto land or sunk in Biscayne Bay. Large parts of both Miami and Miami Beach were flooded by the exceptionally high storm surge. Some boats torn from their moorings floated for blocks into the interior of Miami on the floodwaters, where they became marooned. Tent cities and tourist camps, hastily built to house the people who arrived during the famous Miami land boom of the 1920s, were leveled.

Moralists, who had come to accept Miami as a modern Sodom, believed the hurricane was retribution. Although the land boom had begun to decline months before the hurricane, a fundamentalist preacher in New York City was quoted as saying; "And yonder is beautiful Florida. How beautiful. But how she did depart from God's way? She turned after the worship of Mammon. Racetrack gamblers were welcomed. The Sunday sermons were forgotten in the mad rush for gold. But God did not forget them. It is to be hoped that Florida will return to God, and it seems now she will."

Although Miami suffered the worst loss of property, most deaths were along the south shore of Lake Okeechobee, which was at that time rapidly being developed for agriculture. Several hundred residents were drowned when waves driven by the strong winds lashed a weak dike along the lake's southern shore, forcing it to give way and flooding a densely populated farming area.

In the debate that followed, some felt the state was derelict because it acceded to the wishes of boatmen on Lake Okeechobee who wanted the level of the water to remain high. Farmers had protested this policy in the belief, which proved correct, that heavy rains would overflow the dike. In September 1928, Lake Okeechobee was being maintained at a low level but not low enough to prevent a far worse disaster than that which took place two years earlier. On September 16, a strong hurricane with winds gusting to an estimated 150 miles per hour came ashore at Palm Beach. Although loss of life and even property damage were not great along the coast, when the storm reached Lake Okeechobee, water driven by the wind again breached the dike along the southern shore. Once again, the agricultural settlements behind the dike were flooded.

The loss of life in 1928 was horrendous. The estimate was 1,836, but many people were never accounted for (Mykle, 2002). Three-quarters of the victims were blacks, many from the Bahamas who had come as seasonal labor to work on the vegetable farms. In the scramble to seek shelter above the floodwaters, many in the farming area climbed into trees, only to encounter snakes, including the poisonous water moccasin. A number of people died from snakebites. Bodies were driven so far into the Everglades by the storm that years passed before workers found the skeletons while clearing land for agriculture.

The enormity of the 1928 disaster did bring change to the area around Lake Okeechobee. Dikes were lengthened, heightened, and made stronger. Existing canals were widened and deepened, and new ones were built. A pumping system was installed that could quickly move massive amounts of water to the ocean, to conservation areas that were laid out in the Everglades, or even back into the lake. Today, this system, expanded to several thousand miles of canals throughout South Florida and more than 200 installations that monitor and move water to large water impoundment areas, is operated by the South Florida Water Management District (fig. 5.8). Water drainage is so well managed that officials are confident that a hurricane, even a very wet one, would incur neither the number of deaths nor the water damage of previous ones.

Since 1970, federal, state, and county agencies have taken many measures to minimize the impact of a hurricane. These include evacuation plans, rigid building codes to ensure that new structures can withstand hurricane winds, restrictive zoning along the shoreline, set-back lines to limit beach development, and flood protection and educational programs to inform residents and visitors. To lessen the damage from storm surge along Florida coastlines, homes near the shoreline are required to be elevated on well-anchored stilts to a prescribed height.

Storm surges often are the major cause of death and property damage during storms (fig. 5.9). In the United States, more than 8,000 deaths resulted from a storm surge during the 1900 hurricane in Galveston, Texas. The second worst was the 1928 hurricane that caused Lake Okeechobee to overflow the dikes on its southern shore, killing about 1,836.

A surge is a rise in sea level as the storm's wind drives water onto the land. The height of this tide depends upon the depth of water offshore, the shape of the coastline, the forward speed of the storm, the direction and strength of its winds, the stage of the normal tide at the time of arrival, and the air pressure within the storm. Air of low pressure causes the water below it to dome upward; the lower the pressure, the higher the dome. The worst possibility is for a fast-moving hurricane with very low pressure to reach shore at high tide along a shallow coastline and to drive water directly up a bay or estuary.

The September 1926 hurricane drove water up Miami's Biscayne Bay, a lagoon that is narrow on its northern side, causing a surge in several places slightly higher than 12 feet above mean sea level. A large part of the young cities of Miami and Miami Beach were flooded. Today a surge of

Fig. 5.8. Growth of the South Florida water control system, 1920–70. Almost 2,000 people died in 1928 when Lake Okeechobee overflowed its southern bank during a hurricane. Government response to the tragedy was to build an elaborate flood control system, which today is useful not only in controlling excessive rain but in apportioning water during periods of drought. *Source:* Fernald and Patton, 1984.

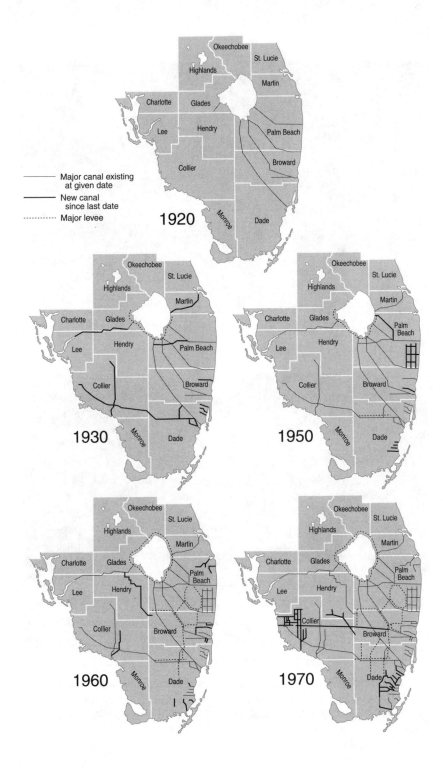

Major canal existing
at given date

New canal
since last date

Major levee

1920

Okeechobee
Highlands
St. Lucie
Martin
Charlotte
Glades
Lee
Hendry
Palm Beach
Collier
Broward
Monroe
Dade

Okeechobee
Highlands
St. Lucie
Martin
Charlotte
Glades
Lee
Hendry
Palm Beach
Collier
Broward
Monroe
Dade

1930

Okeechobee
Highlands
St. Lucie
Martin
Charlotte
Glades
Lee
Hendry
Palm
Beach
Collier
Broward
Monroe
Dade

1950

Okeechobee
Highlands
St. Lucie
Martin
Charlotte
Glades
Palm
Beach
Lee
Hendry
Collier
Broward
Monroe
Dade

1960

Okeechobee
Highlands
St. Lucie
Martin
Charlotte
Glades
Palm
Beach
Lee
Hendry
Collier
Broward
Monroe
Dade

1970

a.

b.

Figs. 5.9a, 5.9b. When Hurricane Eloise struck the Panhandle in 1975, it brought with it an especially damaging surge that destroyed many buildings near the shore. These before and after shots illustrate the amount of damage that results from surges. *Source:* NOAA.

that height would bring floodwaters to areas with hundreds of thousands of residents. Hurricane-induced storm surges on Lake Okeechobee during the 1920s caused the floods that spread death and destruction. When Hurricane Donna came ashore on the southern side of Everglades National Park in 1960, the surge reached nearly 11 feet, devastating the vegetation along the unoccupied coast.

In the event of a high surge, the evacuation of densely populated Miami Beach would be especially difficult, since it is built on an island and the causeways connecting it to the mainland could easily be blocked. In addition, evacuation would be complicated because many of those who would be evacuated are retirees, some in poor health. Problems of removing people from the path of a storm are so complex here that it has been proposed to engage in vertical evacuation. Under this approach, instead of moving people to shelters on the mainland, they would be transported to high-rise buildings that have been identified as well built.

Many other Florida cities besides Miami have been built along the shores of bays and estuaries and face storm-related problems similar to those in the Miami area. The State's Division of Emergency Management has estimated that about 25 percent of the state's population resides in areas vulnerable to storm surges that could be produced by a category three hurricane or stronger (Florida Department of Community Affairs, 1984). The inhabitants of the Gulf coast south of St. Petersburg would be at particular peril because almost 90 percent live on land that would be submerged by a high surge. Fortunately, except for Collier County, the risk of a hurricane striking along this coast is low compared with the Keys, the coast of Miami-Dade County, and the coast of extreme northwest Florida.

Counties have drawn up evacuation plans to be implemented on the arrival of a hurricane. There was a large-scale evacuation of Panama City when Eloise came ashore in 1975. Elena, a category three hurricane that meandered through the Gulf of Mexico in early September 1983 but never reached the Florida coast, caused the largest evacuation in the state's history up until then and one of the largest for any reason in the nation. Over 600,000 people along the Gulf were evacuated, one-third seeking shelter in public facilities. In November 1985, Hurricane Kate caused the evacuation of 100,000 along the panhandle coast. In 1992, as Hurricane Andrew approached, an estimated 55,000 were evacuated from the Florida Keys. In Miami-Dade County, 517,000 people either left or went to shelters. The figure was 300,000 in Broward County, 315,000 in Palm Beach County, and 15,000 in St. Lucie County. Much smaller numbers left or sought shelter along the west coast of the state, recognizing that it would be the hurricane's exit point. Floyd, a 1999 category four hurricane that passed Florida offshore as it proceeded up the Atlantic coast, also caused a large evacuation.

The estimated time to clear residents from the path of a hurricane varies greatly. Florida's Division of Emergency Management has made estimates for the five hurricane categories. Using category three hurricanes as an example, for Key West (Monroe County), whose only land connection to the mainland is the Overseas Highway, evacuation time is estimated to be 36 hours. Densely populated St. Petersburg–Clearwater and nearby Tampa require 17 hours. For coastal West Florida cities, it also is quite long; for Pensacola it is almost 24 hours, and for those between that city and Panama City it is around 21 hours. Naples has the longest clearance time at 50 hours. Lightly populated Dixie County would require 6 hours.

Jay Baker, a Florida State University geographer, has studied residents' response to hurricane evacuation orders. His findings are somewhat discouraging, since he discovered that many people choose to ignore them (2002). Although compliance was unusually high for Andrew, since it approached directly and was announced as an exceptionally powerful storm, the response to the approach of Hurricane Floyd in 1999, almost the same strength as Andrew, was much poorer. Floyd, however, paralleled the Florida coastline and went ashore in North Carolina. He believes that many residents along the coast have inaccurate perceptions about their vulnerability and are not clear that the evacuation orders apply to them.

The National Weather Service begins releasing information on tropical disturbances that might develop into hurricanes when they are first detected. Advisories are released by the National Hurricane Center at six-hour intervals. Aimed mainly at maritime and aviation interests, advisories indicate location, wind speeds, central air pressure, and expected movement in the next 12 to 24 hours. If the disturbance grows into a tropical storm, advisories become more comprehensive. As the hurricane approaches land, advisory information focuses on its possible effects on the coastline and interior. The six-hour advisories are then supplemented with intermediate ones.

A hurricane watch announcement is made when the storm appears to be within 36 hours of striking the coast. It is important to realize that a hurricane watch indicates a strong possibility that the hurricane will make landfall, but there still is considerable uncertainty. Furthermore, the place of landfall cannot be accurately identified. If it is expected that the hurricane will make landfall within 24 hours, the watch is upgraded and renamed a warning. The warning identifies coastal areas where hurricane conditions are expected to occur. Advisories containing hurricane warnings also state probable flood danger in coastal and inland areas and the expectation of hurricane-spawned tornadoes.

Hurricane Andrew

All these preparations were put to the test in August 1992 with the arrival of Hurricane Andrew (Rappaport, 1993). Originally, when Andrew came ashore in the southern half of Miami-Dade County, its strength was categorized as a four, but 10 years later, following extensive investigation, NOAA changed the category to five. This placed it alongside the 1935 Labor Day hurricane, which crossed the Keys, and Hurricane Camille, which came ashore in Mississippi in 1969. These are the three most powerful hurricanes on record in the United States.

When it came ashore in the early morning of August 24 along the shore of southern Miami-Dade County, Andrew was a small but extremely powerful hurricane (fig. 5.10). The National Hurricane Center had been following its progress by satellite from its birth on August 14 as a tropical depression off the coast of Africa near the Cape Verde Islands. On August 17 in the mid-Atlantic, it became a tropical storm and acquired its name. It also began to change its course from west to west-northwest, and as a consequence it spared the Lesser Antilles. Andrew reached hurricane strength on the morning of August 22 about 500 miles almost directly east of South Florida. From there it continued on a nearly due westward course, crossing the Bahamas on August 23. It crossed Florida on August 24 and reached southern Louisiana on August 25, where it also wrought damage and fatalities (eight directly from the storm, and nine indirectly). After it entered Louisiana, it turned eastward and rapidly lost its strength. Nonetheless, it brought heavy rains to states between Mississippi and Virginia.

Hurricane Andrew
NOAA-12 AVHRR HRPT
Multi-spectral False Color Image
August 23, 1992 @ 12:31 UTC

Fig. 5.10. Hurricane Andrew, which came ashore in southern Miami-Dade County in August 1992, became the nation's most costly weather event, a dubious record it still holds. This satellite photo reveals the counterclockwise circulation of winds and a well-developed eye. *Source:* NOAA.

Casualties were comparatively light in Florida: 15 directly related to the storm, and 29 indirectly. The National Hurricane Center, the military, Florida's Division of Emergency Management, numerous county and municipal agencies, and many nongovernment agencies deserve credit for that. Warnings were clear, and since the path of the storm remained almost constant, as time passed warnings became increasingly geographically specific. Also, compliance to evacuation orders was unusually high.

Despite Hurricane Andrew's being relatively dry, and the storm surge along Miami-Dade County's shoreline not being excessively high, property damage was incredibly high. Estimates vary, but in 2002 dollars Andrew damaged $35 billion in property, making it the most costly natural disaster in the nation's history. Several billion dollars more must be added as the indirect costs incurred from the temporary loss of employment and retail sales. Andrew reportedly destroyed 8,000 single-family homes, damaged another 49,000 sufficiently that the owners had to leave until repairs were made, and left perhaps 100,000 homes severely damaged but livable. More than 10,000 apartments were destroyed. Over 90 percent of all mobile homes in southern Miami-Dade County, or 9,000, were lost (fig. 5.11). More than 13,000 apartments had to be abandoned until repairs could be made. Although the surge damaged few homes, boats accounted for approximately $500 million of property damage (fig. 5.12). Clearing the debris alone cost over $2 billion, and by weight there was at least three times more debris than the total removed from the site of New York's World Trade Center towers after they were destroyed by terrorists on September 11, 2001.

A natural disaster of the magnitude of Hurricane Andrew brings out the best in a community, and in South Florida there were countless examples of family, friends, and strangers who came to the assistance of those who had lost their homes, at least temporarily. Unfortunately, there were many who took advantage of the calamity to enrich themselves. Looting became a serious problem until a curfew was imposed. Some retailers, landlords, and hotels seized the opportunity to engage in price gouging (Provenzo and Provenzo, 2002).

Fig. 5.11. Hurricane Andrew destroyed nearly 90 percent of mobile homes in southern Miami-Dade County. *Source:* Florida State Archives.

Fig. 5.12. Although the tidal surge from Andrew was not especially high compared with other hurricanes, small boats sustained considerable damage. Many boats at the marina Gables by the Sea were swept onto the shore. *Source:* NOAA.

The most costly fraud, however, was perpetrated by a significant minority of property owners who saw the disaster as an opportunity to defraud their insurance companies. There were numerous examples of homes and apartments that were only lightly damaged by the hurricane, but afterwards their owners purposely damaged them to get a new roof, new carpets, or interior furnishings. Some damaged their homes so severely that they were reimbursed sufficiently to rebuild or buy a home elsewhere. Tens of thousands of roofs had been damaged, and local roofers could not meet the demand for their services. As a consequence, roofers came from all over the nation to find work. This led to the term *roofers from hell,* because so many took advances for the job and never came back to complete it.

Damage to property would have been considerably less but for another type of fraud: weak enforcement of the building code. In the aftermath of the storm it was determined that the degree of damage to property did not correspond to the intensity of the storm at a particular location. Homes built after 1980 typically sustained triple the damage of those built before that year. Many buildings suffered damage that was directly traceable to code violations and shoddy workmanship. Some building inspectors either had been negligent or had been bribed during construction. Many builders found ways to comply with the letter of the building code but ignored its intent. Although it was a costly lesson, building in the county today is said to be more closely scrutinized than before the hurricane. The state legislature has passed bills that have led to more uniform building codes. These codes are designed to produce a more hurricane-resistant building. New mobile homes must conform to more rigid construction requirements that will make it possible to withstand much stronger winds than previously.

Preparing for Hurricanes

The American Red Cross suggests the following steps be taken in the event of an approaching hurricane.

Know What Hurricane Watch and Warning Mean

- A *watch* means that hurricane conditions are *possible* in the specified area of the watch, usually within 36 hours.
- A *warning* means that hurricane conditions are *expected* in the specified area of the warning, usually within 24 hours.

Prepare a Personal Evacuation Plan

- Identify ahead of time a place to go if you were told to evacuate. Choose several places: a friend's home in another town, a motel, or a shelter.
- Prepare a list of the telephone numbers of these places as well as a road map of your locality. You may need to take alternative or unfamiliar routes if major roads are closed or clogged.
- Listen to NOAA Weather Radio or local radio or TV stations for evacuation instructions. If advised to evacuate, do so immediately.

What to Take Along When Evacuating

- Prescription medications and medical supplies.
- Bedding and clothing, including sleeping bags and pillows.
- Bottled water, battery-operated radio and extra batteries, first aid kit, flashlight.
- Car keys and maps.
- Documents, including driver's license, Social Security card, proof of residence, insurance policies, wills, deeds, birth and marriage certificates, tax records, etc.

Assemble a Disaster Supplies Kit

- First aid kit and essential medications.
- Canned food and can opener.
- At least three gallons of water per person.
- Protective clothing, rainwear, and bedding or sleeping bags.
- Battery-powered radio, flashlight, and extra batteries.
- Special items for infants and elderly or disabled family members.
- Written instructions on how to turn off electricity, gas, and water if authorities advise you to do so. (Remember, you will need a professional to turn them back on.)

Prepare for High Winds

- Install hurricane shutters or purchase precut ½" outdoor plywood boards for each window of your home. Install anchors for the plywood and predrill holes in the plywood so that you can put it up quickly.
- Make trees more wind-resistant by removing diseased and damaged limbs, then strategically removing branches so that wind can blow through.

What to Do When a Hurricane Watch Is Issued

- Listen to NOAA Weather Radio or local radio or TV stations for up-to-date storm information.
- Prepare to bring inside lawn furniture, outdoor decorations or ornaments, trash cans, hanging plants, and anything else that can be picked up by the wind.

- Prepare to cover all windows of your home. If shutters have not been installed, use procured plywood as described above. Tape does not prevent windows from breaking, so its use is not recommended.
- Fill your car's gas tank.
- Recheck manufactured home tie-downs.
- Check batteries and stock up on canned food, first aid supplies, drinking water, and medications.

What to Do When a Hurricane Warning Is Issued

- Listen to the advice of local officials, and leave if they tell you to do so.
- Complete preparation activities.
- If you are not advised to evacuate, stay indoors, away from windows.
- Be aware that the calm "eye" is deceptive: The storm is not over. The worst part of the storm will happen once the eye passes over and the winds blow from the opposite direction. Trees, shrubs, buildings, and other objects damaged by the first winds can be broken or destroyed by the second winds.
- Be alert for tornadoes, which can happen during a hurricane and after it passes over. Remain indoors, in the center of your home, in a closet or bathroom without windows.
- Stay away from floodwaters. If you come upon a flooded road, turn around and go another way. If you are caught on a flooded road and waters are rising rapidly around you, get out of the car and climb to higher ground.

What to Do After a Hurricane Passes

- Keep listening to NOAA Weather Radio or local radio or TV stations for instructions.
- If you had to evacuate, return home when local officials tell you it is safe to do so.
- Inspect your home for damage.
- Use flashlights in the dark. Do not use candles.

www.redcross.org/services/disaster

Appendix Tables

Table A. Weekly weather averages and percentages for selected Florida cities (based on National Weather Service data, 1966–95)

Sea temperatures are monthly averages in warm months and every two months in cooler months. Where no data were available, temperature of nearest station was used.

A.1. Daytona Beach. Volusia County. Elevation 32 feet.

Week beginning	Avg. max. t.	Avg. min. t.	% of days max t. 70–85	Avg. precipitation (in.)	% chance of precipitation				Sea water t.
					.01"+	.10"+	.50"+	1.0"+	
Jan 1	70	50	.52	.66	.25	.15	.06	.02	
Jan 8	68	48	.49	.75	.25	.14	.05	.02	
Jan 15	68	46	.47	.46	.21	.16	.03	.01	61
Jan 22	68	46	.47	.82	.23	.16	.05	.03	
Jan 29	69	48	.50	.51	.19	.12	.03	.02	
Feb 5	68	47	.43	1.02	.29	.19	.09	.06	
Feb 12	70	49	.57	.73	.24	.15	.07	.03	
Feb 19	71	50	.54	.68	.27	.18	.06	.02	59
Feb 26	71	49	.59	.51	.20	.12	.05	.02	
March 5	74	53	.69	.90	.27	.19	.09	.05	
March 12	74	54	.62	.59	.20	.12	.06	.02	65
March 19	76	54	.72	.52	.21	.12	.05	.03	
March 26	77	57	.76	.88	.24	.18	.09	.03	
April 2	77	56	.76	.90	.20	.13	.07	.05	
April 9	79	59	.85	.62	.17	.11	.05	.02	70
April 16	81	60	.79	.47	.14	.08	.03	.02	
April 23	82	61	.69	.27	.14	.09	.02	.01	73
April 30	83	62	.71	.57	.19	.13	.06	.02	
May 7	83	63	.70	.69	.23	.16	.07	.03	
May 14	85	65	.54	.73	.23	.15	.06	.03	75
May 21	85	66	.54	.99	.30	.21	.10	.04	
May 28	86	68	.38	1.02	.31	.20	.10	.05	78

June 4	88	70	.33	1.82	.34	.27	.14	.08	79
June 11	88	71	.33	1.02	.41	.27	.10	.02	
June 18	89	72	.22	1.32	.40	.27	.12	.05	80
June 25	89	72	.19	1.63	.45	.28	.15	.07	
July 2	90	72	.10	1.09	.38	.25	.10	.04	
July 9	91	72	.05	1.05	.31	.21	.10	.05	80
July 16	90	73	.05	1.29	.37	.27	.14	.06	
July 23	90	73	.04	1.37	.44	.32	.14	.06	80
July 30	90	73	.05	1.35	.41	.31	.13	.06	
Aug 6	90	73	.04	1.13	.35	.24	.14	.04	80
Aug 13	89	73	.06	1.54	.47	.33	.15	.06	
Aug 20	89	73	.07	1.56	.50	.33	.13	.07	81
Aug 27	88	73	.13	1.63	.40	.29	.13	.06	
Sept 3	88	73	.19	1.54	.41	.29	.13	.09	83
Sept 10	88	72	.16	1.27	.34	.26	.09	.06	
Sept 17	87	72	.22	1.14	.34	.22	.10	.05	82
Sept 24	86	71	.44	1.95	.46	.34	.16	.10	
Oct 1	85	69	.59	1.01	.30	.20	.10	.06	79
Oct 8	83	67	.75	1.36	.37	.22	.10	.06	
Oct 15	82	65	.78	1.06	.27	.18	.08	.05	76
Oct 22	80	63	.90	.61	.27	.17	.05	.03	
Oct 29	79	63	.90	.85	.32	.21	.08	.02	
Nov 5	77	58	.82	.64	.21	.13	.05	.01	
Nov 12	75	55	.78	.72	.21	.12	.04	.01	
Nov 19	75	56	.78	.66	.21	.13	.04	.02	71
Nov 26	75	55	.73	.49	.21	.14	.04	.01	
Dec 3	73	52	.70	.38	.21	.10	.04	.01	
Dec 10	71	51	.62	.83	.22	.16	.06	.03	
Dec 17	69	48	.49	.60	.26	.16	.06	.02	
Dec 24	69	48	.52	.54	.21	.15	.05	.02	65
Year avg.	80	61	.49	48.52	.29	.19	.08	.04	

A.2. Ft. Myers. Lee County. Elevation 15 feet.

Week beginning	Avg. max. t.	Avg. min. t.	% of days max t. 70–85	Avg. precipitation (in.)	% chance of precipitation				Sea water t.
					.01"+	.10"+	.50"+	1.0"+	
Jan 1	76	56	.72	.46	.19	.12	.04	.02	
Jan 8	74	54	.70	.58	.19	.12	.05	.03	
Jan 15	74	53	.74	.66	.16	.12	.06	.03	66
Jan 22	74	53	.71	.49	.19	.11	.06	.01	
Jan 29	75	54	.73	.38	.14	.10	.03	.01	
Feb 5	74	53	.67	.61	.20	.12	.07	.03	
Feb 12	76	55	.78	.54	.20	.13	.05	.02	66
Feb 19	77	56	.77	.52	.20	.13	.04	.02	
Feb 26	76	54	.75	.56	.14	.11	.05	.02	
March 5	79	58	.78	.85	.20	.15	.07	.03	
March 12	79	58	.72	.55	.18	.10	.03	.03	71
March 19	80	58	.80	.58	.15	.10	.05	.03	
March 26	82	61	.70	.79	.15	.10	.05	.02	
April 2	82	61	.66	.42	.12	.09	.04	.01	
April 9	84	62	.60	.33	.11	.09	.04	.01	
April 16	85	63	.45	.34	.11	.07	.04	.01	77
April 23	86	64	.39	.38	.13	.07	.04	.02	
April 30	87	65	.33	.46	.17	.13	.05	.01	
May 7	88	67	.19	.76	.18	.14	.08	.02	
May 14	89	68	.12	.98	.22	.13	.07	.03	
May 21	89	69	.13	.92	.28	.19	.06	.03	82
May 28	90	71	.09	1.17	.32	.24	.10	.05	
June 4	91	73	.10	2.00	.42	.30	.17	.10	
June 11	91	73	.04	2.13	.47	.32	.16	.10	86
June 18	90	74	.08	2.98	.56	.42	.26	.16	
June 25	91	74	.06	2.41	.48	.36	.20	.11	

July 2	91	74	.02	2.21	.59	.41	.21	.10	87
July 9	92	75	.02	1.63	.50	.38	.14	.07
July 16	91	75	.06	2.13	.53	.40	.24	.10
July 23	92	75	.02	1.82	.55	.39	.17	.07
July 30	91	75	.03	2.12	.53	.42	.23	.10
Aug 6	92	75	.02	2.47	.56	.45	.22	.11	87
Aug 13	92	75	.04	2.04	.61	.42	.19	.09
Aug 20	91	75	.04	2.59	.57	.43	.24	.11
Aug 27	91	75	.03	2.21	.51	.42	.20	.11
Sept 3	91	75	.09	2.13	.54	.39	.18	.09
Sept 10	90	75	.09	1.99	.46	.33	.14	.08	86
Sept 17	91	74	.05	1.78	.46	.34	.15	.07
Sept 24	89	73	.17	1.18	.36	.26	.10	.06
Oct 1	88	72	.23	1.12	.35	.23	.11	.06
Oct 8	87	70	.24	.69	.21	.12	.05	.03	81
Oct 15	86	68	.35	.66	.20	.13	.05	.03
Oct 22	85	67	.51	.52	.16	.12	.04	.02
Oct 29	84	66	.54	.56	.18	.10	.06	.01
Nov 5	82	63	.69	.41	.13	.08	.03	.02
Nov 12	81	61	.71	.32	.13	.09	.02	.01	73
Nov 19	80	60	.75	.25	.13	.09	.01	.01
Nov 26	79	60	.73	.25	.13	.08	.01	.00
Dec 3	78	57	.83	.32	.10	.06	.02	.00
Dec 10	77	57	.80	.39	.12	.07	.03	.02
Dec 17	75	54	.79	.38	.17	.11	.04	.02	68
Dec 24	75	54	.72	.37	.05	.03	.01	.01
Year avg.	84	65	.41	54.18	.29	.20	.09	.05

A.3. Fort Pierce. St. Lucie County. Elevation 25 feet.

Week beginning	Avg. max. t.	Avg. min. t.	% of days max t. 70–85	Avg. precipitation (in.)	% chance of precipitation				Sea water t.
					.01"+	.10"+	.50"+	1.0"+	
Jan 1	75	54	.79	.61	.31	.16	.06	.02	
Jan 8	74	52	.71	.71	.30	.16	.06	.03	
Jan 15	73	51	.71	.56	.24	.11	.04	.02	67
Jan 22	73	50	.73	.64	.25	.16	.05	.02	
Jan 29	74	51	.72	.52	.21	.09	.04	.02	
Feb 5	73	51	.62	.66	.31	.18	.07	.01	
Feb 12	75	53	.78	.76	.26	.14	.07	.03	
Feb 19	76	54	.69	.97	.28	.19	.08	.04	66
Feb 26	75	52	.75	.68	.22	.16	.09	.02	
March 5	77	56	.82	.85	.25	.18	.07	.03	
March 12	78	57	.78	.48	.25	.13	.05	.01	70
March 19	79	56	.77	.61	.18	.14	.05	.02	
March 26	81	60	.79	.98	.25	.16	.08	.03	
April 2	80	60	.84	.60	.20	.14	.07	.01	71
April 9	81	61	.86	.49	.19	.10	.05	.02	
April 16	83	62	.79	.57	.21	.13	.04	.02	74
April 23	84	63	.67	.45	.22	.11	.04	.01	
April 30	84	65	.62	.56	.22	.15	.05	.02	
May 7	85	66	.59	.71	.29	.19	.06	.03	
May 14	87	68	.47	1.06	.29	.19	.09	.06	75
May 21	87	68	.41	1.30	.35	.24	.12	.06	
May 28	88	69	.24	1.50	.43	.28	.15	.08	78
June 4	88	71	.18	1.50	.44	.30	.14	.06	
June 11	89	71	.10	1.36	.38	.26	.13	.05	79
June 18	89	71	.10	1.62	.53	.35	.17	.07	

June 25	90	71	.08	1.47	.45	.27	.15	.07	79
July 2	90	72	.05	1.10	.42	.24	.10	.05	79
July 9	91	72	.01	1.10	.37	.20	.09	.06	79
July 16	91	72	.02	1.24	.46	.30	.11	.05	
July 23	91	72	.02	1.68	.48	.31	.14	.08	79
July 30	91	72	.05	1.55	.48	.32	.15	.06	
Aug 6	91	73	.01	1.37	.48	.33	.13	.05	
Aug 13	90	72	.03	1.55	.47	.31	.15	.06	80
Aug 20	91	72	.02	1.31	.42	.27	.11	.04	
Aug 27	90	73	.02	1.19	.44	.27	.12	.05	80
Sept 3	90	72	.04	1.78	.47	.35	.13	.08	
Sept 10	89	72	.12	1.75	.45	.35	.18	.06	81
Sept 17	89	72	.10	1.89	.52	.31	.13	.06	
Sept 24	88	72	.14	1.88	.52	.36	.14	.10	80
Oct 1	87	70	.28	1.97	.47	.33	.18	.10	
Oct 8	86	69	.41	1.28	.42	.26	.11	.03	79
Oct 15	85	67	.54	1.63	.42	.28	.15	.07	
Oct 22	84	66	.66	.78	.33	.20	.08	.03	77
Oct 29	83	65	.74	1.15	.39	.23	.10	.05	
Nov 5	81	61	.81	.67	.31	.15	.06	.04	
Nov 12	79	59	.86	.84	.29	.14	.07	.04	
Nov 19	79	59	.89	.97	.35	.18	.08	.04	75
Nov 26	79	59	.82	.52	.24	.13	.06	.04	
Dec 3	78	56	.83	.46	.25	.13	.04	.00	
Dec 10	76	54	.80	.49	.23	.13	.03	.01	
Dec 17	75	53	.80	.55	.24	.12	.05	.01	70
Dec 24	73	52	.70	.54	.24	.14	.06	.02	
Year avg.	83	63	.49	53.24	.34	.21	.09	.04	

A.4. Gainesville. Alachua County. Elevation 96 feet.

Week beginning	Avg. max. t.	Avg. min. t.	% of days max t. 70–85	Avg. precipitation (in.)	% chance of precipitation			
					.01"+	.10"+	.50"+	1.0"+
Jan 1	69	45	.45	.95	.29	.22	.10	.04
Jan 8	66	43	.41	.96	.27	.21	.08	.04
Jan 15	67	42	.45	.63	.21	.16	.04	.02
Jan 22	68	43	.48	.82	.27	.20	.09	.03
Jan 29	70	44	.57	.96	.26	.18	.08	.04
Feb 5	68	43	.43	1.19	.31	.22	.12	.06
Feb 12	71	45	.60	1.02	.24	.18	.09	.06
Feb 19	72	47	.60	1.11	.28	.20	.12	.06
Feb 26	74	47	.62	.75	.24	.17	.06	.05
March 5	75	49	.67	1.11	.28	.20	.12	.05
March 12	77	51	.68	.87	.24	.19	.07	.05
March 19	77	51	.82	.66	.21	.16	.06	.03
March 26	79	54	.85	1.12	.23	.19	.11	.05
April 2	80	54	.73	.94	.20	.14	.08	.05
April 9	81	55	.74	.86	.18	.15	.08	.04
April 16	83	56	.60	.29	.16	.08	.02	.01
April 23	84	58	.59	.68	.17	.12	.05	.02
April 30	85	60	.50	.49	.17	.11	.05	.01
May 7	87	62	.28	.54	.16	.11	.04	.01
May 14	88	63	.21	.99	.23	.18	.08	.04
May 21	89	65	.18	1.29	.32	.24	.10	.06
May 28	90	66	.15	.92	.32	.23	.08	.03
June 4	90	68	.14	1.23	.31	.23	.09	.05
June 11	91	69	.10	1.23	.36	.25	.10	.05
June 18	91	70	.10	1.92	.43	.32	.16	.08
June 25	91	70	.06	1.88	.47	.36	.17	.07

July 2	92	71	.02	1.04	.43	.28	.10	.03
July 9	92	71	.07	1.61	.48	.36	.17	.07
July 16	91	71	.05	1.36	.48	.30	.10	.05
July 23	91	71	.08	1.67	.52	.40	.17	.07
July 30	91	72	.04	2.00	.56	.42	.20	.06
Aug 6	92	72	.07	1.92	.53	.38	.18	.07
Aug 13	91	71	.10	1.68	.51	.34	.16	.09
Aug 20	92	71	.08	1.64	.48	.32	.16	.07
Aug 27	91	71	.07	1.55	.40	.29	.14	.07
Sept 3	90	71	.09	1.53	.40	.26	.11	.06
Sept 10	89	70	.16	1.60	.41	.32	.12	.07
Sept 17	88	69	.19	1.12	.36	.23	.10	.06
Sept 24	87	68	.25	1.17	.30	.23	.09	.06
Oct 1	86	64	.39	.44	.22	.12	.04	.01
Oct 8	84	62	.51	.57	.18	.13	.06	.02
Oct 15	83	60	.63	.38	.14	.10	.04	.01
Oct 22	81	57	.82	.28	.17	.09	.03	.00
Oct 29	79	58	.86	.74	.21	.15	.09	.02
Nov 5	77	52	.81	.64	.21	.15	.06	.03
Nov 12	76	51	.81	.33	.12	.08	.03	.01
Nov 19	75	51	.79	.53	.19	.10	.05	.02
Nov 26	73	50	.70	.67	.21	.17	.04	.02
Dec 3	72	46	.64	.62	.19	.11	.04	.03
Dec 10	71	48	.62	.87	.23	.17	.09	.04
Dec 17	68	44	.49	.58	.21	.12	.06	.02
Dec 24	70	46	.55	.71	.21	.12	.06	.03
Year avg..	81	58	.42	50.94	.29	.21	.09	.04

A.5. Jacksonville. Duval County. Elevation 31 feet.

Week beginning	Avg. max. t.	Avg. min. t.	% of days max t. 70–85	Avg. precipitation (in.)	% chance of precipitation				Sea water t.
					.01"+	.10"+	.50"+	1.0"+	
Jan 1	66	44	.36	.73	.29	.20	.06	.02	
Jan 8	63	42	.30	1.04	.27	.20	.10	.05	
Jan 15	63	41	.30	.74	.25	.16	.06	.03	57
Jan 22	65	41	.37	.88	.26	.19	.10	.03	
Jan 29	67	43	.41	.80	.23	.17	.07	.03	
Feb 5	64	42	.32	.97	.28	.21	.10	.05	
Feb 12	67	44	.43	.84	.26	.18	.08	.04	
Feb 19	69	46	.48	.88	.28	.18	.08	.04	56
Feb 26	70	45	.55	.65	.19	.13	.05	.02	
March 5	72	48	.60	1.16	.30	.20	.10	.06	
March 12	73	50	.56	.63	.22	.16	.07	.03	61
March 19	75	51	.67	.48	.23	.14	.05	.01	
March 26	76	53	.74	1.41	.27	.22	.11	.08	
April 2	77	53	.70	.82	.20	.15	.07	.03	
April 9	78	55	.78	.84	.21	.17	.09	.05	68
April 16	81	56	.72	.35	.18	.09	.03	.00	
April 23	82	58	.58	.57	.19	.12	.06	.01	71
April 30	83	60	.65	.82	.21	.15	.08	.02	
May 7	83	61	.60	.81	.21	.15	.07	.04	
May 14	86	63	.44	.82	.25	.16	.07	.03	74
May 21	86	64	.38	.88	.26	.21	.09	.03	
May 28	88	66	.26	1.00	.31	.17	.09	.02	77
June 4	89	69	.24	1.60	.38	.30	.11	.06	
June 11	89	69	.24	1.24	.41	.25	.10	.05	80
June 18	90	70	.16	1.38	.40	.31	.12	.05	
June 25	90	71	.10	1.28	.44	.31	.11	.05	81

167

July 2	92	72	.06	1.50	.38	.31	.11	.07	83
July 9	93	72	.07	1.29	.34	.26	.10	.05	84
July 16	92	73	.04	1.40	.44	.32	.12	.06	
July 23	92	73	.04	1.37	.47	.30	.12	.07	83
July 30	92	73	.04	1.79	.46	.33	.16	.08	83
Aug 6	91	72	.04	1.47	.40	.32	.14	.07	
Aug 13	90	72	.10	1.42	.45	.29	.13	.05	83
Aug 20	91	73	.11	1.84	.43	.30	.16	.10	
Aug 27	90	72	.11	2.17	.47	.32	.18	.08	82
Sept 3	89	71	.19	1.94	.44	.33	.16	.09	
Sept 10	88	71	.24	1.50	.36	.29	.13	.07	78
Sept 17	88	70	.22	1.35	.33	.22	.10	.05	
Sept 24	85	67	.47	1.77	.40	.28	.13	.09	72
Oct 1	83	64	.56	1.31	.24	.18	.09	.07	
Oct 8	81	62	.77	.92	.33	.24	.07	.03	
Oct 15	80	59	.72	.57	.19	.12	.06	.03	
Oct 22	78	58	.87	.64	.22	.12	.07	.03	67
Oct 29	77	57	.87	.87	.28	.16	.06	.03	
Nov 5	74	52	.72	.68	.20	.12	.05	.04	
Nov 12	73	48	.67	.33	.17	.10	.03	.01	
Nov 19	72	49	.68	.44	.14	.10	.03	.02	
Nov 26	72	49	.63	.56	.19	.13	.06	.03	
Dec 3	69	46	.50	.51	.24	.10	.04	.02	60
Dec 10	68	45	.48	.68	.25	.16	.06	.02	
Dec 17	65	43	.37	.50	.18	.12	.05	.01	
Dec 24	65	42	.37	.52	.20	.14	.05	.01	
Year avg. .	79	58	.42	52.18	.29	.20	.09	.04	

A.6. Key West. Monroe County. Elevation 10 feet.

Week beginning	Avg. max. t.	Avg. min. t.	% of days max t. 70–85	Avg. precipitation (in.)	% chance of precipitation				Sea water t.
					.01"+	.10"+	.50"+	1.0"+	
Jan 1	76	67	.88	.38	.23	.14	.03	.00	
Jan 8	75	65	.78	.79	.21	.13	.04	.04	
Jan 15	74	65	.78	.44	.17	.10	.03	.01	69
Jan 22	75	64	.79	.67	.19	.09	.04	.01	
Jan 29	75	65	.83	.30	.14	.07	.02	.01	
Feb 5	74	64	.80	.41	.18	.12	.03	.02	
Feb 12	76	66	.88	.47	.18	.10	.04	.02	70
Feb 19	76	67	.85	.48	.20	.12	.04	.02	
Feb 26	76	65	.87	.41	.14	.09	.05	.02	
March 5	78	68	.94	.65	.19	.12	.06	.01	
March 12	78	68	.93	.41	.13	.10	.03	.02	75
March 19	79	69	.94	.33	.12	.05	.03	.02	
March 26	80	71	.96	.26	.15	.10	.02	.00	
April 2	81	71	.95	.26	.11	.06	.02	.00	
April 9	81	72	.92	.73	.14	.10	.05	.02	
April 16	82	73	.88	.23	.11	.06	.02	.01	78
April 23	83	74	.82	.56	.13	.10	.06	.03	
April 30	83	74	.78	.88	.18	.13	.06	.04	
May 7	84	75	.62	.48	.15	.08	.04	.03	
May 14	85	76	.49	.55	.23	.14	.05	.02	
May 21	86	77	.41	.97	.29	.20	.08	.03	82
May 28	86	77	.29	1.34	.34	.23	.12	.06	
June 4	87	78	.21	1.16	.34	.23	.10	.05	
June 11	88	78	.15	1.35	.38	.26	.11	.07	85
June 18	88	79	.10	1.25	.35	.23	.11	.05	
June 25	89	79	.07	1.32	.34	.26	.12	.05	

July 2	89	79	.02	.94	.34	.22	.09	.04	
July 9	89	80	.04	.66	.30	.17	.05	.02	
July 16	89	80	.03	.94	.36	.22	.09	.04	87
July 23	89	80	.03	.69	.33	.20	.07	.01	
July 30	89	80	.02	.93	.35	.24	.08	.02	
Aug 6	90	79	.02	1.08	.38	.24	.10	.05	
Aug 13	89	79	.05	1.34	.40	.29	.14	.05	
Aug 20	89	79	.03	.94	.41	.25	.07	.03	
Aug 27	89	79	.05	1.30	.43	.26	.11	.06	87
Sept 3	89	79	.05	1.14	.49	.29	.11	.04	
Sept 10	88	79	.08	1.05	.48	.34	.10	.02	
Sept 17	88	79	.08	1.22	.48	.30	.11	.04	
Sept 24	87	78	.21	1.64	.50	.34	.13	.06	86
Oct 1	87	78	.25	1.39	.41	.27	.11	.04	
Oct 8	86	77	.40	1.10	.37	.21	.08	.03	
Oct 15	84	75	.64	1.37	.33	.24	.11	.07	82
Oct 22	83	75	.78	1.02	.25	.19	.08	.03	
Oct 29	83	74	.83	.49	.24	.15	.02	.02	
Nov 5	81	72	.91	.55	.20	.12	.06	.03	
Nov 12	80	71	.94	1.13	.20	.10	.04	.02	
Nov 19	79	71	.96	.39	.17	.10	.02	.01	76
Nov 26	79	71	.95	.48	.20	.11	.03	.01	
Dec 3	78	69	.95	.51	.15	.07	.03	.01	
Dec 10	77	68	.91	.50	.21	.12	.03	.03	72
Dec 17	76	66	.87	.50	.16	.10	.03	.02	
Dec 24	75	65	.81	.35	.20	.11	.01	.01	
Year avg.	83	73	53.00	39.61	.26	.17	.06	.03	

A.7. Leesburg. Lake County. Elevation 120 feet.

Week beginning	Avg. max. t.	Avg. min. t.	% of days max t. 70–85	Avg. precipitation (in.)	% chance of precipitation			
					.01"+	.10"+	.50"+	1.0"+
Jan 1	72	52	.61	.68	.22	.12	.06	.04
Jan 8	69	49	.53	.80	.24	.16	.07	.03
Jan 15	69	48	.50	.66	.22	.17	.06	.03
Jan 22	70	48	.60	.75	.22	.14	.06	.03
Jan 29	71	49	.60	.44	.17	.13	.04	.01
Feb 5	70	48	.53	.88	.26	.19	.08	.05
Feb 12	73	50	.68	.79	.21	.16	.07	.04
Feb 19	74	52	.70	.68	.24	.15	.06	.02
Feb 26	75	51	.77	.53	.19	.14	.05	.02
March 5	77	54	.76	.84	.25	.19	.07	.03
March 12	78	55	.72	.91	.22	.17	.07	.05
March 19	79	56	.80	.60	.18	.13	.05	.03
March 26	81	58	.75	1.13	.23	.16	.11	.05
April 2	82	57	.72	.60	.17	.11	.05	.04
April 9	83	59	.65	.52	.16	.11	.04	.01
April 16	85	60	.52	.21	.10	.07	.02	.00
April 23	85	61	.48	.43	.14	.10	.04	.02
April 30	87	63	.37	.65	.17	.15	.07	.02
May 7	87	64	.32	.86	.20	.14	.08	.05
May 14	89	66	.20	.81	.26	.18	.08	.04
May 21	88	66	.24	1.00	.28	.21	.10	.04
May 28	89	68	.16	1.50	.34	.27	.14	.05
June 4	90	70	.13	1.73	.39	.32	.15	.08
June 11	91	70	.05	1.27	.40	.28	.12	.05
June 18	90	71	.11	2.57	.56	.41	.24	.11

June 25	90	71	.09	1.97	.49	.38	.18	.09
July 2	91	71	.05	1.46	.42	.34	.13	.05
July 9	92	72	.02	1.66	.48	.34	.17	.06
July 16	91	72	.03	1.78	.64	.45	.19	.06
July 23	91	72	.03	1.58	.49	.36	.15	.08
July 30	91	72	.05	1.86	.57	.40	.17	.08
Aug 6	91	72	.07	1.92	.50	.40	.21	.08
Aug 13	91	72	.07	1.59	.47	.31	.14	.07
Aug 20	91	73	.07	1.40	.45	.33	.13	.04
Aug 27	90	72	.07	1.93	.42	.31	.17	.08
Sept 3	90	72	.09	1.90	.42	.36	.19	.08
Sept 10	89	72	.13	1.35	.38	.30	.10	.04
Sept 17	89	71	.13	.84	.30	.19	.08	.03
Sept 24	87	70	.26	1.51	.36	.26	.12	.07
Oct 1	86	68	.36	.87	.26	.20	.08	.04
Oct 8	84	67	.55	.72	.20	.11	.06	.03
Oct 15	83	64	.69	.37	.16	.10	.04	.01
Oct 22	81	63	.81	.47	.20	.13	.04	.01
Oct 29	80	62	.89	.84	.20	.13	.07	.03
Nov 5	77	58	.88	.33	.14	.09	.02	.01
Nov 12	76	56	.85	.41	.12	.08	.04	.01
Nov 19	76	56	.83	.65	.17	.11	.04	.02
Nov 26	75	56	.78	.33	.20	.10	.03	.00
Dec 3	73	53	.73	.37	.15	.09	.03	.01
Dec 10	72	52	.68	.54	.24	.14	.04	.02
Dec 17	70	49	.58	.38	.17	.11	.04	.00
Dec 24	70	50	.59	.62	.16	.10	.05	.02
Year avg.	82	62	.51	51.04	.28	.20	.09	.04

A.8. Melbourne. Brevard County. Elevation 35 feet.

Week beginning	Avg. max. t.	Avg. min. t.	% of days max t. 70–85	Avg. precipitation (in.)	% chance of precipitation				Sea water t.
					.01"+	.10"+	.50"+	1.0"+	
Jan 1	73	54	.66	.54	.20	.14	.06	.02	
Jan 8	71	52	.60	.69	.21	.12	.07	.02	
Jan 15	70	50	.56	.60	.21	.12	.05	.02	57
Jan 22	71	50	.60	.47	.20	.13	.04	.02	
Jan 29	72	51	.63	.37	.17	.10	.03	.01	
Feb 5	71	50	.53	.80	.31	.15	.08	.03	
Feb 12	73	52	.66	.61	.23	.17	.04	.01	
Feb 19	73	53	.65	.74	.26	.15	.07	.02	56
Feb 26	73	52	.69	.46	.18	.12	.04	.02	
March 5	75	55	.76	.83	.22	.17	.06	.03	
March 12	76	56	.70	.69	.23	.14	.04	.02	61
March 19	77	55	.77	.50	.14	.10	.04	.03	
March 26	79	60	.78	.70	.23	.14	.08	.04	
April 2	79	59	.79	.48	.17	.10	.04	.01	
April 9	79	60	.89	.52	.17	.10	.06	.01	68
April 16	81	62	.84	.33	.14	.09	.04	.01	
April 23	82	62	.73	.41	.14	.10	.05	.01	71
April 30	83	64	.74	.45	.17	.12	.04	.01	
May 7	84	65	.67	.87	.23	.16	.06	.04	
May 14	85	68	.52	.60	.23	.14	.05	.02	74
May 21	85	68	.50	1.34	.34	.21	.12	.06	
May 28	86	69	.44	1.28	.40	.25	.14	.07	77
June 4	88	71	.34	1.63	.38	.29	.16	.08	
June 11	88	71	.22	1.06	.31	.22	.10	.05	80
June 18	88	71	.18	1.87	.45	.36	.18	.08	
June 25	89	71	.17	1.49	.43	.28	.12	.07	81

July 2	89	72	.15	1.05	.35	.26	.10	.05	83
July 9	90	72	.05	.96	.34	.23	.12	.03	
July 16	90	72	.03	1.34	.39	.30	.15	.05	84
July 23	90	73	.05	1.27	.40	.28	.13	.06	
July 30	90	73	.03	1.34	.33	.21	.11	.04	
Aug 6	90	73	.07	1.55	.37	.24	.14	.09	83
Aug 13	89	73	.10	1.20	.39	.26	.11	.06	
Aug 20	89	73	.08	1.32	.38	.29	.15	.03	83
Aug 27	89	73	.11	.96	.35	.26	.08	.03	
Sept 3	88	73	.13	1.40	.34	.21	.12	.06	83
Sept 10	88	72	.17	1.75	.47	.32	.16	.06	
Sept 17	88	72	.21	1.31	.38	.25	.12	.05	82
Sept 24	87	72	.36	1.97	.39	.29	.16	.09	
Oct 1	85	71	.52	.94	.35	.26	.09	.04	
Oct 8	84	69	.64	1.35	.39	.25	.10	.05	78
Oct 15	83	67	.77	1.21	.35	.20	.11	.06	
Oct 22	82	66	.85	.49	.24	.12	.03	.02	72
Oct 29	81	65	.89	1.23	.35	.23	.09	.03	
Nov 5	79	61	.92	.45	.21	.12	.04	.02	
Nov 12	77	58	.86	.68	.17	.10	.05	.02	67
Nov 19	77	59	.85	.70	.25	.12	.04	.02	
Nov 26	77	59	.79	.63	.21	.14	.05	.02	
Dec 3	75	55	.78	.42	.17	.10	.03	.02	
Dec 10	74	54	.73	.41	.20	.11	.04	.01	
Dec 17	72	52	.69	.67	.22	.13	.07	.03	60
Dec 24	71	50	.59	.38	.20	.08	.02	.01	
Year avg.	81	63	.52	48.10	.28	.18	.08	.04	

A.9. Miami. Miami-Dade County. Elevation 12 feet.

Week beginning	Avg. max. t.	Avg. min. t.	% of days max t. 70–85	Avg. precipitation (in.)	% chance of precipitation				Sea water t.
					.01"+	.10"+	.50"+	1.0"+	
Jan 1	77	62	.86	.41	.23	.12	.03	.00	
Jan 8	76	60	.81	.71	.23	.13	.06	.03	
Jan 15	75	59	.83	.51	.22	.15	.05	.01	70
Jan 22	75	59	.80	.50	.25	.13	.03	.02	
Jan 29	76	60	.83	.40	.19	.08	.04	.02	
Feb 5	76	59	.82	.37	.19	.12	.02	.00	
Feb 12	77	61	.90	.65	.18	.11	.06	.03	
Feb 19	78	62	.85	.65	.21	.15	.04	.02	73
Feb 26	78	61	.87	.45	.18	.10	.02	.02	
March 5	79	63	.93	.52	.20	.10	.05	.02	
March 12	80	64	.88	.64	.21	.14	.04	.02	75
March 19	80	64	.86	.44	.13	.10	.03	.02	
March 26	81	67	.81	.90	.24	.15	.09	.05	
April 2	81	67	.85	.52	.15	.09	.05	.02	
April 9	82	68	.83	.79	.22	.15	.07	.02	78
April 16	83	69	.76	.46	.16	.10	.04	.02	
April 23	84	69	.68	1.35	.21	.15	.07	.04	78
April 30	84	71	.63	1.01	.19	.14	.08	.02	
May 7	85	72	.54	.93	.27	.18	.08	.05	
May 14	86	73	.45	1.05	.30	.19	.08	.04	80
May 21	86	73	.41	1.80	.43	.35	.15	.08	
May 28	87	74	.36	2.34	.44	.33	.15	.11	
June 4	88	75	.22	2.07	.49	.37	.17	.09	81
June 11	88	75	.23	2.20	.47	.37	.17	.09	
June 18	88	75	.18	2.28	.55	.39	.21	.11	84
June 25	89	76	.12	2.26	.53	.37	.18	.12	85

July 2	89	77	.08	1.47	.52	.38	.13	.06	86
July 9	89	76	.07	1.26	.51	.37	.11	.03	86
July 16	89	77	.07	1.37	.46	.33	.10	.06	
July 23	90	77	.05	1.14	.44	.25	.10	.05	86
July 30	90	77	.04	1.76	.55	.40	.17	.08	
Aug 6	90	77	.06	2.16	.58	.43	.19	.06	86
Aug 13	90	77	.06	1.72	.52	.31	.14	.08	
Aug 20	90	77	.04	1.71	.55	.35	.19	.08	84
Aug 27	89	77	.08	1.94	.53	.39	.17	.08	
Sept 3	89	76	.10	1.69	.53	.39	.15	.07	84
Sept 10	88	76	.15	1.86	.55	.39	.20	.07	
Sept 17	88	76	.11	1.62	.53	.37	.14	.07	83
Sept 24	87	75	.28	2.43	.53	.42	.22	.13	
Oct 1	87	75	.31	1.46	.52	.35	.15	.06	83
Oct 8	86	73	.40	1.61	.41	.28	.13	.06	
Oct 15	84	72	.63	1.28	.38	.26	.10	.06	79
Oct 22	84	71	.71	1.26	.37	.20	.10	.06	
Oct 29	83	71	.73	1.03	.37	.20	.08	.03	
Nov 5	81	68	.85	.96	.32	.17	.08	.03	76
Nov 12	80	66	.90	1.02	.27	.16	.06	.04	
Nov 19	80	66	.94	.50	.23	.11	.03	.02	
Nov 26	79	66	.94	.41	.22	.10	.03	.02	
Dec 3	79	64	.94	.52	.18	.09	.04	.02	
Dec 10	78	62	.91	.33	.19	.10	.03	.01	73
Dec 17	76	60	.87	.44	.16	.08	.03	.02	
Dec 24	75	60	.84	.28	.16	.10	.03	.00	
Year avg.	83	69	.55	58.39	.34	.23	.10	.05	

A.10. Naples. Collier County. Elevation 5 feet.

Week beginning	Avg. max. t.	Avg. min. t.	% of days max t. 70–85	Avg. precipitation (in.)	% chance of precipitation				Sea water t.
					.01"+	.10"+	.50"+	1.0"+	
Jan 1	78	56	.85	.39	.21	.12	.02	.01	
Jan 8	76	54	.80	.42	.21	.12	.02	.01	
Jan 15	76	53	.82	.69	.17	.12	.05	.03	66
Jan 22	76	53	.79	.58	.21	.12	.04	.02	
Jan 29	77	53	.82	.46	.16	.10	.04	.02	
Feb 5	76	53	.78	.45	.20	.12	.04	.02	
Feb 12	78	54	.87	.55	.20	.13	.05	.02	
Feb 19	78	56	.84	.69	.24	.11	.06	.04	66
Feb 26	78	54	.84	.53	.19	.13	.05	.02	
March 5	80	57	.80	.75	.20	.13	.06	.03	
March 12	80	58	.76	.45	.14	.08	.03	.02	71
March 19	81	58	.85	.51	.16	.10	.04	.03	
March 26	83	61	.74	.51	.18	.09	.04	.02	
April 2	83	60	.65	.37	.13	.08	.04	.01	
April 9	84	61	.59	.37	.15	.07	.04	.01	
April 16	85	62	.52	.28	.12	.06	.03	.00	77
April 23	86	64	.46	.60	.12	.09	.07	.02	
April 30	87	64	.35	.39	.17	.09	.03	.01	
May 7	87	66	.22	.92	.19	.13	.08	.06	
May 14	88	67	.14	.87	.27	.15	.07	.04	
May 21	88	68	.13	1.22	.32	.26	.10	.06	82
May 28	89	69	.05	1.74	.35	.22	.11	.07	
June 4	90	71	.06	1.82	.42	.29	.17	.08	
June 11	91	71	.03	1.64	.44	.32	.15	.08	
June 18	90	72	.07	2.23	.55	.37	.21	.09	86
June 25	91	73	.05	2.40	.46	.33	.20	.13	

July 2	91	72	.04	2.07	.53	.38	.18	.11	
July 9	92	72	.02	1.64	.49	.34	.17	.07	
July 16	91	72	.01	2.06	.55	.46	.22	.09	87
July 23	92	72	.00	1.85	.53	.36	.14	.09	
July 30	92	73	.01	1.43	.50	.34	.13	.05	
Aug 6	92	73	.00	2.25	.57	.43	.23	.11	
Aug 13	92	73	.03	1.87	.57	.43	.18	.07	87
Aug 20	92	73	.01	1.73	.53	.37	.16	.08	
Aug 27	91	73	.03	2.38	.54	.43	.21	.10	
Sept 3	91	73	.04	1.76	.58	.39	.19	.07	
Sept 10	91	73	.03	2.61	.55	.42	.19	.10	
Sept 17	91	73	.01	1.56	.49	.38	.17	.06	86
Sept 24	90	72	.06	1.46	.45	.30	.12	.08	
Oct 1	89	71	.08	1.36	.36	.26	.12	.05	
Oct 8	88	69	.13	.95	.27	.18	.07	.04	
Oct 15	87	67	.23	.80	.30	.15	.07	.03	81
Oct 22	86	66	.38	.47	.21	.11	.05	.01	
Oct 29	85	65	.42	.52	.21	.13	.05	.02	
Nov 5	83	62	.64	.46	.17	.10	.04	.01	
Nov 12	82	60	.72	.42	.16	.10	.03	.02	
Nov 19	81	60	.81	.30	.17	.10	.02	.00	73
Nov 26	81	60	.75	.38	.15	.10	.03	.01	
Dec 3	80	57	.87	.34	.15	.06	.02	.02	
Dec 10	79	56	.80	.31	.13	.07	.03	.01	
Dec 17	77	54	.84	.33	.19	.09	.03	.01	68
Dec 24	76	54	.78	.34	.16	.08	.03	.00	
Year avg.	85	64	.42	53.20	.30	.20	.09	.04	

A.11. Orlando. Orange County. Elevation 58 feet.

Week beginning	Avg. max. t.	Avg. min. t.	% of days max t. 70–85	Avg. precipitation (in.)	% chance of precipitation			
					.01"+	.10"+	.50"+	1.0"+
Jan 1	74	52	0.72	0.49	0.20	0.11	0.04	0.02
Jan 8	73	50	0.69	0.58	0.21	0.12	0.05	0.03
Jan 15	72	48	0.67	0.48	0.23	0.13	0.04	0.01
Jan 22	73	48	0.69	0.54	0.24	0.13	0.05	0.02
Jan 29	74	50	0.72	0.52	0.19	0.09	0.06	0.02
Feb 5	73	48	0.63	0.80	0.27	0.15	0.07	0.02
Feb 12	75	51	0.80	0.68	0.28	0.17	0.05	0.02
Feb 19	76	52	0.77	0.80	0.26	0.18	0.08	0.05
Feb 26	76	51	0.79	0.51	0.19	0.11	0.06	0.02
March 5	78	54	0.80	0.79	0.25	0.18	0.08	0.03
March 12	78	55	0.70	0.56	0.18	0.13	0.04	0.02
March 19	80	55	0.81	0.60	0.22	0.12	0.05	0.02
March 26	81	58	0.76	0.88	0.21	0.16	0.10	0.04
April 2	81	57	0.77	0.43	0.19	0.11	0.04	0.01
April 9	83	58	0.74	0.43	0.16	0.10	0.05	0.02
April 16	84	60	0.62	0.45	0.14	0.08	0.04	0.02
April 23	85	61	0.51	0.52	0.14	0.11	0.04	0.01
April 30	86	62	0.40	0.52	0.17	0.10	0.05	0.02
May 7	86	64	0.40	0.87	0.26	0.18	0.08	0.04
May 14	88	66	0.25	0.75	0.25	0.15	0.07	0.03
May 21	88	66	0.22	1.00	0.29	0.21	0.10	0.04
May 28	89	68	0.16	1.04	0.36	0.23	0.09	0.05
June 4	90	70	0.09	1.78	0.44	0.31	0.15	0.09
June 11	91	71	0.04	1.14	0.37	0.26	0.11	0.06
June 18	90	71	0.07	1.52	0.50	0.34	0.14	0.07
June 25	90	71	0.08	1.83	0.46	0.34	0.19	0.08

July 2	91	72	0.03	1.65	0.52	0.33	0.13	0.07
July 9	92	72	0.03	1.21	0.39	0.27	0.13	0.06
July 16	91	72	0.01	1.97	0.57	0.38	0.19	0.07
July 23	92	72	0.01	1.54	0.51	0.39	0.15	0.07
July 30	91	73	0.03	1.60	0.52	0.37	0.16	0.07
Aug 6	91	73	0.03	1.83	0.51	0.36	0.15	0.08
Aug 13	91	73	0.04	1.50	0.46	0.36	0.14	0.06
Aug 20	91	73	0.02	1.52	0.48	0.30	0.11	0.05
Aug 27	91	72	0.04	1.21	0.49	0.30	0.10	0.04
Sept 3	90	72	0.04	1.37	0.47	0.35	0.13	0.03
Sept 10	90	72	0.10	1.45	0.48	0.32	0.14	0.06
Sept 17	90	71	0.08	1.30	0.33	0.23	0.11	0.05
Sept 24	88	70	0.18	1.71	0.39	0.28	0.15	0.07
Oct 1	87	68	0.32	1.04	0.29	0.22	0.08	0.03
Oct 8	86	67	0.45	0.94	0.29	0.20	0.08	0.04
Oct 15	84	65	0.54	0.47	0.23	0.13	0.05	0.01
Oct 22	83	63	0.72	0.42	0.20	0.11	0.04	0.01
Oct 29	82	62	0.85	0.64	0.24	0.15	0.07	0.02
Nov 5	80	58	0.90	0.49	0.19	0.10	0.04	0.03
Nov 12	79	56	0.89	0.42	0.14	0.07	0.03	0.01
Nov 19	78	56	0.86	0.55	0.19	0.09	0.04	0.03
Nov 26	78	56	0.86	0.53	0.22	0.12	0.05	0.01
Dec 3	76	53	0.85	0.40	0.16	0.10	0.04	0.02
Dec 10	75	51	0.81	0.60	0.18	0.11	0.06	0.03
Dec 17	73	50	0.74	0.46	0.21	0.13	0.04	0.02
Dec 24	73	49	0.74	0.42	0.18	0.10	0.03	0.02
Year avg.	83	62	46.00	48.35	0.30	0.19	0.08	0.04

A.12. Panama City. Bay County. Elevation 10 feet.

Week beginning	Avg. max. t.	Avg. min. t.	% of days max t. 70–85	Avg. precipitation (in.)	% chance of precipitation				Sea water t.
					.01"+	.10"+	.50"+	1.0"+	
Jan 1	69	42	.21	1.28	.31	.23	.14	.07	
Jan 8	68	40	.20	1.61	.34	.27	.13	.05	
Jan 15	66	38	.22	1.15	.26	.18	.10	.06	56
Jan 22	62	38	.22	1.64	.33	.24	.15	.10	
Jan 29	63	42	.32	1.12	.26	.21	.11	.05	
Feb 5	62	38	.28	1.40	.31	.24	.10	.08	
Feb 12	66	42	.39	1.32	.26	.23	.13	.06	58
Feb 19	68	46	.49	1.02	.33	.21	.11	.05	
Feb 26	68	44	.46	1.64	.18	.16	.11	.09	
March 5	70	46	.59	1.41	.24	.20	.09	.08	
March 12	71	49	.68	.96	.22	.17	.09	.04	63
March 19	73	50	.71	.90	.25	.20	.07	.04	
March 26	74	53	.80	1.79	.29	.24	.18	.10	
April 2	74	51	.77	1.30	.18	.16	.08	.05	
April 9	77	54	.93	1.27	.22	.16	.12	.08	
April 16	79	56	.90	.63	.15	.13	.06	.02	71
April 23	80	57	.90	.70	.16	.13	.06	.02	
April 30	81	58	.86	.63	.17	.12	.03	.02	
May 7	82	60	.80	1.10	.29	.19	.11	.04	
May 14	84	62	.63	.49	.17	.11	.04	.01	
May 21	85	64	.49	1.22	.24	.21	.12	.05	78
May 28	87	66	.27	.85	.24	.19	.08	.04	
June 4	88	69	.22	1.36	.27	.20	.10	.06	
June 11	89	68	.11	1.35	.26	.21	.11	.05	84
June 18	89	70	.14	1.77	.38	.29	.14	.08	
June 25	89	71	.13	1.81	.41	.30	.18	.08	

July 2	90	71	.09	1.84	.41	.35	.20	.09	
July 9	91	72	.03	1.35	.33	.24	.13	.04	
July 16	90	72	.07	2.06	.49	.42	.22	.10	
July 23	90	72	.13	2.65	.52	.45	.22	.12	85
July 30	90	72	.13	2.43	.52	.42	.20	.08	
Aug 6	90	72	.10	1.43	.46	.35	.14	.04	
Aug 13	90	72	.13	2.10	.46	.38	.19	.08	86
Aug 20	90	72	.10	1.52	.39	.33	.15	.05	
Aug 27	90	71	.13	1.58	.45	.36	.17	.06	
Sept 3	89	70	.17	1.09	.40	.25	.10	.03	
Sept 10	89	70	.13	1.79	.32	.27	.15	.10	82
Sept 17	88	67	.21	1.29	.29	.23	.13	.05	
Sept 24	85	64	.46	.93	.25	.14	.08	.05	
Oct 1	83	60	.66	1.25	.23	.18	.10	.07	
Oct 8	82	58	.67	.72	.19	.13	.07	.04	74
Oct 15	80	55	.77	.71	.14	.11	.07	.05	
Oct 22	79	53	.83	.34	.13	.09	.04	.01	
Oct 29	77	54	.84	1.09	.23	.19	.11	.06	
Nov 5	74	49	.72	.91	.21	.18	.09	.04	
Nov 12	72	47	.67	.77	.21	.17	.07	.03	
Nov 19	72	48	.70	1.35	.28	.18	.13	.06	65
Nov 26	69	46	.57	1.16	.29	.23	.14	.03	
Dec 3	68	43	.46	.92	.24	.16	.08	.04	
Dec 10	66	42	.40	1.24	.29	.22	.12	.05	58
Dec 17	63	40	.33	.67	.24	.16	.05	.04	
Dec 24	63	40	.31	.74	.22	.16	.07	.04	
Year avg.	78	56	.43	65.78	.30	.23	.12	.06	

A.13. Pensacola. Escambia County. Elevation 110 feet.

Week beginning	Avg. max. t.	Avg. min. t.	% of days max. t. 70–85	Avg. precipitation (in.)	% chance of precipitation				Sea water t.
					.01"+	.10"+	.50"+	1.0"+	
Jan 1	60	43	.14	1.15	.34	.25	.13	.04	
Jan 8	59	42	.15	1.10	.27	.17	.11	.06	
Jan 15	59	41	.14	.77	.27	.18	.08	.03	56
Jan 22	62	42	.21	1.50	.31	.25	.12	.05	
Jan 29	62	43	.26	1.30	.30	.22	.09	.05	
Feb 5	61	41	.18	1.52	.32	.24	.13	.06	
Feb 12	64	46	.27	1.05	.31	.21	.10	.04	58
Feb 19	66	47	.36	1.18	.26	.21	.12	.06	
Feb 26	66	47	.38	1.80	.25	.19	.13	.07	
March 5	68	49	.43	1.45	.26	.22	.13	.09	
March 12	69	51	.56	1.32	.28	.20	.09	.04	63
March 19	71	52	.66	.88	.25	.18	.09	.04	
March 26	72	54	.70	1.40	.29	.22	.13	.08	
April 2	74	54	.79	.79	.21	.15	.06	.03	
April 9	75	57	.88	1.13	.23	.18	.11	.05	
April 16	78	60	.94	.64	.21	.11	.06	.01	71
April 23	79	61	.92	.90	.16	.12	.08	.04	
April 30	80	63	.91	.75	.22	.15	.05	.03	
May 7	81	64	.87	1.37	.25	.18	.10	.06	
May 14	83	66	.70	1.04	.21	.16	.10	.05	
May 21	85	67	.58	1.02	.23	.17	.09	.06	78
May 28	86	69	.45	1.10	.26	.16	.08	.06	
June 4	88	71	.25	1.68	.27	.19	.09	.05	
June 11	89	72	.15	1.28	.26	.20	.09	.06	
June 18	90	73	.14	1.69	.34	.25	.12	.07	84
June 25	90	73	.09	1.55	.39	.28	.12	.07	

July 2	90	74	.12	1.71	.42	.31	.17	.08	
July 9	91	75	.07	1.12	.35	.22	.10	.04	
July 16	90	74	.12	1.73	.40	.30	.16	.09	85
July 23	90	75	.09	1.77	.47	.37	.14	.05	
July 30	90	74	.15	2.44	.46	.35	.21	.10	
Aug 6	89	74	.14	1.65	.41	.32	.13	.09	
Aug 13	89	74	.11	1.90	.39	.30	.16	.08	
Aug 20	90	74	.10	1.63	.35	.31	.16	.09	86
Aug 27	89	73	.18	1.21	.34	.24	.12	.06	
Sept 3	88	73	.25	1.99	.36	.27	.16	.10	
Sept 10	88	72	.23	1.00	.24	.16	.07	.04	
Sept 17	87	70	.32	1.35	.25	.18	.11	.06	82
Sept 24	85	67	.47	.59	.24	.14	.05	.02	
Oct 1	82	63	.67	1.20	.18	.16	.09	.06	
Oct 8	81	62	.76	.90	.14	.11	.09	.03	
Oct 15	79	59	.84	.63	.14	.11	.04	.01	74
Oct 22	77	57	.86	.92	.15	.13	.05	.04	
Oct 29	75	56	.84	1.77	.22	.17	.12	.08	
Nov 5	71	51	.62	.65	.21	.14	.05	.02	
Nov 12	70	50	.58	.61	.20	.13	.06	.02	
Nov 19	69	50	.60	.81	.24	.20	.09	.02	65
Nov 26	68	49	.47	1.22	.30	.20	.11	.08	
Dec 3	66	46	.32	.71	.23	.17	.06	.04	
Dec 10	64	46	.34	1.20	.30	.20	.12	.05	58
Dec 17	62	44	.29	.73	.22	.15	.05	.02	
Dec 24	61	43	.21	.92	.26	.19	.08	.05	
Year avg.	77	59	.42	61.96	.28	.20	.10	.05	

A.14. Sarasota. Sarasota County. Elevation 8 feet.

Week beginning	Avg. max. t.	Avg. min. t.	% of days max t. 70–85	Avg. precipitation (in.)	% chance of precipitation				Sea water t.
					.01"+	.10"+	.50"+	1.0"+	
Jan 1	73	53	.69	.47	.21	.11	.04	.02	
Jan 8	71	51	.64	.58	.21	.10	.05	.02	
Jan 15	71	50	.59	.69	.21	.14	.08	.02	58
Jan 22	71	51	.61	.66	.24	.15	.05	.03	
Jan 29	72	51	.69	.40	.17	.10	.04	.00	
Feb 5	72	50	.61	.64	.21	.15	.06	.03	
Feb 12	73	52	.73	.49	.23	.11	.04	.01	60
Feb 19	73	53	.71	.68	.22	.13	.07	.03	
Feb 26	74	53	.73	.55	.21	.12	.06	.03	
March 5	76	56	.82	.88	.20	.13	.08	.04	
March 12	77	58	.89	.94	.19	.12	.06	.06	66
March 19	77	57	.87	.43	.15	.10	.04	.02	
March 26	79	60	.89	.81	.16	.10	.06	.04	
April 2	80	59	.90	.57	.17	.11	.06	.03	
April 9	81	61	.81	.63	.14	.10	.04	.03	
April 16	83	62	.71	.15	.09	.06	.01	.00	73
April 23	83	63	.74	.22	.12	.06	.03	.00	
April 30	84	64	.69	.30	.12	.08	.03	.01	
May 7	85	66	.50	.33	.16	.09	.02	.01	
May 14	87	67	.37	.67	.18	.11	.05	.03	
May 21	87	68	.32	.76	.27	.19	.07	.05	80
May 28	88	70	.16	1.04	.26	.20	.10	.05	
June 4	89	71	.12	1.20	.27	.20	.11	.06	
June 11	90	72	.03	1.20	.34	.25	.11	.06	84
June 18	89	72	.09	2.38	.41	.33	.17	.08	
June 25	90	74	.04	1.87	.38	.29	.13	.05	

Date									
July 2	91	73	.03	1.21	.37	.26	.11	.05	
July 9	91	73	.02	1.37	.40	.30	.15	.07	
July 16	90	73	.08	2.12	.52	.39	.21	.08	86
July 23	91	73	.00	1.18	.46	.32	.10	.03	
July 30	91	73	.02	1.67	.46	.37	.14	.06	
Aug 6	91	73	.03	1.93	.49	.38	.20	.07	
Aug 13	91	73	.03	1.80	.49	.34	.17	.08	86
Aug 20	91	74	.03	1.75	.50	.38	.19	.08	
Aug 27	91	73	.03	2.29	.51	.40	.22	.11	
Sept 3	90	73	.07	2.05	.45	.35	.19	.09	
Sept 10	90	73	.09	1.89	.46	.30	.18	.09	83
Sept 17	90	72	.05	1.29	.38	.29	.11	.05	
Sept 24	89	72	.12	1.56	.38	.29	.11	.07	
Oct 1	87	69	.22	1.18	.30	.20	.10	.07	
Oct 8	87	68	.30	.72	.21	.15	.08	.03	76
Oct 15	84	65	.54	.67	.22	.14	.08	.03	
Oct 22	83	63	.61	.62	.21	.12	.06	.02	
Oct 29	83	63	.70	.54	.22	.13	.04	.02	
Nov 5	80	60	.87	.47	.15	.10	.04	.02	
Nov 12	79	58	.80	.46	.12	.08	.05	.02	66
Nov 19	78	57	.88	.37	.16	.09	.04	.02	
Nov 26	78	57	.85	.39	.21	.12	.04	.02	
Dec 3	76	55	.80	.51	.16	.08	.04	.02	
Dec 10	75	54	.75	.56	.18	.11	.06	.03	60
Dec 17	72	52	.68	.53	.19	.11	.05	.02	
Dec 24	72	51	.61	.29	.19	.08	.03	.00	
Year avg.	82	63	.47	49.41	.27	.18	.09	.04	

A.15. Tallahassee. Leon County. Elevation 55 feet.

Week beginning	Avg. max. t.	Avg. min. t.	% of days max t. 70–85	Avg. precipitation (in.)	%chance of precipitation			
					.01"+	.10"+	.50"+	1.0"+
Jan 1	64	42	.31	1.19	.31	.24	.10	.06
Jan 8	61	39	.22	1.54	.30	.23	.14	.09
Jan 15	62	37	.27	1.08	.26	.18	.09	.05
Jan 22	64	38	.30	1.40	.31	.26	.14	.09
Jan 29	66	40	.40	1.03	.33	.23	.10	.03
Feb 5	64	38	.30	1.69	.32	.24	.15	.08
Feb 12	67	41	.46	1.35	.30	.21	.12	.06
Feb 19	69	43	.50	.78	.22	.17	.07	.03
Feb 26	69	41	.54	1.63	.22	.14	.11	.07
March 5	72	45	.63	1.96	.28	.20	.14	.10
March 12	74	47	.66	.96	.24	.19	.08	.05
March 19	76	47	.75	.95	.21	.16	.09	.05
March 26	77	50	.82	1.72	.29	.22	.14	.10
April 2	77	48	.74	1.09	.23	.17	.08	.05
April 9	80	52	.80	1.15	.23	.16	.10	.07
April 16	82	54	.70	.43	.18	.12	.04	.01
April 23	83	55	.63	.74	.16	.10	.07	.04
April 30	84	56	.63	.54	.16	.12	.04	.02
May 7	85	59	.51	1.34	.25	.19	.11	.05
May 14	87	61	.32	1.03	.26	.17	.08	.04
May 21	87	63	.29	1.40	.32	.22	.12	.07
May 28	89	65	.18	1.20	.28	.20	.11	.05
June 4	90	68	.12	1.60	.33	.25	.12	.07
June 11	91	68	.11	1.47	.35	.24	.12	.07

Date								
June 18	91	69	.08	2.07	.44	.30	.18	.10
June 25	92	69	.06	1.57	.48	.33	.15	.06
July 2	91	71	.10	1.90	.49	.40	.20	.07
July 9	93	71	.07	1.57	.46	.32	.12	.06
July 16	92	72	.08	1.95	.50	.38	.19	.09
July 23	91	72	.12	2.22	.53	.37	.21	.09
July 30	91	72	.11	2.12	.54	.40	.17	.09
Aug 6	91	72	.09	1.58	.45	.30	.17	.08
Aug 13	91	71	.09	1.82	.47	.31	.18	.09
Aug 20	91	71	.10	1.39	.39	.29	.15	.08
Aug 27	91	71	.14	1.45	.44	.32	.14	.07
Sept 3	90	70	.14	1.40	.38	.27	.10	.06
Sept 10	89	69	.20	.97	.25	.18	.10	.06
Sept 17	89	68	.39	1.46	.24	.19	.09	.04
Sept 24	86	64	.52	.95	.24	.17	.08	.04
Oct 1	84	61	.62	1.04	.20	.14	.08	.06
Oct 8	83	59	.73	.74	.16	.13	.06	.03
Oct 15	81	55	.82	.67	.15	.11	.05	.03
Oct 22	79	53	.84	.36	.13	.10	.03	.01
Oct 29	77	53	.71	1.04	.21	.16	.10	.04
Nov 5	74	47	.69	.71	.20	.14	.08	.04
Nov 12	73	44	.68	.66	.16	.10	.04	.03
Nov 19	71	46	.56	.93	.19	.15	.08	.05
Nov 26	70	45	.48	1.28	.28	.21	.11	.05
Dec 3	68	42	.41	.82	.20	.15	.07	.03
Dec 10	66	42	.35	1.24	.29	.20	.12	.05
Dec 17	64	39	.34	.82	.24	.16	.07	.04
Dec 24	64	39	.40	.89	.23	.16	.09	.05
Year avg.	79	55		62.64	.29	.21	.11	.06

A.16. Tampa. Hillsborough County. Elevation 19 feet.

Week	Avg.	Avg.	% of days	Avg.	% chance of precipitation			
beginning	max. t.	min. t.	max t. 70–85	precipitation (in.)	.01"+	.10"+	.50"+	1.0"+
Jan 1	72	53	.60	.47	.18	.12	.05	.03
Jan 8	70	50	.57	.54	.19	.13	.05	.01
Jan 15	69	49	.54	.51	.21	.14	.06	.01
Jan 22	70	49	.54	.47	.22	.14	.05	.01
Jan 29	71	51	.63	.47	.15	.10	.05	.02
Feb 5	70	49	.51	.89	.24	.18	.08	.03
Feb 12	72	51	.65	.73	.24	.17	.07	.03
Feb 19	73	53	.70	.56	.22	.13	.05	.02
Feb 26	73	51	.69	.48	.17	.13	.06	.01
March 5	75	55	.77	.81	.24	.16	.08	.04
March 12	76	56	.80	.58	.18	.12	.06	.02
March 19	77	56	.86	.43	.16	.11	.03	.02
March 26	79	60	.87	.81	.19	.11	.07	.04
April 2	79	59	.86	.46	.17	.13	.04	.01
April 9	81	60	.82	.33	.13	.08	.03	.01
April 16	83	62	.69	.24	.10	.05	.02	.01
April 23	83	63	.66	.26	.15	.08	.02	.01
April 30	85	64	.50	.24	.10	.06	.03	.00
May 7	86	66	.37	.79	.17	.12	.05	.01
May 14	88	68	.22	.68	.18	.11	.04	.03
May 21	88	68	.22	.77	.23	.17	.07	.03
May 28	89	70	.12	.95	.24	.18	.07	.04
June 4	89	72	.10	1.13	.31	.21	.10	.06
June 11	90	73	.04	.79	.29	.20	.06	.03
June 18	89	74	.09	1.49	.41	.29	.14	.05

June 25	89	74	.10	1.88	.43	.33	.17	.09
July 2	90	74	.07	1.02	.39	.25	.10	.04
July 9	91	74	.03	1.70	.40	.29	.18	.08
July 16	90	74	.06	1.81	.45	.34	.20	.08
July 23	90	75	.03	1.32	.47	.34	.12	.04
July 30	90	75	.07	1.70	.52	.40	.16	.06
Aug 6	91	75	.06	1.57	.49	.32	.14	.09
Aug 13	90	74	.07	1.85	.51	.37	.20	.08
Aug 20	90	75	.06	1.83	.49	.36	.18	.10
Aug 27	90	74	.05	1.88	.50	.36	.19	.10
Sept 3	90	74	.08	2.13	.47	.37	.20	.11
Sept 10	89	74	.10	1.23	.39	.26	.10	.05
Sept 17	90	73	.08	.97	.32	.20	.07	.04
Sept 24	88	72	.20	1.07	.31	.20	.10	.05
Oct 1	87	70	.32	.77	.23	.17	.07	.04
Oct 8	86	68	.43	.55	.22	.13	.04	.03
Oct 15	84	65	.55	.45	.17	.09	.03	.02
Oct 22	83	63	.72	.34	.15	.09	.01	.01
Oct 29	82	63	.84	.66	.20	.13	.04	.03
Nov 5	79	59	.80	.27	.14	.08	.03	.00
Nov 12	78	56	.79	.30	.13	.08	.03	.00
Nov 19	77	57	.84	.44	.15	.09	.03	.02
Nov 26	76	57	.79	.36	.19	.11	.03	.00
Dec 3	75	54	.77	.27	.13	.08	.02	.01
Dec 10	73	53	.68	.62	.20	.15	.06	.02
Dec 17	71	51	.59	.43	.20	.12	.03	.01
Dec 24	71	50	.57	.46	.20	.10	.03	.01
Year avg.	82	63	.44	47.38	.26	.18	.08	.03

A.17. Titusville. Brevard County. Elevation 14 feet.

Week beginning	Avg. max. t.	Avg. min. t.	% of days max t. 70–85	Avg. precipitation (in.)	% chance of precipitation				Sea water t.
					.01"+	.10"+	.50"+	1.0"+	
Jan 1	72	51	.59	.60	.24	.14	.06	.03	
Jan 8	70	49	.55	.47	.19	.14	.04	.01	
Jan 15	70	46	.55	.64	.20	.12	.07	.02	57
Jan 22	70	46	.52	.57	.24	.13	.05	.03	
Jan 29	72	49	.59	.52	.20	.12	.05	.03	
Feb 5	70	47	.47	.86	.27	.17	.08	.03	
Feb 12	72	49	.61	.85	.27	.18	.07	.04	
Feb 19	74	51	.64	.59	.26	.16	.05	.01	56
Feb 26	74	49	.70	.60	.19	.11	.07	.01	
March 5	76	53	.71	.74	.26	.18	.08	.02	
March 12	77	55	.67	.86	.25	.17	.09	.04	61
March 19	79	55	.71	.42	.19	.09	.02	.01	
March 26	80	58	.75	.95	.21	.19	.08	.04	
April 2	80	56	.73	.59	.17	.12	.06	.04	
April 9	81	58	.82	1.07	.21	.16	.08	.05	68
April 16	83	60	.61	.47	.15	.08	.05	.02	
April 23	85	61	.53	.44	.15	.08	.05	.02	71
April 30	85	62	.49	.52	.15	.11	.05	.03	
May 7	86	64	.43	.65	.21	.13	.05	.03	
May 14	88	65	.34	.91	.25	.18	.10	.03	74
May 21	87	66	.37	.96	.31	.23	.08	.05	
May 28	88	68	.26	1.06	.35	.25	.10	.05	77
June 4	89	69	.16	1.91	.38	.30	.14	.08	
June 11	90	70	.15	1.54	.41	.34	.14	.08	80
June 18	90	71	.12	1.88	.49	.35	.18	.08	
June 25	90	70	.10	1.88	.46	.35	.18	.09	81

July 2	92	71	.06	1.59	.40	.29	.14	.07	83
July 9	92	71	.02	1.57	.38	.29	.15	.07	
July 16	92	72	.03	1.91	.47	.36	.18	.09	84
July 23	92	71	.03	2.01	.44	.35	.19	.09	
July 30	92	72	.02	1.67	.44	.31	.16	.09	
Aug 6	92	72	.03	1.51	.42	.35	.15	.07	83
Aug 13	92	71	.03	1.78	.45	.34	.17	.07	
Aug 20	91	71	.04	1.99	.47	.36	.18	.06	83
Aug 27	90	71	.05	1.31	.41	.30	.12	.07	
Sept 3	90	71	.06	1.79	.44	.34	.15	.10	83
Sept 10	89	71	.07	1.52	.43	.34	.12	.07	
Sept 17	89	70	.14	1.26	.35	.27	.13	.05	82
Sept 24	87	70	.34	1.92	.46	.34	.15	.09	
Oct 1	86	68	.37	1.80	.35	.28	.16	.07	78
Oct 8	85	66	.53	1.03	.38	.28	.11	.04	
Oct 15	83	64	.67	1.14	.35	.24	.09	.05	72
Oct 22	82	62	.82	.60	.28	.17	.05	.02	
Oct 29	81	62	.83	1.26	.34	.28	.12	.06	
Nov 5	79	58	.86	.61	.19	.12	.06	.02	
Nov 12	77	55	.76	.69	.19	.15	.04	.02	
Nov 19	76	56	.80	.79	.28	.16	.06	.02	67
Nov 26	76	55	.76	.62	.20	.13	.05	.04	
Dec 3	74	53	.75	.51	.20	.12	.05	.01	
Dec 10	74	51	.73	.64	.25	.15	.04	.02	
Dec 17	71	49	.59	.57	.25	.16	.06	.02	60
Dec 24	71	48	.61	.35	.20	.10	.02	.01	
Year avg.	82	61	.45	54.62	.30	.21	.10	.05	

A.18. West Palm Beach. Palm Beach County. Elevation 18 feet.

Week beginning	Avg. max. t.	Avg. min. t.	% of days max t. 70–85	Avg. precipitation (in.)	% chance of precipitation				Sea water t.
					.01"+	.10"+	.50"+	1.0"+	
Jan 1	76	59	.86	.76	.30	.19	.08	.02	
Jan 8	75	57	.77	.97	.30	.21	.07	.04	
Jan 15	74	56	.78	1.06	.24	.13	.05	.04	70
Jan 22	74	56	.76	.64	.24	.14	.04	.03	
Jan 29	75	56	.78	.46	.20	.10	.04	.02	
Feb 5	74	56	.72	.50	.26	.16	.06	.01	
Feb 12	76	58	.86	.59	.21	.16	.04	.02	
Feb 19	77	59	.81	.93	.29	.19	.09	.04	73
Feb 26	76	57	.82	.66	.21	.13	.07	.02	
March 5	78	61	.88	1.02	.27	.17	.07	.05	
March 12	78	61	.84	.76	.24	.18	.08	.04	75
March 19	79	61	.84	.93	.21	.13	.06	.03	
March 26	81	65	.80	.97	.24	.16	.08	.03	
April 2	81	64	.84	.60	.18	.13	.07	.01	
April 9	81	65	.88	.84	.23	.15	.06	.04	78
April 16	83	66	.80	.63	.16	.10	.05	.03	
April 23	84	67	.67	.91	.20	.14	.07	.03	78
April 30	84	68	.64	1.03	.23	.14	.06	.04	
May 7	85	70	.57	1.07	.29	.17	.09	.05	
May 14	86	71	.45	1.10	.31	.22	.12	.05	80
May 21	86	71	.43	1.78	.42	.30	.15	.08	
May 28	87	72	.28	1.93	.45	.34	.17	.09	81
June 4	88	73	.21	2.12	.44	.38	.20	.10	
June 11	88	73	.21	1.38	.40	.30	.12	.06	84
June 18	88	73	.14	2.57	.59	.42	.23	.11	
June 25	89	74	.08	2.09	.45	.38	.20	.13	85

July 2	89	74	.06	1.52	.44	.30	.16	.07	86
July 9	90	75	.03	1.27	.40	.28	.11	.05	
July 16	90	75	.05	1.43	.44	.32	.13	.03	86
July 23	90	75	.02	1.19	.45	.32	.11	.05	
July 30	90	75	.03	1.48	.49	.38	.15	.06	
Aug 6	90	75	.03	1.65	.52	.37	.13	.07	86
Aug 13	90	75	.04	1.32	.45	.30	.10	.06	
Aug 20	90	75	.04	2.04	.53	.35	.15	.06	84
Aug 27	89	75	.04	1.37	.50	.29	.12	.04	
Sept 3	89	75	.06	1.70	.55	.38	.17	.08	84
Sept 10	89	75	.10	2.02	.48	.38	.18	.10	
Sept 17	89	74	.07	1.92	.52	.33	.15	.08	83
Sept 24	87	74	.20	2.29	.57	.41	.20	.10	
Oct 1	87	73	.32	1.75	.44	.31	.12	.06	83
Oct 8	86	72	.48	1.20	.39	.28	.13	.04	
Oct 15	84	70	.67	1.52	.36	.23	.15	.07	79
Oct 22	84	69	.77	1.19	.32	.22	.10	.05	
Oct 29	83	68	.77	1.48	.39	.26	.10	.05	
Nov 5	81	65	.88	1.50	.30	.21	.09	.06	76
Nov 12	80	64	.90	1.06	.25	.15	.08	.05	
Nov 19	79	63	.93	1.03	.29	.17	.04	.04	
Nov 26	79	64	.90	.51	.27	.16	.04	.01	
Dec 3	78	62	.91	.67	.22	.12	.06	.02	73
Dec 10	77	60	.88	.55	.21	.14	.05	.02	
Dec 17	75	57	.82	.71	.23	.14	.05	.02	
Dec 24	75	57	.80	.67	.25	.16	.05	.02	
Year avg.	83	67	.53	61.13	.34	.23	.10	.05	

Table B.1. Hurricanes that made landfall in Florida or passed within 50 miles of Florida, 1900–2002

Year	Date of landfall	Assigned hurricane category[a]	Florida landfall (approx.)	Florida coast	Area of origin of storm	Landfall wind speed (mph)	Names
1903	12 Sep	2	Jupiter	se	Atlantic	86	
1906	17 Jun	2	Cape Sable	sw	Atlantic	75	
1906	18 Oct	4	Key West	sw	Caribbean	127	
1909	11 Oct	3	Key West	sw	Caribbean	104	
1910	18 Oct	3	Key West	sw	Caribbean	115	
1911	11 Aug	1	Pensacola	nw	Caribbean	81	
1915	4 Sep	2	Apalachicola	nw	Caribbean	81	
1916	18 Oct	3	Pensacola	nw	Caribbean	75	
1916	15 Nov	1	Keys	sw	Caribbean	81	
1917	29 Sep	3	Off Ft. Walton	nw	Atlantic	98	
1919	10 Sep	4	Key West	sw	Atlantic	132	
1921	26 Oct	4	St. Petersburg	sw	Caribbean	98	
1924	15 Sep	1	Panama City	nw	Gulf	75	
1924	21 Oct	3	Naples	sw	Caribbean	92	
1925	2 Dec	2	Sarasota	sw	Caribbean	75	
1926	28 Jul	4	Jupiter	se	Atlantic	92	
1926	18 Sep	4	Miami	se	Atlantic	138	
1926	21 Oct	4	Keys	sw	Caribbean	109	
1928	8 Aug	2	Stuart	se	Atlantic	98	
1928	17 Sep	5	Palm Beach	se	Atlantic	134	
1929	30 Sep	4	Marathon	sw	Atlantic	75	
1933	30 Jul	1	Jupiter	se	Atlantic	81	
1933	1 Sep	3	Off the Keys	sw	Atlantic	104	
1933	4 Sep	4	Jupiter	se	Atlantic	127	
1933	5 Oct	4	Keys	sw	Caribbean	132	
1935	3 Sep	5	Keys	sw	Atlantic	161	
1935	29 Sep	3	Off Miami	se	Caribbean	115	
1935	4 Nov	1	Miami	se	Atlantic	75	
1936	31 Jul	1	Ft. Walton	nw	Atlantic	92	
1939	11 Aug	1	Ft. Pierce	se	Atlantic	75	
1941	6 Oct	3	Miami	se	Atlantic	121	
1944	19 Oct	3	Sarasota	sw	Caribbean	75	
1945	26 Jun	3	Cedar Key	nw	Caribbean	92	

Year	Date	Category	Location	Direction	Ocean		Name
1945	16 Sep	4	Homestead	se	Atlantic	132	
1946	8 Oct	4	Sarasota	sw	Caribbean	75	
1947	17 Sep	5	Pompano Beach	se	Atlantic	155	
1947	12 Oct	1	Cape Sable	sw	Caribbean	86	
1948	21 Sep	3	Key West	sw	Caribbean	121	
1948	5 Oct	4	Key West	sw	Caribbean	127	
1949	26 Aug	4	Palm Beach	se	Atlantic	150	
1950	31 Aug	3	Pensacola	nw	Atlantic	86	Baker
1950	5 Sep	3	Tarpon Springs	sw	Caribbean	121	Easy
1950	18 Oct	3	Miami	se	Caribbean	104	King
1953	26 Sep	3	Panama City	nw	Caribbean	81	Florence
1956	25 Sep	1	Ft. Walton	nw	Caribbean	75	Flossy
1960	10 Sep	5	Keys	sw	Atlantic	132	Donna
1964	26 Aug	5	Miami	se	Atlantic	92	Cleo
1964	9 Sep	4	St. Augustine	ne	Atlantic	109	Dora
1964	15 Oct	3	Naples	sw	Caribbean	127	Isbell
1965	8 Sep	5	Miami	se	Atlantic	127	Betsy
1966	9 Jun	3	Alligator Point	nw	Caribbean	92	Alma
1966	4 Oct	4	Upper Keys	sw	Atlantic	86	Inez
1968	18 Oct	1	Cedar Key	nw	Caribbean	81	Gladys
1972	19 Jun	1	Port St. Joe	nw	Caribbean	75	Agnes
1975	23 Sep	3	Ft. Walton	nw	Atlantic	127	Eloise
1979	3 Sep	5	Jupiter	se	Atlantic	92	David
1979	13 Sep	4	West of Pensacola	nw	Atlantic	132	Frederic
1985	2 Sep	3	Off Port St. Joe	nw	Atlantic	121	Elena
1985	22 Nov	3	Port St. Joe	nw	Atlantic	92	Kate
1987	12 Oct	1	Key West	sw	Caribbean	75	Floyd
1992	24 Aug	5	Miami	se	Atlantic	138	Andrew
1995	2 Aug	1	Melbourne	ne	Atlantic	86	Erin
1995	5 Oct	4	Niceville	nw	Caribbean	92	Opal
1997	19 Jul	1	Pensacola	nw	Gulf	75	Danny
1998	3 Sep	2	Panama City	nw	Gulf	75	Earl
1998	25 Sep	5	Key West	sw	Atlantic	81	Georges
1999	15 Oct	2	Cape Sable	sw	Caribbean	104	Irene
2000	18 Sep	1	Off Cedar Key	nw	Caribbean	75	Gordon

Source: Unisys, 2002.

a. Category at its height, not when it reached Florida.

Table B.2. The nation's 30 most deadly and costly hurricanes and tropical storms, 1900–2000.

(Storms that made a Florida landfall and those that seriously affected the state are in bold.)

	Most deadly				Most costly			
	Hurricane	Year	Category	Deaths	Hurricane	Year	Category	Damage ($bill.)[a]
1	TX (Galveston)	1900	4	8,000	**Andrew (FL/LA)**	**1992**	5	**35.0**
2	**FL (SE/L. Okeechobee)**	**1928**	4	1,836	Hugo (SC)	1989	4	9.7
3	**FL (Keys/TX)**	**1919**	4	600	**Agnes (FL/NE U.S.)**	**1972**	1	**8.6**
4	New England	1938	3	600	**Betsy (FL/LA)**	**1965**	5	**8.5**
5	**FL (Keys)**	**1935**	5	408	Camille (MS/LA/VA)	1969	5	7.0
6	Audrey (LA/TX)	1957	4	390	Diane (NE U.S.)	1955	1	5.5
7	NE U.S.	1944	3	390	Frederic (AL/MS)	1979	3	5.0
8	LA	1909	4	350	**Floyd (E. seaboard)**	**1999**	2	**4.7**
9	LA	1915	4	275	New England	1938	3	4.6
10	TX	1915	4	275	Fran (NC)	1996	3	3.7
11	Camille (MS/LA/VA)	1969	5	256	**Opal (FL/AL)**	**1995**	3	**3.5**
12	**FL (Miami) MS/AL**	**1926**	4	243	Alicia (TX)	1983	3	3.4
13	Diane (NE U.S.)	1955	1	184	Carol (NE U.S.)	1954	3	3.1
14	SE FL	1906	2	164	Carla (TX)	1961	4	2.6
15	**FL/MS/AL (Pensacola)**	**1906**	4	134	**Georges (FL/MS/AL)**	**1998**	5	**2.5**
16	**Agnes (FL/NE U.S.)**	**1972**	1	122	Juan (LA)	1985	1	2.4
17	Hazel (SC/NC)	1954	4	95	**Donna (FL/E U.S.)**	**1960**	5	**2.4**
18	**Betsy (FL/LA)**	**1965**	5	75	Celia (TX)	1970	3	2.0
19	Carol (NE U.S.)	1954	3	60	**Elena (FL/MS/AL)**	**1985**	3	**2.0**
20	Floyd (E. seaboard)	1999	2	56	Bob (NC/NE U.S.)	1991	2	2.0
21	**SE FL/LA/MS**	**1947**	4	51	Hazel (SC/NC)	1954	4	1.9

22	Donna (FL/E. U.S.)	1960	5	50	FL/MS/AL	1926	4	1.7
22	GA/SC/NC	1940	2	50	TX	1915	4	1.5
24	Carla (TX)	1961	4	46	Dora (FL)	1964	4	1.5
25	TX	1909	3	41	Eloise (FL)	1975	3	1.5
26	TX	1932	4	40	Gloria (E. U.S.)	1985	3	1.5
26	TX	1933	3	40	NE US	1944	3	1.2
28	Hilda (LA)	1964	3	38	Beulah (TX)	1967	3	1.1
29	LA	1918	3	34	FL/LA/MS	1947	5	.9
30	SW FL	1910	3	30	TX	1900	4	.9
30	Alberto (FL/GA/AL)	1994	Trop. storm	30				

Source: Jarrell, 2002; Unisys, 2002.

a. Converted to 2000 dollar value.

Table C.1. Fall dates when the first temperature of 32°F or lower will occur: one median, three early, and one late probability[a]

Station	Median	Early	0.25	0.75	Late
Interior North Florida					
Chipley (Washington)	Nov 13	Oct 20	Nov 6	Nov 26	Dec 31
Cross City (Dixie)	Nov 9	Oct 28	Nov 4	Dec 12	Dec 31
Lake City (Columbia)	Nov 23	Nov 1	Nov 13	Dec 1	Dec 22
Madison (Madison)	Nov 26	Oct 21	Nov 13	Dec 3	Dec 31
Milton (Santa Rosa)	Nov 14	Oct 20	Nov 5	Nov 29	Dec 26
Monticello (Jefferson)	Nov 14	Oct 21	Nov 5	Nov 29	Dec 31
Palatka (Putnam)	Dec 7	Nov 3	Nov 30	Dec 17	Dec 25
Quincy (Gadsden)	Nov 17	Oct 12	Nov 11	Nov 29	Dec 16
Tallahassee (Leon)	Nov 14	Oct 18	Nov 5	Nov 26	Dec 29
Interior Peninsula					
Avon Park (Highlands)	Dec 16	Nov 25	Dec 7	Dec 23	Dec 27
Belle Glade (Palm Beach)	Dec 18	Nov 16	Dec 12	Dec 23	Dec 31
Bushnell (Sumter)	Dec 4	Nov 10	Nov 16	Dec 13	Dec 26
Clermont (Lake)	Dec 16	Nov 24	Dec 8	Dec 23	Dec 28
Lake Alfred (Polk)	Dec 12	Nov 16	Nov 30	Dec 20	Dec 30
Lakeland (Polk)	Dec 19	Nov 24	Dec 12	Dec 23	Dec 27
Orlando (Orange)	Dec 25	Dec 19	Dec 21	Dec 26	Dec 28
St. Leo (Pasco)	Dec 11	Nov 15	Nov 30	Dec 18	Dec 26
Coastal Florida					
Everglades (Collier)	Dec 18	Dec 12	Dec 12	Dec 23	Dec 26
Fernandina Beach (Nassau)	Dec 6	Nov 3	Nov 25	Dec 15	Dec 26
Jacksonville (Duval)	Dec 1	Nov 3	Nov 18	Dec 10	Dec 25
Miami (Miami-Dade)	Too few freezes to calculate				
Pensacola (Escambia)	Dec 7	Oct 31	Nov 27	Dec 14	Dec 24
Tampa (Hillsborough)	Dec 16	Nov 16	Dec 1	Dec 23	Dec 27
Titusville (Brevard)	Dec 15	Nov 16	Dec 9	Dec 19	Dec 31

Source: Southeast Regional Climate Center, 2002.
a. Period of observation 1970–2001.

Table C.2. Spring dates when the last temperature of 32°F or lower will occur: one median, three early, and one late probability[a]

Station	Median	Early	0.25	0.75	Late
Interior North Florida					
Chipley (Washington)	Mar 8	Jan 1	Feb 21	Mar 17	Apr 4
Cross City (Dixie)	Mar 16	Jan 8	Mar 5	Mar 26	Apr 16
Lake City (Columbia)	Mar 2	Jan 20	Feb 16	Mar 15	Mar 29
Madison (Madison)	Feb 24	Jan 1	Feb 11	Mar 11	Mar 31
Milton (Santa Rosa)	Mar 11	Feb 8	Feb 25	Mar 22	Apr 11
Monticello (Jefferson)	Mar 10	Jan 2	Mar 1	Mar 18	Apr 1
Palatka (Putnam)	Feb 15	Jan 1	Jan 27	Feb 26	Mar 24
Quincy (Gadsden)	Mar 5	Jan 28	Feb 20	Mar 13	Mar 27
Tallahassee (Leon)	Mar 18	Feb 2	Mar 7	Mar 25	Apr 23
Interior Peninsula					
Avon Park (Highlands)	Feb 10	Jan 1	Jan 21	Feb 25	Mar 15
Belle Glade (Palm Beach)	Feb 5	Jan 2	Jan 20	Feb 25	Mar 4
Bushnell (Sumter)	Feb 23	Jan 2	Feb 9	Mar 9	Apr 17
Clermont (Lake)	Feb 4	Jan 1	Jan 19	Feb 21	Mar 15
Lake Alfred (Polk)	Feb 10	Jan 2	Jan 25	Feb 23	Apr 6
Lakeland (Polk)	Jan 31	Jan 4	Jan 19	Feb 12	Mar 4
Orlando (Orange)	Feb 5	Jan 3	Jan 19	Feb 18	Mar 3
St. Leo (Pasco)	Feb 2	Jan 1	Jan 19	Feb 15	Mar 15
Coastal Florida					
Everglades (Collier)	Jan 20	Jan 3	Jan 14	Jan 29	Mar 12
Fernandina Beach (Nassau)	Feb 21	Jan 1	Jan 31	Mar 6	Mar 27
Jacksonville (Duval)	Feb 26	Jan 2	Feb 9	Mar 7	Mar 31
Miami (Miami-Dade)	Too few freezes to calculate				
Pensacola (Escambia)	Feb 26	Jan 22	Feb 16	Mar 4	Mar 22
Tampa (Hillsborough)	Feb 1	Jan 1	Jan 19	Feb 14	Mar 4
Titusville (Brevard)	Feb 7	Jan 2	Jan 20	Mar 2	Mar 22

Source: Southeast Regional Climate Center, 2002.
a. Period of observation 1970–2001.

Table D.1. Average number of days with heavy fog

	Winter			Spring			Summer			Fall			
	Dec	Jan	Feb	Mar	Apr	May	Jun	Jul	Aug	Sep	Oct	Nov	Total
Daytona Beach (58)	5	5	3	3	2	2	1	1	1	1	2	3	28
Ft. Myers (3)	4	4	6	2	1	0	1	1	1	1	2	2	23
Gainesville (18)	7	6	5	3	3	4	3	2	2	3	3	5	44
Jacksonville (57)	6	6	4	3	3	3	1	1	2	2	3	6	39
Key West (54)	0	0	0	0	0	0	0	0	0	0	0	0	1
Miami (53)	1	1	1	1	1	0	0	0	0	0	0	1	6
Orlando (53)	5	5	3	3	1	1	1	1	1	1	2	3	26
Pensacola (31)	5	5	5	5	4	2	1	1	0	1	2	4	32
Tallahassee (40)	6	7	5	5	5	5	3	2	2	2	3	5	50
Tampa (55)	4	5	3	3	1	0	0	0	0	0	1	3	20
Vero Beach (18)	2	3	2	2	1	1	1	0	0	0	0	1	12
West Palm Beach (58)	1	2	1	1	1	0	0	0	0	0	0	1	8

Source: Based on data from U.S. Dept. of Commerce, Local Climatological Data, 2001.
Note: Number of years of observation in parentheses. All data rounded to nearest whole number.

Table D.2. Average number of days with thunderstorms

	Winter			Spring			Summer			Fall			
	Dec	Jan	Feb	Mar	Apr	May	Jun	Jul	Aug	Sep	Oct	Nov	Total
Daytona Beach (58)	1	1	2	3	3	7	13	17	15	9	3	1	77
Ft. Myers (3)	0	1	0	3	1	4	17	18	17	10	2	0	73
Gainesville (18)	1	2	2	4	3	6	14	18	15	8	3	1	76
Jacksonville (60)	1	1	2	3	4	6	12	16	13	7	2	1	67
Key West (54)	1	1	1	2	2	4	10	13	14	11	4	1	65
Miami (52)	1	1	1	2	3	6	12	15	16	12	5	1	74
Orlando (57)	1	1	2	3	3	8	15	19	18	10	3	1	82
Pensacola (31)	3	2	3	4	4	5	10	15	14	6	2	2	68
Tallahassee (40)	2	2	2	4	4	7	14	19	16	8	2	2	80
Tampa (55)	1	1	2	3	3	5	14	20	20	11	3	1	83
Vero Beach (18)	0	2	2	4	4	6	13	15	14	10	4	1	75
West Palm Beach (58)	1	1	1	2	4	8	13	16	16	11	4	2	79

Source: Based on data from U.S. Dept. of Commerce, *Local Climatological Data 2001.*
Note: Number of years of observation in parentheses. All data rounded to nearest whole number.

Table D.3. Average wind speed (mph) and prevailing direction

		Winter			Spring			Summer			Fall			
		Dec	Jan	Feb	Mar	Apr	May	Jun	Jul	Aug	Sep	Oct	Nov	Annual
Daytona Beach	Sp	(37)a		8	9	9	10	9	9	8	7	7	8	9
	Dir	(22)		NW	N	N	WSW	WSW	ESE	E	WSW	ESE	ENE	ENE
Ft. Myers	Sp	(3)		7	7	7	8	8	7	6	6	6	7	8
	Dir	(3)		*	*	*	*	*	*	*	*	*	*	*
Gainesville	Sp	(17)		7	7	7	8	7.	7	6	6	5	6	6
	Dir	(18)		WNW	NW	W	W	W	WSW	WSW	W	WSW	E	NE
Jacksonville	Sp	(50)		8	8	9	9	9	8	8	7	7	8	8
	Dir	(34)		N	WNW	NW	WSW	WSW	SE	WSW	WSW	SW	ENE	NE
Key West	Sp	(30)		12	12	12	12	12	10	10	9	9	10	11
	Dir	(22)		N	N	N	ESE	ESE	SE	SE	ESE	SW	ESE	ENE
Miami	Sp	(49)		9	10	10	11	11	9	8	8	8	8	9
	Dir	(33)		NNW	NNW	N	SE	ESE	E	ESE	ESE	ESE	ESE	ENE
Orlando	Sp	(47)		8	8	8	9	9	8	7	6	6	7	8
	Dir	(36)		N	N	N	S	ESE	E	S	S	S	ENE	N
Pensacola	Sp	(24)		10	10	10	11	12	10	9	8	7	9	9
	Dir	(20)		N	N	N	S	SE	S	S	S	S	N	N
Tallahassee	Sp	(42)		6	7	7	8	7	6	5	5	5	6	6
	Dir	(26)		N	N	N	N	SE	S	S	SSW	SSW	ENE	N
Tampa	Sp	(49)		8	9	9	10	9	9	8	7	7	8	8
	Dir	(33)		ENE	N	N	S	S	W	WSW	S	E	ENE	ENE
Vero Beach	Sp	(17)		8	9	9	10	10	9	8	7	7	7	9
	Dir	(18)		ENE	NW	N	E	E	W	W	W	E	E	ENE
West Palm Beach	Sp	(39)		10	10	10	11	11	10	8	8	8	9	10
	Dir	(23)		NW	NW	N	SE	SE	SE	ESE	ESE	ESE	E	ENE

Source: Based on data from the U.S. Dept. of Commerce, *Local Climatological Data, 2001.*

Notes: Wind direction is from the source. All data rounded to nearest whole number. * = no data.

a. Period of observation in parentheses.

Table D.4. Average amount of sunshine (% possible amount)

	Winter			Spring			Summer			Fall			Total
	Dec	Jan	Feb	Mar	Apr	May	Jun	Jul	Aug	Sep	Oct	Nov	
Jacksonville (49)	56	58	62	68	73	71	65	65	64	58	60	60	63
Key West (37)	71	74	77	82	84	82	76	77	76	72	71	71	76
Miami (20)	63	66	68	74	76	72	68	72	71	70	70	67	70
Pensacola (5)	49	53	53	61	63	67	67	57	58	60	71	64	60
Tampa (49)	61	63	66	71	75	75	67	62	61	61	65	64	66

Source: Based on data from U.S. Dept. of Commerce, *Local Climatological Data, 2001.*
Notes: Number of years of observation in parentheses; all data rounded to nearest whole number.

Table D.5. Average number of days with various sky conditions

	January			April			July			October		
	CR	PC	CD	CR	PC	CD	CR	PC	CD	CR	PC	CD
Daytona Beach (43)	10	9	12	11	11	9	4	15	12	9	11	11
Ft. Myers (45)	11	1	8	11	13	6	2	18	11	11	13	8
Jacksonville (38)	9	8	14	10	10	9	5	4	12	10	9	12
Key West (38)	11	12	9	14	11	5	3	17	11	8	13	10
Miami (37)	10	13	8	9	15	7	3	17	11	7	14	11
Orlando (38)	9	11	11	10	12	8	3	17	11	9	12	10
Pensacola (20)	8	7	16	10	9	11	5	16	10	13	9	9
Tallahassee (25)	6	7	15	10	11	9	3	17	11	13	8	10
Tampa (40)	10	10	11	11	11	8	2	16	13	11	11	9
West Palm Beach (44)	8	11	12	9	13	8	4	14	14	6	14	11

Source: Based on data from U.S. Dept. of Commerce, Local Climatological Data, 2001.
Notes: Number of years of observation in parentheses.
CR= clear; PC= partly cloudy; CD= cloudy.

Table D.6. Average relative humidity (%)

	January				April			
	1A.M.	7A.M.	1P.M.	7P.M.	1A.M.	7A.M.	1P.M.	7P.M.
Daytona Beach	84	85	59	75	81	84	51	65
Ft. Myers	86	89	56	72	84	89	47	64
Gainesville	87	89	61	75	87	90	50	62
Jacksonville	84	86	58	74	84	88	48	63
Key West	80	81	69	76	75	76	63	69
Miami	81	84	59	69	76	80	53	64
Orlando	84	87	56	68	83	87	46	58
Pensacola	79	81	62	71	82	85	56	66
Tallahassee	85	87	58	72	88	91	47	56
Tampa	84	86	58	73	82	86	50	62
Vero Beach	85	87	59	75	80	84	52	65
West Palm Beach	81	83	59	72	76	79	54	65

	July				October			
	1A.M.	7A.M.	1P.M.	7P.M.	1A.M.	7A.M.	1P.M.	7P.M.
Daytona Beach	87	88	64	76	83	85	61	75
Ft. Myers	90	90	60	77	87	90	57	73
Gainesville	94	94	63	78	91	92	62	80
Jacksonville	89	90	60	74	89	91	59	80
Key West	76	76	66	71	79	81	69	75
Miami	82	84	63	72	82	86	62	72
Orlando	89	91	59	75	87	88	55	74
Pensacola	86	88	64	71	80	84	55	69
Tallahassee	93	94	61	74	88	91	52	72
Tampa	85	88	63	73	85	89	56	71
Vero Beach	89	89	65	78	83	87	62	77
West Palm Beach	85	85	64	75	80	83	62	74

Source: U.S. Dept. of Commerce, *Local Climatological Data, 2001.* Period of observation 1972–2001.

Table E. A comparison of average weather between coastal humid subtropical weather stations in similar latitudes

Station	Latitude	Hottest month	Coldest month	Annual precipitation
Daytona Beach	29.13 N	81°F	57°F	48 inches
Durban, S. Africa	29.52 S	76	64	45
Grafton, Australia	29.41 S	78	57	35
Uruguaiana, Brazil	29.42 S	80	56	52
Wenchow, China	29.01 N	84	45	67

Table F. Heating (H)[a] and cooling (C)[b] degree-days

		Winter			Spring			Summer			Fall			
		Dec	Jan	Feb	Mar	Apr	May	Jun	Jul	Aug	Sep	Oct	Nov	Total
Daytona Beach	H	207	282	205	112	21	0	0	0	0	0	0	82	909
	C	55	50	37	90	150	301	432	502	496	432	265	109	2919
Ft. Myers	H	100	153	108	32	0	0	0	0	0	0	0	25	418
	C	119	116	103	160	247	412	501	552	558	510	378	199	3855
Gainesville	H	310	384	282	138	30	0	0	0	0	0	22	150	1316
	C	31	34	24	61	117	279	417	487	477	390	184	69	2570
Jacksonville	H	331	421	296	169	37	0	0	0	0	0	31	149	1434
	C	25	31	22	48	97	260	423	515	502	393	179	56	2551
Key West	H	19	44	30	7	0	0	0	0	0	0	0	0	100
	C	221	196	184	279	360	484	543	601	598	549	465	318	4798
Miami	H	41	88	51	14	0	0	0	0	0	0	0	6	200
	C	168	156	149	221	306	425	492	546	552	507	412	264	4198
Orlando	H	164	234	164	65	5	0	0	0	0	0	0	54	686
	C	74	70	58	117	191	369	483	536	543	480	316	144	3381
Pensacola	H	371	471	331	184	38	0	0	0	0	0	39	183	1617
	C	20	25	12	42	116	295	459	530	512	402	172	51	2639
Tallahassee	H	389	471	344	191	59	0	0	0	0	0	48	203	1705
	C	23	21	13	42	98	267	438	505	505	399	163	44	2518
Tampa	H	171	234	160	81	7	0	0	0	0	0	0	72	725
	C	84	76	62	130	196	384	489	539	539	477	304	147	3427
Vero Beach	H	127	186	138	56	7	0	0	0	0	0	0	34	548
	C	87	81	74	124	196	335	435	499	505	453	326	163	3278
West Palm Beach	H	74	122	85	27	0	0	0	0	0	0	0	15	323
	C	149	125	119	182	252	391	468	533	543	498	397	234	3891

Source: Based on data from U.S. Dept. of Commerce, Local Climatological Data, 2001.
Years of observation 1972–2001.
a. Heating degree days: Total number of degrees for the days in the month that the mean temperature falls below 65°F.
b. Cooling degree days: Total number of degrees for the days in the month that the mean temperature rises above 65°F.

References

Attaway, John A. 1997. *A History of Florida Citrus Freezes*. Lake Alfred: Florida Science Sources.

———. 1999. *Hurricanes and Florida Agriculture*. Lake Alfred: Florida Science Sources.

Baker, Earl J. 2002. *Southeast Florida Hurricane Evacuation Behavioral Analysis*. Tallahassee: Hazard Management Group (prepared for U.S. Corps of Engineers, Jacksonville).

Barnes, Jay. 1998. *Florida's Hurricane History*. Chapel Hill: University of North Carolina Press.

Benson, M. A., and R. A. Gardner. 1974. *The 1971 Drought in South Florida and Its Effect on the Hydrologic System*. Tallahassee: U.S. Geological Service Investigation, 74–12.

Blanchard, David O., and Raul E. Lopez. 1985. "Spatial Patterns of Convection in South Florida." *Monthly Weather Review* 113, 3: 1282–99.

Bradley, James T. 1973. "Snow in Florida." *Weatherwise* 26: 72–73.

———. 1975. *Freeze Probabilities in Florida*. Publication no. 777. Gainesville: University of Florida Institute of Food and Agricultural Sciences.

Brenner, James. 1999. "Southern Oscillation Anomalies and Their Relation to Florida Wildlife." http://flame.doacs.state.fl.us/Env/enso/html

Burpee, Robert W. 1979. "Peninsula-Scale Convergence in the South Florida Sea Breeze." *Monthly Weather Review* 107, 7: 852–60.

Burpee, Robert W., and Lawrence N. Lahiff. 1984. "Area-Average Rainfall Variations on Sea-Breeze Days in South Florida." *Monthly Weather Review* 112, 3: 520–34.

Byers, Horace R., and Harriet R. Rodebush. 1948. "Causes of Thunderstorms of the Florida Peninsula." *Journal of Meteorology* 5: 275–85.

Changnon, Stanley. 2000. *El Niño, 1997–1998: The Climate Event of the Century*. New York: Oxford University Press.

Doesken, Nolan, and William P. Eckrich. 1987. "How Often Does It Rain Where You Live?" *Weatherwise* 40: 200–203.

Drye, Willie. 2002. *Storm of the Century: The Labor Day Hurricane of 1935*. Washington, D.C.: National Geographic.

Elsner, James B., and A. Birol Kara. 1999. *Hurricanes of the North Atlantic: Climate and Society*. New York: Oxford University Press.

Everling, Anna. 1987. "Waterspouts." *Weatherwise* 40: 207–8.

Fagan, Brian M. 2000. *The Little Ice Age: How Climate Made History 1300–1850*. New York: Basic Books.

Fernald, Edward A., and Donald J. Patton, eds. 1984. *Water Resources Atlas of Florida*. Tallahassee: Florida State University Institute of Science and Public Affairs.

Florida Climate Center. 2001. *Torrential Rain Study*. www.coaps.fsu.edu

———. 2000. *Winter Weather Outlook, 2000–2001*. www.coaps.fsu.edu

Florida Department of Community Affairs. 1984. *Florida Hazards Analysis*. Tallahassee: Division of Emergency Management.

Florida Department of Environmental Regulation. 1993–2002. *Air Monitoring Reports*. www.dep.state.fl.us/air.

Glantz, Michael H. 1996. *Currents of Change: El Niño's Impact on Climate and Society*. New York: Cambridge University Press.

Golden, Joseph H. 1971. "Waterspouts and Tornadoes over South Florida." *Monthly Weather Review* 99: 146–53.

———. 1973. "Some Statistical Aspects of Waterspout Formation." *Weatherwise* 26: 108–17.

———. 1974. "Life Cycle of Florida Keys Waterspouts I." *Journal of Applied Meteorology*. 13: 676–92.

Grazulis, Thomas P. 1993. *Significant Tornadoes, 1980–1991*. St. Johnsbury, Vt.: Environmental Films.

Hagemeyer, B. C. 1997. "Peninsular Florida Tornado Outbreaks." *Weather and Forecasting* 12: 399–427.

Hansen, James W., and James W. Jones. 1999. "El Niño–Southern Oscillation Impacts on Winter Vegetable Production in Florida." *Journal of Climate* 12: 92–102.

Henry, James A., Kenneth M. Portier, and Jan Coyne. 1994. *The Climate and Weather of Florida*. Sarasota: Pineapple Press.

Hodanish, Stephen, David Sharp, Waylon Collins et al. 1997. "A 10-Year Monthly Lightning Climatology of Florida, 1986–95." *Weather and Forecasting* 12: 439.

Jarrell, Jerry D. et al. 2002. *The Deadliest, Costliest, and Most Intense United States Hurricanes from 1900 to 2000*. Washington, D.C.: NOAA Technical Memorandum NWS TPC-1 (available on the Internet).

Johnson, Warren O. 1954. "Florida Freezes." *Weatherwise* 7: 7–10.

———. 1970. *Minimum Temperatures in the Agricultural Areas of Peninsular Florida: Summary of 30 Winter Seasons 1937–1967*. Publication no. 9. Gainesville: University of Florida Institute of Food and Agricultural Sciences.

Jones, Catherine Stephens, Jay F. Shriver, and James J. O'Brien. 1999. "The Effect of El Niño on Rainfall and Fire in Florida." *Florida Geographer* 30: 55–69.

Jordan, Charles L. 1984. "Florida's Weather and Climate: Implications for Water." In *Water Resources Atlas of Florida*, ed. Edward A. Fernald and Donald J. Patton. Tallahassee: Florida State University Institute of Science and Public Affairs.

Kahn, Jennifer. 2002. "Rain, Rain, Go Away: A Superabsorbent Polymer Reinvigorates an Old Dream." *Discover,* September, 64–66.

Karl, Thomas R., and Richard W. Knight. 1998. "Secular Trends of Precipitation Amount, Frequency, and Intensity in the United States." *Bulletin of the American Meteorological Society* 79, 2: 231–41.

LeComte, Douglas. 1999. "The Weather of 1998: A Warm, Wet, and Stormy Year." *Weatherwise* 52: 19–28.

Lemley, Brad. 2002. "The Next Ice Age." *Discover* 23: 34–40.

Lericos, Todd P., Henry E. Fuelberg, and Andrew I. Watson. 2002. "Warm Season Lightning Distributions over the Florida Peninsula as Related to Synoptic Patterns." *Weather and Forecasting* 17: 83–98.

Ludlum, David M. 1958. "Snowfall in Florida." *Weatherwise* 11: 55, 67.

———. 1982. *The American Weather Book.* Boston: Houghton Mifflin.

Mykle, Robert. 2002. *Killer'cane: The Deadly Hurricane of 1928.* New York: Cooper Square Press.

National Oceanic and Atmospheric Administration (NOAA). www.noaa.gov.

National Weather Service. 1998. *Service Assessment: Central Florida Tornado Outbreak, February 22–23, 1998.* Washington, D.C.: National Weather Service.

O'Brien, J. J., D. F. Zierden, D. Legler, J. W. Hanson, J. W. Jones, A. G. Smajstrla, G. P. Podestá, and D. Letson. 1999. *El Niño, La Niña, and Florida's Climate: Effects on Agriculture and Forestry.* The Florida Consortium (Florida State University, University of Florida, and University of Miami).

Pardue, Leonard, and Jessie Freeling. 1982. *Who Knows the Rain? Nature and Origin of Rainfall in South Florida.* Coconut Grove: Friends of the Everglades.

Pielke, Roger A. 1975. "Ice Fall from a Clear Sky in Fort Pierce, Florida." *Weatherwise* 28: 157–59.

Pielke, Roger A., et al. 1991. "The Predictability of Sea-Breeze Generated Thunderstorms." *Atmosphera* 4: 65–78.

———. 1999. "The Influence of Anthropogenic Landscape Changes on Weather in South Florida." *Monthly Weather Review* 127: 1663–72.

Pinellas County Department of Environmental Management. 2001. *Determination of the 8–Hour Ozone Nonattainment Boundary for the Tampa Bay Area.*

Provenzo, Eugene F., Jr., and Asterie Baker Provenzo. 2002. *In the Eye of Hurricane Andrew.* Gainesville: University Press of Florida.

Rappaport, Ed. 1993. *Preliminary Report: Hurricane Andrew, 16–28 August 1992.* Miami: National Hurricane Center.

Schneider, Stephen H., and Terry L. Root, eds. 2002. *Wildlife Response to Climate Change: North American Case Studies.* Washington, D.C.: Island Press.

Schwartz, Barry E., and Lance F. Bosart. 1979. "The Diurnal Variability of Florida Rainfall." *Monthly Weather Review* 107: 1535–45.

Schwartz, Glenn E. 1977. "The Day It Snowed in Miami." *Weatherwise* 30: 50, 95.

Soon, Willie, Craig Idso, Sherwood Idso, and David R. Legates. 2003. "Reconstructing Climatic and Environmental Changes of the Past 1000 Years." *Energy and Environment* 14, 2 and 3: 233–96.

Tartaglione, Carissa A. 2002. "Regional Effects of ENSO on U.S. Hurricane Landfall." Thesis, Florida State University.

Titus, James G., and Charlie Richman. 2001. "Maps of Lands Vulnerable to Sea Level Rise: Modeled Elevations along U.S. Atlantic and Gulf Coasts." *Climate Research* 18, 3: 205–28.

Uman, Martin. 1987. *The Lightning Discharge.* Orlando: Academic Press.

Union of Concerned Scientists. 2003. www.ucsusa.org/gulf.

U.S. Department of Commerce. 1978. *Climate of Florida.* Climatography of the United States, no. 60. Asheville, N.C.: National Oceanic and Atmospheric Administration, National Climatic Data Center.

———. 2002. *Local Climatological Data, 2001.* Washington, D.C.: NOAA.

U.S. Environmental Protection Agency. 1997. *Climate Change and Florida.* Washington, D.C.: EPA 230–F-97–008i (available on the Internet).

Unisys. 2002. *Atlantic Tropical Storm Tracking by Year.* www.weather.unisys.com/hurricane/atlantic.

University of Florida Department of Otolaryngology. 2002. www/ent.health.ufl.edu/forms/allergies.

USPIRG. 2002. *Danger in the Air, August 2002.* //uspirg.org/reports/dangerintheair 2002.

Waller, Bradley G. 1985. *Drought of 1980–82 in Southeast Florida with Comparison to the 1961–62 and 1970–71 Droughts.* Tallahassee: U.S. Geological Survey Water Resource Investigation Report 85–4152.

Weeks, Jerry Woods. 1977. *Florida Gold: The Emergence of the Florida Citrus Industry, 1865–1895.* Ann Arbor, Mich.: University Microfilms.

Williams, Dansy T. 1974. "Predicting the Atlantic Sea Breeze in the Southeast States." *Weatherwise* 27: 106–9.

Williams, Jack. 1985. "Tough Decisions: Calling the Weather Shots for the Space Shuttle." *Weatherwise* 38: 240–47.

Williams, John M., and Iver W. Duedall. 2002. *Florida Hurricanes and Tropical Storms.* Gainesville: University Press of Florida.

Woods, Richard. 1985. "A Dangerous Family: The Thunderstorm and Its Offsprings." *Weatherwise* 38: 131–35.

Newspaper files have been of great help, in particular those of the *Miami Herald, Orlando Sentinel, St. Petersburg Times,* and *Tampa Tribune.*

The web pages of the National Oceanic and Atmospheric Administration, National Climate Data Center, and the Southeastern Regional Climate Center provided most of the climatological data.

Index

Morton D. Winsberg is professor emeritus of geography at Florida State University, where he taught for more than thirty years. While his primary interest has been human geography, his avocation has been weather, and he has maintained a weather station at his home in Tallahassee since 1965. He is the author of *Florida History through Its Places* (UPF, 1997).

Books of Related Interest

Florida Hurricanes and Tropical Storms, 1871–2001, expanded edition, edited by John M. Williams and Iver W. Duedall

In the Eye of Hurricane Andrew, by Eugene F. Provenzo, Jr., and Asterie Baker Provenzo

El Niño in History: Storming Through the Ages, by Cesar N. Caviedes

Florida: A Short History, revised edition, by Michael Gannon

Florida Lighthouses, by Kevin M. McCarthy

Atlas of Florida, revised edition, edited by Edward A. Fernald and Elizabeth Purdum